THE WITHDRAWN
WRITER'S
LEGAL GUIDE

THE

WRITER'S

LEGAL GUIDE

AN AUTHORS GUILD DESK REFERENCE

FOURTH EDITION

KAY MURRAY AND TAD CRAWFORD

ALLWORTH PRESS
NEW YORK

AUTHORS GUILD

Allworth Press books may be purchased in bulk at special discounts for sales promotion, corporate gifts, fund-raising, or educational purposes. Special editions can also be created to specifications. For details, contact the Special Sales Department, Allworth Press, 307 West 36th Street, 11th Floor, New York, NY 10018 or info@skyhorsepublishing.com.

17 16 15 14 13 5 4 3 2 1

Published by Allworth Press, an imprint of Skyhorse Publishing, Inc.
307 West 36th Street, 11th Floor, New York, NY 10018.

Copublished with The Authors Guild, Inc.

Allworth Press® is a registered trademark of Skyhorse Publishing, Inc.®, a Delaware corporation.

www.allworth.com

Cover design by Danielle Ceccolini

Library of Congress Cataloging-in-Publication Data is available on file.
ISBN: 978-1-62153-242-2

Printed in the United States of America

CONTENTS

CHAPTER 1

WRITING IS A BUSINESS

For some writers, practicing their craft is a joy. For some, it is a burden. In either case, writing is also a business—and you, the professional writer, are a sole proprietor. Like any entrepreneur, you need to minimize your financial and legal risks, protect your assets, and make the most of your investments of time and effort. This book is intended to help you make your business a success.

The literary marketplace has fundamentally changed in the decade since the last edition of this book was published, and as of this writing, it is in a state of upheaval. Few of the changes have been advantageous to writers. The traditional print publishers and bricks-and-mortar book retailers that have survived the changes so far are scrambling to adapt their business models to the new economic reality, which is that readers expect instant, inexpensive access to literature. Instead of content being king, it is content aggregators—Amazon, Google, Apple, Facebook, the *Huffington Post*, and their ilk—that reign in today's information industry. Publishers and retailers are cutting costs by squeezing their suppliers, and that means writers. They are more reluctant than ever to take risks on new writers or to try to develop a fledgling or midlist writer's career. They are neither able nor willing to invest in marketing most of the books they publish or sell. With the exception of the handful of blockbuster writers who perennially have at least one title on the bestseller lists, even prolific published authors often have to keep their day jobs because advances have shrunk dramatically. Freelance assignments have dried up and print media companies cannot offer the same fees that they used to pay.

On the other hand, the advent of digital delivery systems offers writers new ways to reach a paying audience. Thousands of writers now deal directly with online retailers to sell their work as an ebook, print-on-demand edition, "quick read" or "short," effectively cutting out the middleman, i.e., traditional publishers.[1] Many others are in effect self-publishing by setting up their own blogs and some are even earning a bit of income through advertising. Of course, without a publisher, a self-published writer has to provide her own editing, marketing, and promotion.

Whether you publish through a traditional publisher, directly through an ebook or print-on-demand provider, or in another medium, it is important to learn how to protect your legal and financial interests and to license your intellectual property. There are many reasons why you should do this. To take a common example, when a commercial publisher finally offers its standard contract to a writer who has been looking long and hard for a deal, she will undoubtedly be tempted to sign it right away, no questions asked. Doing so would be a big mistake, one that could haunt her for a good part of her career. Publishers' so-called boilerplate contracts are typically biased in nearly every way in favor of the publisher and against the writer—but they are also negotiable. Within reason, publishers are willing to accommodate many requests to change their terms. Before you sign any contract offered to you, you owe it to yourself and to your work to understand what it means so that you can negotiate what is important to you. If you do not, there is a good chance you will come to regret it.

Operating on a "handshake basis" presents legal pitfalls as well. Copyright law, which is explained in the next several chapters, creates default terms for transactions between parties who do not enter into a contract. If two people work together intending to create one work, for example, the copyright law gives them both equal and independent ownership and control of the work. If a writer contributes to a periodical based on a verbal assignment, the publisher is presumed to have certain limited

---

[1] Amazon's spokespeople have taken to calling traditional publishers "legacy publishers." It is not a compliment. See chapter 14.

rights to reuse the contribution. If a publisher heavily edits your work, you could be sued as legally responsible if the revisions contain a defamatory statement. But all of these results can be changed by agreement. The first aim of this book is to give you the knowledge to understand your publishing deals and make them work for you. A second goal is to help you avoid defamation, copyright infringement, invasion of privacy, and tax problems.

Even if you have a literary agent, you need to be able to understand and work with the relevant laws. Without a doubt, a good agent can be a tremendous ally for a writer. Some agents are lawyers, and many others are experts at finding and negotiating the best possible deal for their clients. But any honest agent would tell you that no writer should abdicate responsibility for her assets and career interests to another person, no matter how trustworthy. A professional agent has interests beyond, even in conflict with, any one client. For the sake of their other clients, agents must preserve their relationships with publishers, sometimes to the detriment of an individual client.[2] You can and should discuss your licenses and contract terms with your agent, but you should not expect her to be a copyright or defamation or contract law expert. An agent markets and sells her clients' work and accounts for the payments; she is not retained to give legal advice. *You* need to be able to spot the issues so that you can seek out legal advice or take protective measures. Finally, it is a fact of life that authors and agents sometimes decide to part ways. If your agency relationship is terminated, you will have to understand your rights and obligations regarding both the agent and your publisher(s).

This book is intended to be a legal reference for anyone who writes literary works for publication in print and online: nonfiction writers, novelists, journalists, freelance contributors to newspapers and magazines, poets, children's book writers and illustrators, and textbook and academic authors. It is structured to cover the legal issues a writer faces in roughly chronological order from the time she begins creating a written work for publication: understanding and securing copyright, avoiding defamation and invasion of privacy, accessing government information, negotiating various kinds of publishing contracts (including the "deal point memos" that precede many

---

[2] Moreover, no license is required to set up shop as an agent and represent authors. Chapter 15 will explain how to find and retain an ethical and appropriate agent and detect poseurs.

negotiations), finding and retaining a literary agent, taxes, and estate planning. It will explain how to get the best possible deal for the various ways a work of literature can be exploited using new technologies, including those as yet unknown. Even if you are writing for purely personal and not financial reasons, or to promote yourself, or your business, or a cause, you can still use the information here to protect your work from piracy and distortion and to minimize your legal risks.

BASIC ADVICE AND INFORMATION FOR NEW WRITERS

Every professional or aspiring writer should join a writers association. Some of the most prominent organizations are described in Appendix A, but you can easily find others, including local groups or branches of national groups, by doing a little research.

Writing is an isolated endeavor. Joining a writers group offers you many benefits that offset the negative effects of working alone. By connecting with other writers, virtually and in person, you become part of a community of people who share your professional interests and from whom you can learn current relevant market information. As the chapters covering contracts illustrate, information equals power in any negotiation. Membership in at least one writers organization will improve your knowledge of the legal and business environment and thereby help you enhance your negotiating position. Even the most successful writers with powerful agents gain from being part of a writing community, and most bestselling authors belong to at least one of the associations listed in the Appendix.

There are numerous organizations for published and aspiring writers of every genre. Each offers varying benefits, such as substantive feedback on ongoing projects, practical advice about the market, writing competitions and awards, networking opportunities with agents and editors, current payment rates and industry information, legal advice and individual advocacy, lobbying for writers' interests, health and liability insurance group plans, website- and blog-building software, self-promotion advice, and discounts to services. In general, membership dues are small and can usually be deducted on tax returns as a business expense against your writing income.

RESOURCES WORTH YOUR INVESTMENT

In order to sell your work at the best price, you need to know what the market is buying and how much it is paying. Because aspiring writers are themselves a market, there are many resources available that promise to help you find an agent and a publisher, promote yourself, and understand the publishing industry. When considering various services, keep in mind that there is *absolutely no need* to spend a lot of money on any service or product that makes these promises. The best ones are not expensive, and many great resources are free. A few of the best and most cost effective are listed here, but this list is not at all comprehensive. You can find many more on the web.

PUBLISHERS LUNCH/PUBLISHERS MARKETPLACE

Publishers Lunch (www.publisherslunch.com) is a daily and weekly email newsletter and a database of reported deals written and compiled by Michael Cader, a former publisher and bookseller, on the *Publishers Marketplace* platform. If you want to be part of the publishing business, then you should join the more than 40,000 editors, agents, booksellers, and writers who subscribe. Each free "Daily Lunch" email gathers key stories from the web and from print media, and also has original reporting, all for the professional trade book community. The "Deluxe" version of *Lunch* at *Publishers Marketplace* (www.publishersmarketplace.com) costs $25 per month. For that, you receive access to resources to help you find an agent or a publisher and learn what the public, and publishers, are buying. Most literary agents and publishers subscribe, and they love to report their deals, proposals, and acquisitions, and that information is all available to other subscribers. Subscribers can search the proprietary database of members' pages, discover who represents which particular writers, and search descriptions of thousands of reported acquisitions and licenses. No other resource provides this information in one place in an easily searchable format. As a member, you can create a webpage on the database displaying your contact information, career highlights, proposals, and a checkbox to show you are looking for an agent. At a minimum, the free daily *Publishers Lunch* is essential. While you are searching for an agent or publisher, consider the $25 monthly fee for *Publishers Lunch Deluxe* a very worthwhile investment.

WRITER'S DIGEST

Writer's Digest magazine and its free website (www.writersdigest.com) provides much helpful information about the industry and many resources to help you improve your writing, including an annual list of the 101 best websites for writers. The annual *Writer's Digest Guide to Literary Agents* (www.guidetoliteraryagents.com) includes a blog that is an excellent source of potential agents, especially when cross-referenced against the database at *Publishers Marketplace*. *Writer's Digest* publishes an annual "Writer's Market" series, which lists book publishers, consumer and trade magazines, contests and awards, literary agents, newspapers, playwriting markets, and screenwriting markets. After registering on its website, you will receive frequent emails offering information and registration (for a fee) to webinars and courses that help improve your craft, find markets for your work, and improve self-promotion tools and skills. *Writer's Digest* also publishes several annual references focused on the novel and short story market, which include current pay rate charts. The "Deluxe Edition" of the *Writer's Market* (about $12 more than the regular edition), provides access to the digital edition of *Writer's Yearbook* featuring the 100 Best Markets, a year-long subscription to *Writer's Digest* magazine online, and other resources.

PUBLISHERS WEEKLY *ONLINE*

Publishers Weekly, the weekly industry magazine, sends several free weekly emails with industry news. Its website (www.publishersweekly.com) makes a searchable database of major reported deals available to subscribers (about $200 per year).

REFERENCE BOOKS

The Literary Marketplace (*"LMP"* to those in the know) lists agents that have at least three references and every publisher currently in business, along with their contact and other information. It is too expensive to consider buying, but it is available in most libraries. Jeff Herman's annually updated *Guide to Book Publishers, Editors, and Literary Agents* is subtitled "Who They Are! What They Want! How to Win Them Over!" The book offers in-depth information about what specific agents and publishers are seeking. The downside to using print resources is that, although they are updated every year, the information in them can become dated quickly.

ESSENTIAL BLOGS

The Book Deal, at www.alanrinzler.com/blog, gives an insider's perspective on how books are published and what is happening behind the scenes in the industry. The author, Alan Rinzler, was an acquiring editor and publisher for more than forty years at several major publishers. His blog describes how writers can exploit the world of digital and print publishing, how books are acquired, developed, and promoted, and how agents and publishers "really" seek the most promising new authors. Experts contribute posts explaining specific aspects of every phase of the publishing process and readers make helpful comments on the posts. The blog also links to numerous articles and posts around the web, casting a wide net to cover many aspects of the industry and the craft of writing.

Nathan Bransford's blog, blog.nathanbransford.com, has dozens of posts by an industry polymath (author, social media manager, and former literary agent) aimed at helping aspiring writers succeed. Posts offer advice on writing well, explain how to seek and query agents, and bring the realities of publishing to life.

LITERARY AGENTS' BLOGS

Nobody understands the book industry better than established literary agents. Many of them publish blogs that tout their writers and also offer practical and accurate insight into the current state of the industry. Several of them focus on advising writers how to increase their chances of getting published successfully and happily. Appendix B to this chapter contains a list of good agencies' blogs.

THE COPYRIGHT OFFICE

The moment you write an original piece of any length, it is governed by the Copyright Act, the law that affects how your work is owned and licensed. The Copyright Office, part of the Library of Congress, administers the Copyright Act by recording registrations and transfers of copyrights, taking deposit copies of registered works, making registrations and transfer records searchable through its website (www.copyright.gov), informing the public about the law, and advising Congress. The Register of Copyrights leads the Copyright Office. Its website offers a wealth of information, including the Office's regulations, registration forms (both online and paper), and numerous circulars and fact sheets that explain specific parts of the law in user-friendly detail. These items can be downloaded individually and are also available by mail (write to the Copyright Office, Library of Congress, Washington, D.C. 20559). The website also contains frequently asked questions about copyright, the complete text of the Copyright Act, pending and new amendments, testimony of the Register, regulations, announcements, and press releases.

CITIZEN MEDIA LAW PROJECT

If you are self-publishing a nonfiction blog or other news website or are working for an online publishing venture, subscribing to the Citizen Media Law Project (www.citimedialaw.org) is a must. The CMLP is a nonprofit resource hosted by the Berkman Center for Internet & Society, a research center founded at Harvard University to promote understanding of the Internet and help pioneer its development. The CMLP helps online journalists and small publishing ventures understand the law as it relates to news reporting so as to minimize their risks of liability. It has many resources to help train and inform journalists and online publishers so they can protect themselves and their First Amendment rights. The CMLP has five core initiatives: a free, downloadable legal guide for journalism ventures; a database of "legal threats," i.e., lawsuits, subpoenas, and cease and desist demands; a media legal network that helps match journalists and publishers to volunteer lawyers and legal clinics; a "Research and Response" initiative through which CMLP advocates and litigates on issues affecting online media; and a blog, regular email, and monthly newsletter addressing issues and legal developments important to online journalists.

DO YOU NEED A LAWYER?

This book encourages writers to think like lawyers when engaged in the business side of writing. It aims to help you negotiate better deals and protect your financial and career interests. It will *not* make you a legal expert on copyright, contracts, tax, defamation, or any of the other topics covered. It is not intended to serve as a substitute for the advice of a lawyer or other expert on specific issues, because there is no substitute for the advice of a knowledgeable expert who can carefully evaluate a unique query. Situations might arise in the course of your career that are best handled in consultation with a lawyer, literary agent, tax or royalty accountant, or other professional.

You should consider consulting a lawyer if:

- ✎ You are negotiating or facing an issue in a contract (signed or unsigned), and you feel you cannot conduct the negotiation on your own behalf.
- ✎ You are being threatened with suit or termination of a contract or a withholding of royalties.
- ✎ You are unsure about the consequences of a document you are asked to sign or do not understand one or more of its provisions.
- ✎ Whenever a large amount of money or other valuable property is at stake in a transaction or dispute.

For questions about the meaning of a contract term, concerns about royalty statements, or problems with a publisher or agent's behavior, the first place to go is to the Authors Guild's Contract Services staff. If you are not a member of the Authors Guild (www.authorsguild.org), then join if you qualify.[3] The seasoned publishing lawyers at the Authors Guild can review and evaluate an entire contract, answer your questions and offer advice on how to proceed, and send demand letters to publishers, agents, or other parties on your behalf. Most publishers and agents take a demand letter from the Authors Guild, the oldest and largest association of professional authors in the country, very seriously. If your matter requires legal representation, the Guild can refer you to a qualified lawyer.

Finding the right lawyer for your specific query is crucial. General practitioners and business lawyers do not necessarily have the expertise to deal with the issues facing writers. A good way to find a lawyer with appropriate experience is to inquire of your network of writing colleagues or writers organizations. If possible, get more than one name and interview

---

[3] To qualify for full membership, within the previous eighteen months you must have published at least one book or three freelance articles with established, paying publishers or have earned at least $5,000 from self-published work. Self-published writers earning at least $500 within the previous eighteen months and those who have received an offer of a book contract from a paying publisher are eligible for associate membership. Associate members can access all the benefits of membership except for voting privileges. Dues are $90 the first year and are based on a sliding scale thereafter, but most members continue to pay $90. The Authors Guild is a copublisher of this book.

each candidate, asking about their fees, experience in matters like yours, and how they intend to approach your matter.

Many lawyers and law students enjoy representing writers and artists more than other kinds of clients. Several law schools have clinics specially focused on representing clients in intellectual property and First Amendment matters, and the Citizen Media Law Project has a legal network of experienced lawyers willing to work at a reduced rate. Many cities have volunteer lawyers for the arts organizations and local bar associations that offer pro bono or reduced-fee legal services to clients who meet certain income requirements. If you cannot afford to pay a lawyer's fees, consider contacting one of these groups. Even if they cannot provide free or low-cost legal services for a specific matter, many of them offer general advice and referrals to knowledgeable attorneys.

DO YOU NEED A LITERARY AGENT?

Most book authors should have a literary agent. If you want to publish a book with a trade book publisher (large or small), or to publish regularly as a freelancer, you are much more likely to succeed if you have a diligent, professional literary agent in your corner. Her primary objective is to place her clients' work with the best possible publisher for the best possible terms and to nurture their professional development. It is the agent's business to understand the industry in depth, which means knowing what editors are currently buying, what publishers are paying, and what new ways to exploit literary works are on the horizon. Your agent will negotiate the financial and other significant terms of your publishing and other related contracts. As explained in chapter 15, your agent is paid a commission, usually 15 percent of what she sells on your behalf, but you are still likely to come out well ahead if she is doing her job.

WHY YOU NEED *THE WRITER'S LEGAL GUIDE*

Successful writers are lucky, as most of them would acknowledge. But they also had a big role in making their own luck. Aside from their years of toil and sacrifice, writers who learn to protect and leverage their property, promote their interests, and negotiate effectively are more likely to succeed. They can earn more income from their work, avoid the waste of time and energy that legal disputes cause, retain control over their careers and their work, and suffer less anxiety because knowing more allows them to worry less. The authors and publishers of this book hope *The Writer's Legal Guide* will help you care for the business side of your writing career so that you can have more self-reliance, confidence, and peace of mind as you build that career.

DISCLAIMER

This book is not a substitute for the advice of a lawyer, accountant, literary agent, or any other expert who has examined the specific facts of a given situation. While every attempt has been made to ensure that the information in this book is thorough, accurate, and current, the authors and publishers cannot warrant that this is the case, especially because the law, the industry, and publishers' practices can—and do—change overnight. In fact, the publishing industry and the state of intellectual property law are in such a state of flux today that it is likely that some of the information in this book will be out of date by the time you read it. For these reasons, the publishers, authors, and their agents, employees, directors, officers, partners, and representatives disclaim all liability for any loss arising out of or in connection with anything that appears or does not appear in this book.

NOTE ABOUT TERMS USED

This book uses the terms "writer" and "author" interchangeably, although the chapters covering copyright use "author" to mean the creator of any kind of work product protected by copyright. Also, following the current convention in legal writing, this book uses the female pronoun to refer to either sex.

CHAPTER 2

COPYRIGHT BASICS

Article I of the US Constitution gives Congress "the power . . . To promote the Progress of Science and useful Arts, by securing for limited Times to Authors and Inventors the exclusive Right to their respective Writings and Discoveries." Promoting the creation of literary works and inventions in the new republic was important to the Founding Fathers, but they also worried about the effect that "exclusive rights" would have on other citizens' freedoms. Letters between Thomas Jefferson and James Madison express their ambivalence about the wisdom of granting a "private monopoly" to anyone. In the end, they acknowledged that copyright was necessary to promote creativity and that exclusive rights granted to private citizens were acceptable because they would be time-limited.

In 1790, Congress used its constitutional power and enacted the first federal copyright law, giving exclusive rights to writers and inventors for a term of fourteen years, optionally renewable for an additional fourteen years.[4] In the ensuing two centuries, copyright protection has expanded

---

[4] Laws protecting literary property rights evolved through English common law and legislation, which the United States adopted. Chapter 6 explores the history of copyright in more detail.

dramatically, far beyond what the Founders could have foreseen. In its current incarnation, copyright covers not just writings and discoveries, but many other kinds of original work product, including software. The length of the term of a copyright is now the life of the author plus 70 years, or at least 95 years for certain works.

Copyright in the United States is designed to give creators an economic incentive by letting them benefit from the fruits of their talent and labor, but its ultimate objective is to promote progress by allowing society to enjoy and build on their creations. The United States Supreme Court has described copyright as grounded in the economic philosophy that the "sacrificial days" devoted to creativity ultimately benefit the general public and therefore must be encouraged by commensurate personal profit. The ongoing struggle by legislators (and the lobbyists who woo them) and courts to keep these private and public interests in balance is the driving force behind the development of copyright law.

THE VALUE OF COPYRIGHT

Think of copyright as the means by which a creative work realizes economic value. Subject to certain specified exceptions, the Copyright Act gives exclusively to the "author"[5] of a work the right to capitalize on it by any of the following methods: reproduction, distribution of copies, public display, public performance, and the creation of derivatives, or adaptations, of the work. Only the author may use or give license to others to use any of these rights, individually or in combination. Publishing contracts are essentially licenses of one or more of the author's exclusive rights under copyright.

THE GOVERNING COPYRIGHT LAW

Until January 1, 1978, copyright in the United States existed in two distinct varieties: common law, which governed unpublished works, and statutory, which governed published works. Common law copyright grew out of judge-made precedent and protected works as soon as they were

---

[5] In the Copyright Act, "author" refers to the creator of any work covered by copyright, and it is used the same way in this chapter.

created, without the need for publication, copyright notice, or registration. Statutory copyright was embodied in federal legislation and protected works only when registered with the Copyright Office or published with a correct copyright notice. Common law copyright lasted for as long as a work remained unpublished or unregistered; statutory copyright lasted for a finite term, whether or not the work was published. Under this system, any work that was published without a copyright notice forfeited copyright protection and entered the public domain.

On January 1, 1978, the current law, known as the Copyright Act of 1976, replaced both the common law and the federal copyright statute that had been in effect since 1909. The 1976 Act significantly reformed the previous system. It eliminated and preempted common law copyright. Most dramatically, the 1976 Act gives automatic copyright protection to any original work created on or after January 1, 1978, from the moment it is fixed in tangible form.[6] Copyright protection is immediate, whether or not the creator wants it, and whether or not she registers the copyright or publishes the work. The 1976 Act, still the exclusive law of copyright in the United States, has constantly evolved since its passage, as courts and Congress attempt to address the challenges of new technologies and new economic realities.

By superseding common law copyright and protecting works without requiring registration, the 1976 Act simplified the copyright system and made it more consistent with the laws of most other developed nations. At the same time, by automatically covering all works that are fixed in a tangible medium, the Act exponentially expanded the universe of works that are exclusively owned by private citizens and therefore not in the public domain. It has been estimated that today, more than 95 percent of the works covered by copyright are not commercially available to the public.

The 1976 Act covers all works created on or after January 1, 1978. If copyright in a pre-1978 work had not expired as of January 1, 1978, the 1976 Act governs the treatment of that copyright.[7] With a few exceptions

---

[6] The statutory language is: "Copyright protection subsists . . . in original works of authorship fixed in a tangible medium of expression, now known or later developed, from which they can be perceived, reproduced or otherwise communicated, either directly or with the aid of a machine or device."

[7] Certain transactions made before January 1, 1978, including grants, licenses, registrations, and renewal registrations, are still governed by the 1909 Act.

explained below, if a work covered under the 1909 law entered the public domain, the 1976 Act did not revive its copyright.

WHAT WORKS ARE COVERED BY COPYRIGHT?

The following kinds of works of original authorship are protected by copyright: literary (i.e., written works, including computer programs), musical (including lyrics), dramatic, architectural (if created on or after 1990), cartographic (i.e., maps), choreographic, pantomimic, pictorial, graphic, sculptural, sound recordings, and audiovisual (including motion picture) creations. With the exception of works made for hire and joint works, explained in chapter 4, the creator of an original work owns the copyright, and only the creator may use or allow others to use the exclusive rights under copyright.

IDEAS AND FACTS

Copyright does not protect ideas (including concepts, principles, general topics, common plots or themes, and stock characters),[8] facts (including discoveries), or any procedure, process, method of operation, or titles, names, slogans, and short phrases.[9] These things are in the public domain, free for the taking by anyone.[10] In contrast, the original *expression* of any of these, an author's creative realization of her ideas or of facts, her fleshing out of common themes or stock characters, is protected. To illustrate, a written description of a discovery is covered by copyright, as is an author's selection, coordination, and arrangement of facts, but anyone else may write about the same discovery and set forth the same facts, independently arranged and coordinated, without infringing on the first writer's copyright.

ORIGINAL WORKS

Copyright protects only "original" works. "Originality" under the Act means simply that the author created the work and did not copy it from another work. One author's work might be similar, or even identical, to

---

[8] But idea theft might be remedied under contract theory, as discussed in Chapter 7.

[9] Titles, slogans, and short phrases might earn trademark protection as explained in Chapter 7.

[10] Works created by the US government (but not works commissioned by the government from private contractors) are also in the public domain.

another's, but if she independently created it and did not actually copy the first work, her creation is "original" and fully protected by the Act. Even if part of a work is not original because it infringes another's copyright or contains public domain material, the author still owns copyright in the part that is original.

The work need not rise to any particular level of quality, but it must show a modicum of creativity or artistic qualities to be considered original and covered by copyright. In 1991, the US Supreme Court held that a residential telephone directory containing nothing more than an alphabetical listing of all the names and addresses in a particular area code failed to demonstrate a "constitutionally mandated" minimum level of originality. *Feist Publications, Inc. v. Rural Telephone Service Company, Inc. Feist* was important in recognizing that some creativity is needed to warrant copyright protection, but the bar it set to demonstrate originality is very low.

COMPILATIONS

Although copyright does not protect the discovery of objective facts, it does protect the original way facts are selected, arranged, and coordinated in a compilation. A copyrightable compilation is formed by collecting and assembling preexisting material in such a way that the result is to some extent original. Examples are magazines and newspapers, the "yellow pages," a selection of poems (even if the poems are all in the public domain), and a list of the best restaurants in a city. Whether copying a compilation is an infringement of the copyright depends on the nature of the collection, the originality of its presentation, and the nature of the appropriation.

The *Feist* ruling overturned a long-standing doctrine protecting "the sweat of the brow." Under that theory, courts recognized a proprietary interest in facts and prohibited others from saving time and effort by copying the facts contained in prior works. After *Feist*, copyright no longer protects raw data, regardless of the time and effort involved in finding and compiling it. Writers can freely copy facts from prior works without infringing copyright, although they should verify the facts copied and must, to avoid infringing, select, arrange, and coordinate them independently.

The Copyright Office can refuse to register a work on the ground that it is not copyrightable, but the federal courts, having exclusive jurisdiction over copyright disputes, may reverse this exercise of the Copyright Office's discretion.

CHARACTERS

The popularity of prequels, sequels, spin-offs, "fan fiction," and retellings raises the question whether specific characters are copyrightable apart from the story containing that character. The courts have determined that stock characters or literary "types"—the superhero masquerading as an ordinary citizen, the hard-bitten private eye, or the wry and resourceful valet—are not copyrightable. But there are many characters in literature and culture—a certain boy wizard, for example—that might be copyrighted. The distinction rests on how well developed the character is, and the bar is higher when the character appears only in literature and not in a visual work. As one court put it in 1931: "The less developed the characters, the less they can be copyrighted: that is the penalty an author must bear for marking them too indistinctly." *Nichols v. Universal Pictures Corp.* A later court went further, holding that a character appearing in literature must have actually "constituted the story being told" to have copyright independent of the story. *Warner Bros. v. CBS.* The bottom line is that the law is still unsettled in this area. Cases considering whether copyright should be recognized in a character require a factual analysis and consideration of the equities involved.

DURATION OF COPYRIGHT

The Constitution mandates that copyright in a work is to exist for *a limited time*. After that time, the work enters the public domain and can be freely used by anyone. When Congress passed the first copyright law, it provided a term of fourteen years and a renewal term of fourteen years. Since then, Congress has extended the term of copyright many times. In 1998, the Copyright Term Extension Act (the "CTEA") extended the term of copyright in the United States for works published on or after January 1, 1978, to the length of the author's life plus 70 years.[11] For works owned by an entity other than a person (such as a corporation) and for pseudonymous or anonymous works, the term is the shorter of 95 years from first publication or 120 years, if not published.[12] The CTEA increased the term by

---

[11] Terms run through December 31 of the year they are scheduled to expire.

[12] If the name of the author of an anonymous or pseudonymous work is recorded with the Copyright Office, the term runs for the writer's life plus 70 years.

20 years, making it match many other countries' terms. A presumption exists that a copyright has expired if 95 years have passed and the records disclose no information indicating that copyright might still be in effect. This does not mean, however, that copyright has expired; the presumption can be rebutted with evidence of the author's continued existence or date of death. The term of copyright for a joint work created by two or more writers with the intention that their contributions be merged is the life of the last surviving writer plus 70 years.

The 1909 Copyright Act provided an original term of 28 years and a second term, called the "renewal term," of 28 years, which arose only if the author filed a renewal registration in the twenty-eighth year of the first term. If the owner did not renew the registration before the original term ended, the work entered the public domain after the first term expired. For the most part, the terms of copyrights that existed on January 1, 1978, were increased to 95 years from first publication (28 years in the first term, 67 years in the renewal term). All works copyrighted between January 1, 1964, and December 31, 1977, automatically had their terms extended to 95 years.

With common law copyright in unpublished works eliminated by the 1976 Act, all works that were protected under common law as of January 1, 1978, were given a copyright term equal to the author's life plus 70 years, except that in no event would a copyright previously protected under common law expire prior to December 31, 2002. If a common law copyrighted work was published, the term was extended until at least December 31, 2047. Appendix C is a chart showing when copyright expires for written works published or created in particular years.

THE EXCLUSIVE RIGHTS OF COPYRIGHT

Prior to passage of the 1976 Act, a copyright owner who licensed her work for any purpose had to transfer the entire copyright to the buyer; she could not license only selected rights. The "indivisibility" of copyright led to unfair results for creators. For example, if a writer sold the right to publish a story to a magazine, the magazine legally became owner of the entire copyright exclusively. If a motion picture studio wanted to purchase the rights to the story, it did so from the magazine publisher; the writer was cut out. The 1976 Act addressed this injustice by making copyright divisible into specific exclusive rights, and the exclusive rights of copyright subdivisible.

The Act gives the owner of a copyright the exclusive rights to exploit the work's value by doing, or authorizing others to do, any of the following: reproduce the work, sell and distribute copies, perform the work publicly, display the work publicly, and prepare derivative works. Copyright is now often described as a bundle of rights, each of which may be licensed separately, exclusively or nonexclusively, by the owner.

In order to best capitalize on the value of your work, you should know how to subdivide the rights you grant to publishers and other parties. Appropriately limiting rights you license can allow you to earn more from your work by granting others the rights to make secondary uses. For example, freelance writers typically license certain rights to publish their stories to periodicals and retain other rights. The writer may subdivide the exclusive publication rights by territory, such as "first North American serial rights," divide them further, for example granting "English-language first North American serial rights" (note that "first publication" rights are exclusive rights), or divide them into nonexclusive rights. All other rights are reserved to the writer.

The 1976 Act contains several exceptions to the exclusive rights of the copyright owner. The most important of these is "fair use," discussed in chapter 5, which allows others to copy and adapt copyrighted works without permission in appropriate cases. Another exception is the "first sale" doctrine, which allows anyone who has purchased a lawfully made copy of a work to resell, trade, or give away that copy (but not to make additional copies). Another exception allows the owner or consignee of an original or copy of a work, such as a museum or art gallery, to display it directly or with the aid of a projector to people present at the place of display. The owner of a copy of an audiovisual work such as a motion picture may publicly *display* the copy without permission defined as showing its images nonsequentially, but may not publicly *perform* it, which means to show its images sequentially.

DERIVATIVE WORKS

Derivative works are defined as distinguishable variations of existing works, including abridgements, adaptations, translations, and renderings in another format. A motion picture version of a book, a revised or expanded edition of a textbook, and a "cover" recording of a song are all derivative works.[13] To the extent they include original contributions, derivative works are themselves distinctly copyrightable. An author who adds new elements to a previously copyrighted work would own the copyright in the new elements. If a work is in the public domain, anyone can create a copyrightable work by adding original elements to it, but only the new elements are protected; others may still freely use the public domain portion.

TRANSFERS AND LICENSES

The 1976 Act requires transfers and licenses of exclusive rights to be made in a writing signed by the licensor (that is, the owner of the rights). An exclusive license, like a transfer, grants to the licensee a right that no one else may exercise. Book, magazine, and newspaper publishers rarely accept rights that are not exclusive. Copyright owners may vary the scope of the rights granted according to the duration of the license, the geographic extent of the license, specific formats, languages, and other limitations that the parties negotiate. A typical book publishing contract, described in chapter 11, contains many specifically delineated licenses.

Nonexclusive licenses allow more than one licensee to exploit a work in the same way, at the same time, in the same place, and are therefore less valuable than exclusive rights. For example, a writer could give two magazines the simultaneous rights to publish an article. Syndication rights, described in chapter 12, are analogous to simultaneous, nonexclusive licenses. Nonexclusive licenses need not be made in writing to be valid and enforceable, so take care not to inadvertently grant to a prospective publisher an implied or verbal nonexclusive license to use your work. Be wary of statements made in conversation, unsigned writings (such as a memorandum on a publisher's letterhead), or email that suggests a party has the right to exploit your work unless you so intend. Before entering a writing competition, scrutinize the application form and contest literature to understand whether the contest organizer is requesting any rights to your entry; it might need limited-time nonexclusive rights to copy and publish the entries, but you should generally not transfer any exclusive rights to

---

[13] The distinction between creating a derivative work, which requires the owner's permission, and making fair use of a work to create a "transformative work," which does not require permission, is discussed in Chapter 5.

the sponsor. In general, make sure any license agreement you enter clearly specifies the rights you are granting and reserves all other rights to you.

An exclusive licensee may file records of transfers of copyrights or exclusive licenses with the Copyright Office, but it is not mandatory to make the license valid. Doing so, however, does help others find the owner of rights in a work.

TERMINATION RIGHTS

In 1940, Jerry Siegel and Joe Schuster sold the rights to their story and character called Superman for $130. Their unfortunate situation is not unusual; most authors sell their rights without knowing their ultimate worth, and many have been excluded from the extraordinary profits their licensees earned from their creations. To right this injustice, the 1976 Act gave authors the right to terminate any grant or transfer of their rights after many years. Under the Act, all authors have an inalienable right to terminate any grant of rights under copyright after 35 years (for post-1977 works) or 56 years (for pre-1978 works). If the license is properly terminated, the licensee may no longer exploit the author's work unless it negotiates anew, but sublicenses made while it had the rights remain in force.

The purpose of the termination right is to give creators a second chance to benefit from work they sold or licensed years before they knew its long-term value. The right to terminate a grant is inalienable; in the words of the Act, it belongs to the original author "notwithstanding any agreement to the contrary." Therefore, an agreement made today in writing and for additional compensation not to exercise the termination right is not enforceable. Should your work succeed beyond your expectations, your termination right could prove extremely valuable to you or your family years from now. The termination right does not apply, however, to works "made for hire" or to transfers made in a will.

Any author who grants exclusive or nonexclusive rights in a copyright after January 1, 1978, may terminate the license(s) during the five-year period starting at the end of 35 years after the execution of the grant (if the grant includes the right of publication, the five-year window begins at the end of 35 years from the date of publication or 40 years from the date of execution of the grant, whichever ends sooner). If before 1978 an author (or her heirs) granted a license for the renewal term of a copyright, that grant may be terminated during the five-year period beginning 56 years after the copyright was first obtained. The mechanics of termination involve giving notice from two to ten years prior to the termination date and complying with requirements listed in Copyright Office Circular 96, *Notice of Termination of Transfers and Licenses.*

The clear-cut mandate of the inalienable termination right is soon to be tested. Recording artists who transferred their copyrights to their record companies in 1978 will be entitled to terminate the transfers beginning in 2013. A number of artists, including Billy Joel and Bruce Springsteen, have signaled their intention to send termination notices. The artists' record companies will understandably be tempted to fight to keep those immensely profitable rights. If the courts recognize any legal theory that weakens the termination right, it could well affect all creators. See Scorpio v. Willis, United States District Court for San Diego California, May 7, 2012 ("Village People" case).

COPYRIGHT AND PERIODICALS AND OTHER COLLECTIVE WORKS

Magazines, newspapers, anthologies, encyclopedias—anything in which a number of separate contributions are combined—are defined in the 1976 Act as "collective works." The law provides that the copyright in each contribution is distinct from the copyright in the entire collective work, and belongs to the author of the contribution. Until the mid-1990s, newspapers and magazines commonly published freelance contributions as part of their collective works without an express agreement on the scope of the rights. The 1976 Act addressed this situation by providing a default license: "In the absence of an agreement, the collective work publisher has only the privilege to reproduce the contribution in (1) the issue of the collective work for which it was contributed, (2) any revision of that collective work, or (3) any later collective work in the same series."

Under this default term, when a freelancer contributes to a magazine based on an editor's verbal assignment, the publisher may use the article in one issue and again in later issues, but it may not publish the piece in a different magazine. In a collective work such as an anthology or an encyclopedia, the publisher may use the article in the original issue and later revisions, but may not include it in a new anthology or different encyclopedia. As well, only nonexclusive rights are transferred, so a writer could theoretically sell the nonexclusive right to publish the work to another publisher at the same time.

After an eight-year legal battle, the Supreme Court ruled in 2001 that the scope of this default license does not give a collective work publisher the right to include the contributions in an electronic database that disaggregates the contributions from the original collective work. Other courts have inferred from this holding that publishers may reproduce a collective work contribution in digital form without the author's permission, if the digital copy appears as it originally appeared in the collective work. Rather than allowing your freelance work to be governed by the Copyright Act, which might not satisfy either your needs or your publisher's needs, it makes better sense to have your work governed by terms agreed upon by both parties. Chapter 12 covers how to negotiate contracts with periodicals.

FOREIGN WORKS AND INTERNATIONAL COPYRIGHT

Most foreign works are protected under US copyright law. If a work is published,[14] US copyright law protects it if one or more of its authors are:

A national or permanent resident of the United States; or

A stateless person; or

A national or a permanent resident of a nation that is a party to a copyright treaty with the United States or covered by a presidential proclamation.

If a work is unpublished, US copyright law protects it regardless of the author's nationality or place of residence. The work need not have been created in the United States to have copyright protection here.

Likewise, works created in the United States or by a US national are protected in most other nations under their national copyright laws.

The United States is a party to several treaties (formally called "conventions") in which the participating nations agree to apply their copyright protection to works published in the other participating nations. Authors automatically obtain protection in the treaty nations when they publish a

---

[14] The definition of "publication" is important because the Copyright Act treats published works differently from unpublished works in several situations. The Copyright Act defines "publication" as public distribution, i.e., when one or more copies of a work are distributed to people who are not restricted from disclosing the content to others. "Distribution" can take place through sale, rental, lending, or other transfer of copies to the public. Offering copies to a group of people for the purpose of review, further distribution, public performance, or public display also constitutes "publication" under the Act.

work in the United States. The Universal Copyright Convention, which dates from 1955, provides that publication in any treaty nation bestows copyright in the United States, and vice versa. Under this treaty, there is one special requirement: the works must contain a copyright notice that includes the symbol ©, the author's full name, and the year of first publication. The author's initials will not suffice for protection under the Universal Copyright Convention. Under an older treaty, the Buenos Aires Convention, which still covers many Western Hemisphere countries, the notice must also contain the phrase "All rights reserved."

The United States joined the larger Berne Convention as of March 1, 1989. As a result, it is no longer necessary for US writers to publish simultaneously in a Berne country to gain protection under the Berne Convention. Indeed, the Berne treaty forbids member countries from imposing copyright formalities—including registration and publishing with notice—as a condition of copyright protection for the works of foreign writers. Joining Berne required the United States to enact changes in its law that favor creators, including eliminating copyright notice as a prerequisite to full protection. Copyright Office Circular 38a, *International Copyright Relations of the United States,* details the international copyright relations of the United States, including a list of every nation and the copyright conventions to which they belong. Many countries belong to both Berne and the Universal Copyright Convention, and some to one or the other, but not both. American authors are automatically protected under both conventions when they publish a work in the United States.

CONCLUSION

The subject of copyright is highly complex and acutely relevant to working writers. The volumes of case law and writings about copyright would probably fill a small library. The following four chapters attempt to provide a comprehensive but necessarily abbreviated survey of the topic, so you can have a workable knowledge of the basics.

CHAPTER 3

COPYRIGHT: NOTICE,

REGISTRATION, AND DEPOSIT

Because copyright exists from the moment a work is fixed in tangible form, an author might well ask why she should bother to register the copyright in her work or to make sure it contains a notice when published. There are several excellent reasons to do so, chief among them are the great advantages the author enjoys if her work is infringed.

PUBLICATION WITH COPYRIGHT NOTICE

As of March 1, 1989, when the United States officially joined the Berne Convention, US copyright law no longer requires a copyright notice to be placed on published works to receive full protection. (Works created before March 1989 are still subject to certain notice requirements.) Most copyright owners, however, continue to publish with copyright notice. Notice warns potential infringers that the work is protected by copyright and thereby precludes the argument that an infringement was innocent. In addition, the Universal Copyright Convention still requires copyright notice and a number of its signatories are not part of the Berne Convention, meaning that full copyright protection in those countries requires published works to contain a proper notice.

FORM OF COPYRIGHT NOTICE

For purposes of the Universal Copyright Convention, the proper form of copyright notice has three elements: © (the spelled out word "copyright" will not do); the author's name or an abbreviation by which the name can be recognized (or an alternative designation by which the author is well known), and the year of publication (or the year of creation, if the work is unpublished). The notice should appear in a conspicuous place on a published work, such as the first page of a book. If the United States government primarily created a work, a statement indicating this fact must be included with the copyright notice, or else the work will be treated as if notice had been omitted. Copyright Office Circular 3, *Copyright Notice*, discusses in detail the proper form and placement of copyright notice.

DEFECTIVE NOTICE

Most works published in the United States before March 1989 without correct copyright notice might have entered the public domain, depending on the circumstances and the date of first publication. Works published without notice before January 1978 are more likely to have forfeited copyright than those published between January 1978 and March 1989.

Under the 1909 Copyright Act, covering pre-1978 works, a missing or defective notice on a published work almost always led to the irrevocable loss of copyright. For example, if the notice gave a year later than the year of first publication, copyright was lost. There are a few exceptions to this harsh rule. The use of a year earlier than the correct year of first publication would reduce the copyright term but would not invalidate the copyright. If notice was omitted from a relatively small number of copies distributed, the copyright would continue to be valid, although an innocent infringer would not be liable for relying on the lack of notice.

Works published between January 1978 and March 1989 did not always forfeit copyright if notice was incorrect or omitted when first published. If the wrong name appeared on the notice, copyright remains and the actual owner may still register it in her own name. If a writer contributed a piece to a collective work such as a magazine but the publisher omitted a copyright notice in the writer's name, the contribution remained protected if the publisher's own notice appeared in the front of the magazine. If an earlier date than the actual date of publication appeared on the notice, the term of copyright is computed from the earlier date. (Note that this penalty affects only copyrights with fixed terms of years, such as those owned by a business entity; if the author is a person the term is measured from the date of the author's death.) If the name or date was omitted from the notice or if the date was more than one year later than the actual date of publication, the work is treated as if notice was completely omitted. In those cases of omission, the copyright is still not forfeited if any one of the following three tests can be met:

Notice was omitted from only a relatively small number of copies distributed to the public; or

Notice was omitted from more than a relatively small number of copies, but copyright then was registered within five years of publication and a "reasonable effort" was made to add notice to the copies distributed in the United States or

Notice was omitted despite the author's written instructions that notice appear on the work.

If none of these conditions apply, then the failure to include notice means the work is in the public domain.

REGISTRATION AND DEPOSIT

All copyrighted works may be registered with the United States Copyright Office, the official repository for copyright registrations, whether or not they have been published. Although book publishers usually contractually agree to register a work in the author's name within three months of publication, authors should consider registering the works they intend to self-publish or otherwise risk that it could be infringed. The right to sue for infringement, evidentiary advantages, and, depending on when the work is registered, attorney's fees and statutory damages all are available only if the owner has registered the work. Registration also allows others to find you or your publisher in the Copyright Office's database. The cost of registering a work is not prohibitive (in most cases, online registration costs $35), the application process is short and straightforward, and groups of works may be registered together.

ADVANTAGES OF REGISTRATION

If your work is infringed, you must register the copyright before you may file a lawsuit in the United States for infringement. The only exception to this requirement is when the infringed work is protected under the Berne Convention and its country of origin is not the United States.[15] Your certificate of registration, if issued within five years of first publication, is presumptive proof in court of the validity of the copyright and the facts stated on the certificate. If you have registered your work within three months of publication or before it is infringed, you are eligible (if you win your suit) to receive from the infringer your attorneys' fees and "statutory" damages (a special kind of damages that an author may elect to receive in lieu of proving any actual loss). Registration also cuts off any defense that an infringement was innocent because of a defective or missing copyright notice.

The 1976 Act and subsequent amendments have made renewal of the registration of pre-1978 works optional, but the same legal advantages that avail new registrations also apply to renewal registrations. As shown on the renewal form, it may be possible to renew a group of works belonging to one owner if they expire in the same year. Circular 15, *Renewal of Copyright,* offers additional information about copyright renewal and Circular 15t, *Extension of Copyright Terms*, discusses the extended terms of copyrights for pre-1978 works, whether the copyright was in its first 28-year term or in its renewal term.

HOW TO REGISTER A COPYRIGHT

Registering a copyright essentially requires a claimant to submit to the Copyright Office relevant information about the nature of the work, who owns it, and when it was created and/or published. It requires the registrant to complete a form, pay a fee, and, if the work has been published, send in the "best copy" for deposit in the Library of Congress. There are two ways to register: electronically and through the mail using a form tailored to the type of work. In 2009 the Copyright Office instituted the electronic registration option. The so-called "eCO" (for "electronic Copyright Office") system makes it easier, cheaper, and faster to register copyright than through the mail. See www.copyright.gov/eco for a tuto-

---

[15] Although authors of foreign works originating in a Berne Convention country other than the United States do not have to register before suing for infringement here, they should consider the other advantages of timely registration.

rial, FAQs, and fee information. If you use eCO, you don't have to choose among various forms, you can pay by credit or debit card or Automated Clearing House, and the fee is $35 versus $65 for using a mail-in form. Processing time is also reduced, from an average of five to eight months for mailed registrations, three to four and one-half months for eCO as of this writing. If your work is unpublished, you may upload a digital deposit copy at the time you register. If the work is published, eCO allows you to print a shipping slip to include with the work.

To register by mail, you must first choose the correct form (available at www.copyright.gov/forms) based on the kind of work you are registering. Form TX (for "text") is used for all nondramatic literary works, including books, poetry, articles and other contributions to collective works, and short stories. Periodicals or serial issues (not to be confused with contributions to periodicals) are registered with Form SE. Works meant to be performed, such as songs, scripts, and plays, use Form PA. Each form has corresponding step-by-step instructions. Along with the completed form, the filing fee of $65 and deposit copies of the work must be mailed in one package to the Copyright Office. In the event of litigation, it is important that the work deposited with the Copyright Office show all of the features for which the copyright is claimed. Also, make sure that the deposit copies are not likely to fade or alter with time. Review Circular 1c, *Make Sure Your Application Will Be Acceptable.*

Upon processing, the Copyright Office will mail you the official copyright certificate. Although it might take several months to a year or more to receive the certificate, the official registration dates back to when the Copyright Office received the application, deposit copy, and fee. Because the date of registration might determine whether a claimant can win statutory damages and attorneys' fees from an infringer, it is prudent to send a mailed registration by certified mail and request a return receipt.

After receipt of your registration, the office will assign an examiner to process your registration. If the examiner finds problems with the registration, the Copyright Office will contact you. Depending on the nature of the problem and your response to it, the official registration date will likely date back to the Copyright Office's original receipt of the application. To correct a mistake or amplify information contained in a completed registration, you should use Form CA for supplementary registration, but only after the office has issued a registration certificate. This could take many months, so take care that your registration is as comprehensive and correct as you can make it.

GROUP REGISTRATION

Unpublished and published works may each be registered in groups, which can save significant time and money. The rules are different for published and for unpublished works.

UNPUBLISHED WORKS

Authors may register an unlimited number of unpublished pieces as a single work, even if they are unrelated. Doing so saves significant time and money compared to registering each work in the collection individually. To qualify for group registration for an unpublished collection, the following conditions must be met:

The deposit materials are assembled in an orderly form;

The collection bears a single title identifying the whole, such as "Collected Writing of Jane Doe, January, 2013";

The person claiming copyright in each work forming part of the collection is also the person claiming copyright in the entire collection; and

All the works in the collection are by the same person or, if by different persons, at least one of them has contributed copyrightable material to each work in the collection.

A work registered when unpublished need not be registered again when it is published (although if it adds substantial new material or is substantially different, it should be registered when published to protect it fully).

PUBLISHED WORKS

Freelance contributors should register their published contributions even if their publishers register the periodical as a collective work. Registering the collective work does not confer the benefits of registration on each individual contribution to it. A writer may register as a group all contributions to any number of collective works published within a twelve-month period, as long as each contribution has the same copyright claimant (and, if published before March 1, 1989, had a proper copyright notice). Currently, group registration for published contributions can only be made on paper and through the mail, so the fee is $65. The registrant completes both the basic application form (Form TX for literary works) and Form GR/CP. Form GR/CP and its instructions are available at the Copyright Office website.

Although a writer may register an entire year's works at one time, it is better to register collectively every three months in order to qualify for attorneys' fees and statutory damages in case of infringement. At $65 for each group registration, the total cost to register a year's work on a quarterly basis is $260. If any of your work is infringed, that investment could pay off many times over. Chapter 5 describes the rules and procedures of an infringement lawsuit.

DEPOSIT COPIES

Along with the registration form and fee, a registrant must "deposit" (i.e., deliver) one complete copy of an unpublished work or two copies of the "best edition" of a published work to the Copyright Office. If editions of differing quality have been published, Copyright Office guidelines explain which edition is considered the "best" (Circular 7b). For works first published outside the United States, only one complete copy of the work must be deposited. If a work is published simultaneously in the United States and abroad, it is treated as if first published in the United States.

For a group registration of published contributions to periodicals, the deposit materials can be one copy of any of the following:

One complete copy of each periodical or section of a newspaper in which the work appeared; or

The entire page(s) containing the contribution; or

The contribution clipped from the collective work; or

One photocopy of the contribution as published.

For a multimedia work first published in the United States, the registrant must deposit one complete copy of the best edition. Circular 55, *Copyright Registration for Multimedia Works*, discusses the deposit requirements and the forms for the different combinations of works that might comprise a multimedia work.

The deposit for works fixed in CD-ROM is one complete copy, including one copy of the disk, one copy of any accompanying operating software and instructional manual, and, if the work is in print as well as on CD-ROM, one printed version of the work.

ALTERNATE DEPOSIT

In certain cases, such as registration of limited editions or fine printings, a registrant might be able to make an alternate deposit instead of a valuable copy of the work. The registrant must make a special request to the Copyright Office for permission to submit "identifying material" rather than full copies of the work. The Copyright Office rules on requests for this "special relief" on a case-by-case basis. Generally, whether a work is published or unpublished, only one set of alternate deposit materials must be sent.

DEPOSIT FOR THE LIBRARY OF CONGRESS

In addition to depositing copies for registration, copies of works published in the United States must be deposited with the Library of Congress. (Certain kinds of works are exempt from the Library of Congress deposit requirement, including contributions to collective works; lectures, speeches, and addresses when published individually and not as a collection, among others.) Delivery of the correct number of deposit copies for registration within three months of publication will satisfy the deposit requirement. If an author registered her work before publication, then within three months of publication two copies of the best edition of the work must be deposited with the Copyright Office for the Library of Congress. The Library of Congress deposit requirement does not affect copyright protection. For example, if a writer registered a work before it was published and failed to deposit two copies upon publication, the Copyright Office might request copies from the writer or publisher, and failure to do so could subject the author to a fine, but the copyright would remain valid.

FILLING OUT THE COPYRIGHT FORMS

The application forms come with directions. Several of the mail-in paper forms are reproduced here. The eCO is the preferred and much faster filing method, but this section is included to present additional filing options in the absence of electronic communication.

1. **Unpublished nondramatic literary work—Form TX**
   Space 1—Fill in the title of the work and the nature of the work, such as fiction, nonfiction, poetry, textbook, advertising copy, or computer program.
   Space 2—State the author's name and indicate [if accurate] that the work is not a work-for-hire. Give the date of the

author's birth nation of citizenship or permanent residence, and indicate [if accurate] that the work is neither anonymous nor written under a pseudonym. Where it asks "Nature of Authorship," briefly explain the author's particular contribution (e.g., "entire text").

Space 3—For an unpublished work, give the year the work was finished; leave blank the date and nation of first publication.

Space 4—The writer's name and address should be shown for the copyright claimant. A claimant is either the writer or the owner of *all* rights who obtained rights from the writer; it is *not* a licensee or an owner of *some* exclusive rights.

Space 5—Answer no, if the writer did not previously register the work, or yes, if the author is registering new material to a work that had been previously registered.

Space 6—If the writer has added new material to a previously registered work, explain what material was added to the prior work to make a derivative work (e.g., "new text" or "revisions"). The registration will cover the new elements of the derivative work.

Space 7—Fill in the information about a deposit account, if the author has one. Give the author's name and address for correspondence purposes.

Space 8—Check the box for author, sign, and then print or type the name.

Space 9—Enter the author's name and address for mailing of the certificate of registration.

2. **Group registration for unpublished nondramatic literary works—Form TX**

   Fill out Form TX as you would for an unpublished nondramatic literary work, except for the following changes:

   Space 1—The collection must have its own title; use it here.

   Space 3—The year in which creation of the work was completed is the year in which the most recently completed work in the collection was completed.

3. **Published nondramatic literary works—Form TX**

   Fill out the form as you would for an unpublished nondramatic literary work, except for the following changes:

Space 3—In addition to the date of creation, give the date and nation of first publication of the work.

4. **Group registration of published contributions to periodicals—Form TX**

   Use Form TX if the contributions are nondramatic literary works, along with the adjunct Form GR/CP. Form TX is filled out as for a published nondramatic literary work, except for the following changes:

   Space 1—In the space for the title, write "See Form GR/CP, attached" and leave the other parts of Space 1 blank.

   Space 3—Give the year of creation of the last work completed and leave blank the date and nation of first publication. Next, fill out **Form GR/CP. Space A**—Mark Form TX as the basic application and give the name(s) as both writer and copyright claimant.

   Space B—For each box, fill in the requested information about the title of each contribution, the title of and other information about the periodical, and the date and nation of first publication. Mail Form GR/CP together with Form TX, the deposit copies, and the filing fee of $65.

5. **Unpublished works in the performing arts—Use Form PA**

   Includes works intended to be performed for an audience that is physically present at the performance and also works delivered indirectly to an audience by means of a device or process. This form is filled out in essentially the same way as for an unpublished nondramatic work.

6. **Published works of the performing arts—Use Form PA**

   This form is filled out essentially the same way as for a published nondramatic literary work.

CHAPTER 4

COPYRIGHT: WORKS MADE

FOR HIRE, JOINT WORKS,

AND COMMUNITY PROPERTY

The Copyright Act automatically recognizes the creator of an original work as the owner of the copyright—except in two cases. When a work is made "for hire," the party for whom the work is written—the author's employer or a commissioning party—is considered the legal "author" and the original owner of the work. A "work for hire" differs from an irrevocable assignment of the copyright. Unlike a writer who assigns her copyright, the creator of a work for hire never owns any interest in the work. Among other things, this means the creator of a work for hire has no right to terminate an assignment after 35 or 56 years under the inalienable termination right. If the owner of a work for hire never publishes or lets it go out of print, the creator still has no right to use the work.

Given these potentially extreme results, the Copyright Act recognizes "work made for hire" only in two situations: (1) when an employee creates copyrightable work within the course and scope of her employment; or (2) when a creator produces one of nine types of specially ordered or commissioned work *and* both parties agree in writing that the commissioned work is made for hire.

There are some situations where a freelance writer does not need or want to own the copyright in a commissioned work, such as a research paper, index, forward or afterward to another's work, a compilation of corporate data, or an instruction booklet, and is willing, for the right price, to sign away all copyright interests in the work. But traditional publishers rarely ask book writers or freelance journalists to write works on a for-hire basis, and these writers should resist doing so if they are asked.[16]

The second case that raises the question of the "author's" identity is when the work is a "joint work." The Copyright Act defines a joint work as one created by two or more authors with the intention, *at the time the work is created*, that their contributions be merged into inseparable or interdependent parts of a unitary whole. Unless they agree otherwise, the authors of a joint work own equal shares in the copyright, regardless of the amount of their respective contributions. Each owner of a joint work may license nonexclusive rights in the work without the other owner's consent, but she must share the proceeds from licensing the work equally with the other. All owners of a joint work must consent to license exclusive rights in it.

WORK FOR HIRE: DEFINING AN "EMPLOYEE"

If an employee creates copyrightable work in the course of her employment, it is work made for hire owned by the employer. In contrast, an independent contractor is not an employee and initially owns the copyright in any work she creates, whether or not done on assignment. Sometimes the distinction between an employee-employer relationship and an independent contractor-client relationship is not clear. Obviously, a writer earning a salary for working on an employer-defined scheduled and site, and under the control, direction, and supervision of the employer, is an employee. Typically, the employer withholds income and payroll taxes from the employee's paychecks and offers some employee benefits. These perquisites of traditional employment are a fair exchange, in the view of lawmakers, for the copyright in the employee's work product.

At the other end of the spectrum, a freelancer is not an employee if she receives an assignment and writes it in her own space, during hours

---

[16] Freelance contributors to periodicals might be presented with a work for hire agreement, which is discussed in Chapter 12.

she sets, in exchange for a fee from which tax is not withheld, who is not offered employee benefits, and who is legally free to accept assignments from unrelated parties. Clearly, she owns the copyright in her work product.

Some writers fall somewhere on the spectrum between these clear cases. Consider, for example, a contributing editor to a periodical, who works as a freelancer in her own space, receives no employment benefits, and pays her own taxes. These are clear indicia of an independent contractor. However, at the publisher's behest, she makes a regular submission of the same length on a defined topic that is regularly published for a set fee. In the 1980s, most courts would have ruled that such a writer, working under the direction and supervision and creating the works at the "instance and expense" of the publisher, was an employee. Even after the 1976 Act passed, courts continued to rely on precedent under the 1909 Act and common law that when a commissioning party exercised sufficient control and direction over a project, the writer became an employee for copyright purposes. Fortunately for freelance creators, the courts have since refined the distinction between an employee and an independent contractor. Writers and publishers now have fairly clear and consistent guidance on this question.

In 1989, the Supreme Court comprehensively laid out the relevant factors. In *Community for Creative Non-Violence v. Reid*, an artist was commissioned to create a sculpture for the Community for Creative Non-Violence (CCNV). CCNV's founder, who envisioned a modern Nativity scene with the Holy Family replaced by a homeless couple and infant, conceived the idea. Titled *Third World America*, the tableau was set on a steam grate with a legend reading "and still there is no room at the inn."

The parties did not enter a contract delineating their respective rights and obligations. Reid created the sculpture without charging a fee, receiving payments only to cover expenses. CCNV built the pedestal and gave Reid ideas and some creative direction as the work progressed. After the work was finished, a dispute over copyright ownership arose.

The Supreme Court ruled that whether someone is an "employee" under the Copyright Act depends on the common law of agency, which is primarily concerned with determining when one party's (the employee's) actions should be legally attributed to another party (the employer). Under the law of agency, a key factor is "the hiring party's right to control the manner and means by which the product is accomplished." The Court then listed the other relevant factors:

> The skill required of the creator
> Which party supplies the instrumentalities and tools used to make the work
> The location in which the work is done
> The length of the relationship between the parties
> Whether the hiring party has the right to assign additional projects to the hired party
> The extent of the hired party's discretion over when and how long to work
> The method of payment
> The hired party's discretion to hire and pay assistants
> Whether the work is part of the regular business of the hiring party
> Whether the hiring party is in business
> Whether the hiring party offers employee benefits to the creator
> The tax treatment of the hired party

Using these factors, Reid was ruled an independent contractor, and at least a joint owner with CCNV of the copyright to *Third World America*. Later courts have trimmed the list of factors to those that actually indicate whether there is an agency relationship in particular circumstances. These five of the *Reid* factors are considered most important:

> The hiring party's right to control the manner and means of creation
> The skill required of the hired person
> The provision of employee benefits
> The tax treatment of the hired party

Whether the hiring party has the right to assign additional projects to the hired party.

Even under this refined test, which most jurisdictions have adopted, the "contributing editor's" status in our example remains uncertain. To avoid disputes over ownership of the writer's work product, the parties ought to define their relationship in a written agreement.

WORK FOR HIRE: SPECIALLY COMMISSIONED OR ORDERED WORKS

An independent contractor can create a work for hire, but only if the work meets the necessary definition under the Act. For specially commissioned or ordered works, the parties must: 1. agree in a writing signed by both that the work is made for hire; and 2. the work must fall into one of the following categories:

A contribution to a collective work, such as a magazine, newspaper, encyclopedia, or anthology.

A contribution used as part of a motion picture or other audiovisual work.

A translation.

A compilation (i.e., a work formed by collecting and assembling pre-existing materials or data).

An instructional text.

A test.

Answer material for a test.

An atlas.

A supplementary work, defined as a work used to supplement another author's work for such purposes as illustrating, explaining, or assisting in the use of the embellished work. Examples include forewords, afterwards, pictorial illustrations, maps, charts, tables, editorial notes, appendixes, and indexes.

A freelance contribution to a collective work such as a magazine or newspaper is one of the nine eligible categories. But even though it is eligible, a freelance contribution cannot be a work for hire unless the parties agree in writing. Therefore, it is crucial that freelance contributors understand the terms to which they agree. Be wary of contract language such as "work-for-hire," "specially commissioned or ordered" work, or work to be done at the "instance and expense" of the publisher. Some courts have ruled that a written agreement creating a work for hire can be entered even after the work has been delivered. This means freelancers should not cash a check with an endorsement saying the payment is for a "work-for-hire" or similar language. Try to clarify the contract terms before starting work, and insist that any check endorsement conform to your understanding of the deal.

If, as an independent contractor, you prepare a specially ordered or commissioned work that is not one of the listed categories, it cannot technically be a work for hire. Similarly, if you create a work that falls into one of the categories, but do so independently of an explicit contract calling it a work for hire, the work cannot be made for hire. Even so, exercise caution in your dealings with commissioning parties. A court will look for ways to make a writer live up to the bargain she struck, so avoid signing an agreement that can reasonably be read to create a work for hire unless you really intend to give up your copyright.

Of course, in some cases, you might be more than willing to agree to create a commissioned work in one of the enumerated categories as a work for hire. If so, remember the consequences of not being the legal author when negotiating your fee. Unless you specifically agree to royalties or secondary use fees, your initial payment will be the only compensation you can expect ever to receive for the work. A basic rule of negotiating for writers is that the more rights in your work the other party wants to own, the more it should have to pay for them. Other negotiating points to consider in a work for hire agreement:

- Make sure that only one particular work is included in the contract. Do not include any future or past works created for the commissioning party.
- Limit the defined work product by describing specifically its length, medium, intended use, and any other distinguishing factors.
- If applicable, reserve the right to make sequels and other supplementary works related to the primary work and to exploit them in other media, such as television or movies.
- Consider providing that you will retain the copyright if the commissioning party rejects the work for any reason, unless it has paid the full agreed fee.
- If attribution of authorship is important to you, even if another party owns the copyright, ensure that it is included; otherwise, the commissioning party has no obligation to credit you.

JOINT WORKS

The question of joint authorship can arise in various creative relationships —with commissioning parties, freelance editors, book doctors, research assistants, dramaturges, and producers. After the 1989 *CCNV v. Reid* decision restricted commissioning parties' claims to authorship of others' works, some publishers and producers began to assert joint ownership with the creators they had retained. Authors of some great successes have faced claims of joint copyright from such professionals.

The Copyright Act defines a "joint work" as "a work prepared by two or more authors with the intention that their contributions be merged into inseparable or interdependent parts of a unitary whole." Examples of "insep-arable parts" of the work are joint contributions to a single novel or painting. Examples of "interdependent parts" are the lyrics and music of a song or the text and artwork in a children's picture book. Unless they agree otherwise, authors who create a joint work are co-owners of the undivided copyright in the work, meaning that each of them owns all the rights in the work, but shares them equally with the other. Each may freely license nonexclusive rights without the other's consent, subject only to the obligation to share equally all proceeds from licensing. But neither joint author is able to license *exclusive* rights to the work without the other's written agreement. The equal ownership of a joint work exists regardless of any difference in amount of the authors' respective contributions. Joint authorship does not, however, confer joint author status in derivative works based on the joint work.

In recent years courts have elaborated on the stark definition of "joint work" in the Act, giving some guidance to parties who make the mistake of collaborating without clarifying ownership rights before starting work. Chapter 16 explains collaboration agreements.

EACH CONTRIBUTION MUST BE COPYRIGHTABLE: THE CHILDRESS RULE

Clarice Taylor, an actress, wanted to produce and star in a play based on the life of the comedienne "Moms" Mabley. Taylor conducted significant his-torical research on which to build the play, but because she was not a writer, she hired Alice Childress to use her research and write the play in exchange for a fee. Throughout their short-lived collaboration, they discussed the play and the scenes together, but Childress alone wrote the script, which was never produced. After their collaboration ended, Taylor retained another writer to produce a play about the same subject. Childress claimed the new play infringed her copyright in the first play. Taylor defended her use of Childress's material by claiming she was a joint owner of the Childress play, and therefore had the right to use it in the second production. Taylor argued that although she did not write any of the first script, her significant research and discussions with the writer were enough of a contribution to entitle her to joint ownership status.

This case raised a fundamental question for courts grappling with joint authorship disputes: must *each* party claiming joint copyright as a coauthor contribute *independently copyrightable* elements to the work. If so, then collaborators who add extensive ideas and factual research—such as Ms. Taylor—have no share of copyright in the work. If not, then editors, peer reviewers who offer ideas and comments, and research assistants could conceivably claim an equal interest in the primary author's copyright. The Copyright Act does not define an "author," so it gives the courts no guidance to answer this question.

In 1991, the influential Second Circuit Court of Appeals decided against Taylor. It concluded that the "spirit of copyright" is better served by requiring all joint authors to make copyrightable contributions. Those making noncopyrightable contributions may protect their rights through contract. Under this logic, Taylor could not be a joint author because she had contributed only ideas and research, neither of which are copyrightable. The so-called Childress Rule is the law in most jurisdictions. Collaborators should not misread the Childress Rule, however. Although each joint author's contribution must be copyrightable, courts have ruled overwhelmingly that contributions need not be qualitatively or quantitatively equal to create joint ownership.

THE JOINT AUTHORS' INTENT

The second requirement to create joint authorship is the intent of *each* putative joint author at the time of creation of the contributions to regard themselves as joint authors. All parties must share this intention at the time of creation, although they need not understand the legal effects of joint authorship. An editor, for example, might meet the *Childress* test by contributing significant amounts of copyrightable material to a book, but neither she nor her author is likely to intend a joint author relationship.

In some cases, intent can be inferred from the coauthors' relatively equal contributions to the work (such as a song with lyrics by one person, music by another). When the respective contributions of each are very unbalanced, courts must consider other factors that illuminate the collaborators' intent. The 1998 case of *Thomson v. Larson* involved such an analysis. Thomson was a dramaturge who worked intensively with the playwright Jonathan Larson on revising his book and libretto for the musical *Rent*. Days before the play opened to great critical acclaim and commercial success, Larson died suddenly at age thirty-six. Thomson claimed she had contributed copyrightable material amounting to 9 percent of the work, and as such was entitled to share the copyright equally with Larson's estate.

The Second Circuit agreed with the trial court that Thomson had contributed significant copyrightable elements to the work, but concluded that Larson never intended to share authorship with his dramaturge. The court reviewed four factors to find the parties' intent. First was the contributors' decision-making authority over what changes were made and what was included in the work. Larson alone indisputably had this authority. Second, the parties' billing or credit was another significant, though not decisive, indicator of their intent, and Larson was named as "author" in every listing, Thomson as "dramaturge." The third factor was the parties' agreements, such as licenses, with third parties. Larson had entered several agreements as the sole author of *Rent* with the theater that had hired Thomson to help him. Thomson was not a party to them. Finally, additional testimony and letters showed that Larson steadfastly intended *Rent* to remain entirely his own project. For these reasons, the requisite intent of both collaborators to create a joint work was lacking, and Thomson's joint authorship claim failed. Instead, the court agreed with her fallback position that her contribution of significant (9 percent) copyrightable portions of the finished product entitled her to a corresponding share of the proceeds.[17]

Authors should try to avoid the kinds of disputes that led to the lawsuits described here. It is not difficult to do, especially compared to the agonizing costs in time and money of a lawsuit. The right time to protect your rights and interests is as early as possible after your intention to collaborate on a work becomes explicit. Whenever you collaborate, make sure at the appropriate time that you agree on who owns what rights in and control over the work. A collaboration agreement is the way to go; see chapter 16.

COPYRIGHT AND COMMUNITY PROPERTY

Community property laws exist in nine states—Arizona, California, Idaho, Louisiana, Nevada, New Mexico, Texas, Washington, and Wisconsin. While there are variations from state to state, community property laws make both spouses equal owners of property acquired during the marriage (with some exceptions, such as gifts or bequests). If you are or were married and now live or previously lived in one of these nine states, any property you acquired while living in one of these states is probably community property.

---

[17] The parties eventually settled.

The remaining forty-one states all provide for some form of "equitable distribution" of property acquired during a marriage upon divorce, which could be more or less than 50 percent of any asset awarded to the parties. If you should divorce, the question whether the copyright in works acquired during the marriage are community property or subject to equitable distribution will arise. The issue is complicated by the special nature of copyright ownership and the fact that the Copyright Act preempts conflicting state laws. Can a divorcing author be forced to become a joint copyright owner with the estranged spouse? If so, which of them would control the licensing and management of the work?

A California case, *In re Marriage of Worth*, examined the issue for the first time in 1987, when a husband argued that books he wrote during the marriage were not community property. The court rejected his argument that the federal Copyright Act, which vests copyright in the author (rather than jointly in the author and the author's spouse), preempts the state's community property laws. The state appellate court ruled:

> Our analysis begins with the general proposition that all property acquired during marriage is community property. Thus, there seems little doubt that any artistic work created during the marriage constitutes community property. . . . Since the copyrights derived from the literary efforts, time and skill of husband during the marriage, such copyrights and related tangible benefits must be considered community property.

Worth left unresolved such questions as who has the right to renew a copyright or terminate a grant of rights once a copyright is designated community property. More recently, in 2000, a federal appeals court resolved those questions in *Rodrigue v. Rodrigue*, when it held that the creator of copyrighted works can maintain all the ownership rights of copyright—that is, control and management of the works—but that the spouse must be awarded the ownership right to receive half of all the economic rewards from the works (including any derivative works). Whether other courts will agree with that court's analysis remains to be seen. The obvious solution to this uncertainty, analogous to a collaboration agreement, is a pre- or postnuptial agreement that provides for the division of proceeds from, and the ownership and control of, copyrights acquired before and during the marriage.

COPYRIGHT: INFRINGEMENT,

LITIGATION, AND FAIR USE

The purposes of copyright—to promote the advancement of culture by providing an economic incentive to create art and literature—require that copyright owners be able to enforce their exclusive rights. With some important exceptions, anyone who exploits an owner's rights without permission commits copyright infringement, and the Copyright Act directs the courts to punish it harshly. The penalties can include a court order restraining further uses of the work, impoundment and/or destruction of unauthorized works, and money damages calculated in various ways, even when the infringer did not intend to infringe. Including infringed material in a book or article may also constitute a material breach of the infringer's publishing contract and may make her liable for her publishers' losses and attorneys' fees as well as for her own.

This chapter describes the procedure followed in an infringement lawsuit, the elements of an infringement claim, and other key legal concepts. It explains how authors can use self-help to stop infringements of their own works on the Internet. It then covers the all-important fair use exception to infringement, how fair use works in practice for writers, and how to obtain permission to use copyrighted works in ways that exceed fair use.

LEGAL PROCEDURE IN INFRINGEMENT SUITS

Similar to every civil litigation, proving infringement and defenses such as fair use requires evidence that the parties gather through pretrial discovery, which can include document exchanges, sworn testimony in deposition questioning conducted by the lawyers, written responses to each others' interrogatories, trial testimony, and the courts' comparisons of the original and alleged infringing works. The plaintiff has the burden of proving the elements of infringement by a preponderance (that is, more than 50 percent) of the evidence; the defendant must prove its defenses, including fair use. If the plaintiff fails to prove its case, the defendant does not need to proffer a defense. The elements of and defenses to infringement present both legal and factual questions. The judge decides legal issues. Fact issues are usually decided by juries, but parties frequently ask judges to step in before the jury's fact finding role and issue a summary judgment before trial, based on the evidence presented, that no genuine issue of material fact exists and a ruling is appropriate as a matter of law. In some cases, a judge might rule at the outset that the plaintiff has failed to state a legally cognizable claim and dismiss the case based solely on deficiencies in the claims raised by the defendant on a motion to dismiss the complaint.

All copyright suits in the United States must be brought in federal district court. The twelve federal appellate courts of the nation, called Courts of Appeals, strongly influence the practice of copyright law because they devise the tests and standards interpreting the statute. The district courts must follow the precedents of the Court of Appeals covering their geographic jurisdictions (called Circuits), and of course all courts must follow the rulings of the ultimate appeals court, the Supreme Court. The appellate courts of the Second and Ninth Circuits, covering New York and the West Coast respectively, deal frequently with copyright cases, and therefore their rulings are influential throughout the country.

THE ELEMENTS OF INFRINGEMENT

In order for a court to find an infringement, it must determine that: (1) the plaintiff owns the copyright or at least one of the exclusive rights in the work; and (2) the alleged infringer actually copied the protected work or exercised an exclusive right held by the plaintiff. To show that the allegedly infringing work was copied, the plaintiff must show that it is "substantially similar" to the original work. Proving the defendant copied some or even most of a work is only part of the battle. The plaintiff still must prove that the alleged infringing work copied enough of the expressive elements of the original work to warrant liability. In other words, the appearance of similar plot elements, stock characters, descriptions of facts, and *scènes à faire*[18] in two works is not, in itself, proof of infringement. Remember, copyright does not protect ideas, facts, discoveries, concepts, processes and procedures, and works in the public domain; it protects only the original expression in which these are embodied. Many writers have sued for infringement only to learn the hard way that the copied elements of their works were unprotected ideas or facts, not protected expression.

OWNERSHIP

The plaintiff must show it owns the copyright or at least one of the exclusive rights of copyright. A licensee of a specific exclusive right under copyright, such as a publisher, has the right to sue for infringement of that particular right, but it may not sue for an unauthorized use that it has not licensed. If the owner registered the copyright within five years of first publication, the certificate of registration serves as presumptive proof of the validity of the owner's copyright and of the facts stated on the certificate. The defendant may rebut that presumption with evidence to the contrary, but the burden of doing so rests on the defendant.

COPYING

Copyright protects against the actual copying of a protected work, but not against the independent creation of a similar or even an identical work. Therefore, infringement cannot have happened unless the defendant actually copied the protected work, whether deliberately or unconsciously. Given the difficulty plaintiffs often face in producing direct proof of actual copying, some courts will accept evidence that the defendant had access to the work and that the alleged infringing work bears enough similarity to the original (known in legal parlance as "probative similarity") that a jury may conclude actual copying must have occurred.

---

[18] A leading court has defined *scènes à faire* as "incidents, characters or settings which are as a practical matter indispensable, or at least standard, in the treatment of a given topic."

ACCESS TO THE ORIGINAL WORK

In some cases, access is not so difficult to prove. If the original work was nationally distributed, broadcast repeatedly, or freely available online, a court might readily accept that a person with a television or Internet connection at the time in question had access to the work. Without direct proof of access, courts can consider circumstantial evidence, such as correspondence to or from a publisher or producer (e.g., submission or rejection letters) to conclude that a defendant had access to the work. In some circuits, courts may infer that a defendant must have copied the original based solely on such a "striking similarity" between the works as to preclude the possibility of independent creation. When a mistake or a deliberately placed non sequitur appears in both the original and the second work, a court is more likely to draw that inference.

SUBSTANTIAL SIMILARITY

Direct proof or striking similarity shows that actual copying took place. But, substantial similarity, needed to show infringement, requires a deeper analysis. It means the appropriation was wrongful, that is, that a substantial amount of original, copyrighted expression was copied. Copyright would be toothless as an incentive to create if it protected only against complete verbatim copying. On the other hand, no copyright owner has a monopoly on the ideas or facts expressed in her work. The amount of copying, both qualitative and quantitative, required to rise to the level of infringement depends in part on the amount of creativity or originality in the protected work. The more creative the original work, the less copying is necessary to make the second work substantially similar. The less creative the original, the more copying is necessary to prove substantial similarity.

In the classic description of the substantial similarity test written in 1930, Judge Learned Hand explained that every work can be abstracted on several levels, from the most general statement of what the work is about to complete verbatim reproduction. Between these abstractions lies the boundary between uncopyrightable ideas and their copyrightable expression and in turn, between an original new work and a substantially similar infringing work:

> Upon any work . . . a great number of patterns of increasing generality will fit equally well, as more and more of the incident is left out. The last may

perhaps be no more than the most general statement of what the [work] is about, and at times might consist of only its title; but there is a point in this series of abstractions where they are no longer protected, since otherwise the [author] could prevent the use of his "ideas," to which, apart from their expression, his property is never extended.

Although no bright line test separates unprotected ideas and protected expression, it is clear that altering some text or visual or aural parts of a work—10, 25, even 75 percent—will not avoid infringement if the jury or judge decides that more than a *de mimimus* amount of the protected elements of the work has been copied. Different courts use several different tests, and sometimes employ expert testimony, to determine substantial similarity. Depending on the nature of the work and of the alleged infringement, courts often use an "ordinary observer" test, that is, whether an average lay observer, comparing the two works, would recognize the alleged copy as having been taken from the original. If the nature of the works is more complex, courts might allow expert testimony on the theory that a specialized group, not the general public, was the intended audience. For narrative works, courts look for similarities in the text, format, plot, structure, sequence, and other protected elements, such as well-developed characters. For works including literary, visual, audio or multimedia, the test might be whether the "total concept and feel" of a work has been copied. The total concept and feel test can be further divided into "extrinsic" and "intrinsic" tests: the "extrinsic" test analytically dissects the expressive elements of each of the two works and often requires expert testimony. The intrinsic test depends again on the reaction of the "ordinary observer."

The choice of test employed by a court, and the makeup of a jury comparing two works, can easily determine the outcome, and any of the tests can err in the result, either by finding infringement because a significant amount of unprotected ideas or facts were copied, or by allowing superficial changes in a second work to mask the misappropriation of expressive elements of the first. Two examples illustrate how courts approach this fundamental issue.

In 2001, author Alice Randall and her publisher were about to release *The Wind Done Gone* ("TWDG"), the story of *Gone With the Wind* ("GWTW") narrated from the point of view of a slave. *TWDG* is a harsh critique of Margaret Mitchell's depiction of slavery and the antebellum

South. Mitchell's estate sued for an order prohibiting the publication of *TWDG*. Although the defendants ultimately proved their work was fair use, their argument that the works were not "substantially similar" failed. The appellate court found that Randall's depiction of fifteen of *GWTW*'s main characters and their relationships, the plot, and several famous scenes, though acidly reimagined, renamed, and retold from the narrator's view, contained enough of Mitchell's protected expression to make the books substantially similar. "While we agree . . . that the characters, setting and plot taken from *GWTW* are vested with a new significance when viewed through the character of [*TWDG*'s narrator], it does not change the fact that they are the very same copyrighted characters, setting and plot."

In another example, the Second Circuit held that *The Seinfeld Aptitude Test*, a novelty book containing more than 600 trivia questions about the characters, scenes, and plots from eighty-four episodes of the long-running TV show *Seinfeld*, substantially copied protected elements of the fictional show. The court chose to view the TV series as a whole, rather than comparing the small quantity of copied elements from each of eighty-four episodes separately. Every reference to any episode of *Seinfeld* was found to have copied from the series. Through this lens, the book was held to be substantially similar to the expressive elements in the series.

DAMAGES FOR INFRINGEMENT

The Copyright Act dictates the required penalties and monetary awards for infringement, and they can be quite significant.[19] A successful plaintiff can recover her own actual market loss caused by the infringement, *plus* any additional profits earned by the infringing work. If the owner registered the work within three months of publication (or for unpublished works, at any time before the infringement), then in lieu of having to prove actual damages she may opt for "statutory damages," which the court has discretion to decide within the range of $750 to $30,000 for each infringed work.[20] Courts may decrease statutory damages to as little

---

[19] Critics of the scope and duration of copyright point to the heavy liabilities required by the Copyright Act to illustrate the chilling effect of copyright on users who might otherwise legitimately employ fair use or other exceptions.

[20] A defendant has the right to ask a jury, not a judge, to determine statutory damages.

as $200 per infringed work if the original work did not have a copyright notice and the infringer shows it did not intend to or know it was infringing, and may increase them to as much as $150,000 for each infringed work if the infringement is found to have been willful. "Willful" is not defined in the statute, but courts have defined it as knowing or reckless. Juries have found that attempting to hide or deny an infringement can amount to willfulness. For example, a jury leveled a verdict of almost $2 million—$80,000 per infringed work—against a woman it found to have willfully infringed twenty-four sound recordings through file-sharing software. The jury decided that she had lied and tried to cover her tracks online when first approached by the plaintiffs.[21]

In addition to money damages, the Act allows for court orders prohibiting additional infringement, impoundment and disposal or destruction of infringing works, court costs, and, for timely registered works, attorneys' fees.[22] Attorneys' fees can amount to hundreds of thousands of dollars or more for cases that go to trial, so registering copyright within three months of publication not only makes it easier for plaintiffs to sue, but also creates a strong deterrent against infringement. The Supreme Court has read the Act also to allow attorneys' fees awards to defendants who prevail in infringement suits.

STATUTE OF LIMITATIONS

The statute of limitations for a copyright infringement claim is three years from the time the claim "accrued." That means that, in most cases, a claim that arose more than three years ago is time-barred and cannot be asserted against the infringer, though a court might "toll" (i.e., extend) the statute if a defendant fraudulently concealed the infringement. Fixing the accrual date of a claim is not only significant for determining whether a claim can be made at all but can make a world of difference in damage calculations when an infringement continued, but was not discovered, for more than three years. Most courts have adopted the "discovery rule," meaning that

---

[21] The judge in the case reduced the award significantly, calling it "monstrous and shocking." The verdict was handed down during a second trial of the case. After a third trial, the Court of Appeals reinstated a $222,000 verdict from an earlier trial. *Capitol v. Thomas-Rasset*, 692 F.3d 899 (8th Cir. 2012). The United States Supreme Court declined to reconsider that decision; certiorari was denied on February 11, 2013.

[22] Moreover, the Act provides criminal penalties for cases of willful infringement prosecuted by the government.

THE WRITER'S LEGAL GUIDE **54**

the clock does not start until the plaintiff discovered, or with reasonable diligence should have discovered, the infringement, even when it began more than three years before suit. Other courts allow claims to be made and damages awarded only for acts that occurred within the three-year window immediately prior to the date of filing.

The best practice for copyright owners is to exercise diligence to detect unauthorized uses; at the very least, set up a Google Alert or other search engine equivalents for your name and for key words or phrases from your work, so you can discover when they appear online.

WHO IS LIABLE FOR INFRINGEMENT? SECONDARY LIABILITY?

Lawyers call copyright infringement a "strict liability" tort, meaning that infringers are liable whether or not they intentionally copied or knew they were infringing.[23] Strict liability means the publisher of an infringing work is liable even when its author guaranteed its authenticity. By the same token, any party who knowingly assists or induces another party to infringe copyright can be held equally liable as a contributor to the infringement. Even a party who does not knowingly help another infringe copyright, but who is in a position to stop the infringement and receives a financial benefit from it, can be held "vicariously liable." For example, a swap meet operator was held to be contributorily liable for the sale of pirated works at the swap meet. The operators of file-sharing systems that enabled the exchange of copyrighted music, both on a peer-to-peer and a centralized basis, were held fully responsible for their users' infringement.[24] But courts do not extend secondary liability to every actor in the chain of infringement. For example, the Ninth Circuit recently affirmed the dismissal of claims by a purveyor of copyrighted photos against the banks that processed payments for websites selling infringing access to the photos.

Liability for infringement damages among co-infringers can be assessed jointly and severally, meaning that each defendant is potentially liable for

---

[23] Intent does affect the calculation of money damages, however.

[24] The Digital Millennium Copyright Act (DMCA) of 1998 exempts Internet service providers and websites from contributory and vicarious liability if they provide a means for copyright owners to notify them of users' infringements through their services and expeditiously remove alleged infringing works. See below for more on the DMCA.

up to the full award. The judgment creditor may choose to collect up to the entire damage award from either the direct infringer or the secondarily liable party, regardless of that party's relative responsibility.[25] For example, a publisher and a printer might each be jointly and severally liable for all damages if the publisher wrongfully authorizes the reprint of a book in which it no longer has rights.

The limited liability normally gained by forming a corporation is not necessarily a shield against individual liability in a copyright infringement lawsuit. When a corporate officer participates in the infringement, uses the corporation to carry out an infringement, or is the dominant influence over the corporation, courts are likely to "pierce the corporate veil" and impose personal liability. Likewise, an employee who commits or causes its employer to commit infringement might be held personally liable, and the employer can still be responsible as a contributory or vicarious infringer.

STATES AND STATE ENTITIES IMMUNE

A series of decisions by the US Supreme Court in the late 1990s significantly increased states' rights by making them immune from lawsuits by private parties to enforce federal rights, including copyright. In 1999, a divided Court ruled that unless states explicitly agree to be sued by private citizens to enforce federal claims—including intellectual property rights—the states' Eleventh Amendment sovereign immunity shields them from such lawsuits. Following the holding, the Fifth Circuit Court of Appeals dismissed an infringement lawsuit against the University of Houston press brought by author Denise Chavez, because the university, as an instrumentality of the state, was immune from liability under Supreme Court precedent. These rulings mean that states, state-owned entities (such as state university presses and educational institutions), and their employees cannot be sued for damages if they infringe copyright. Injured plaintiffs may ask only for injunctive relief against states. Subsequent attempts by Congress to remedy these holdings have been rejected by the Supreme Court as unconstitutional.

---

[25] Contributory or vicarious infringers are generally not responsible for the other defendants' profits, however.

SELF-HELP FOR ONLINE INFRINGEMENT

Have you discovered your work copied in full on an ad-heavy website, read or performed on YouTube, or emailed to untold numbers, without your knowledge, permission, attribution, or compensation? Many writers are happy to have their work widely distributed, but it is reasonable to want to do so on your own terms. It is easy enough to find your work on the web, but ascertaining whether its appearance represents an infringement, and if so, stopping it, requires some work.

After years of lobbying by online service providers concerned that their customers' unfettered infringements could expose them to massive vicarious and contributory liability, Congress amended the Copyright Act in 1998 by passing the Digital Millennium Copyright Act. The DMCA provides safe harbor to online service providers (including Internet service providers, website hosts, social media sites, search engines, and portals) when they passively and unknowingly facilitate their users' infringement. Copyright owners may not sue service providers for money damages or an injunction as long as the service provides a straightforward method to address and stop infringement through their services. They must also publish and enforce a policy of removing repeat infringers from their services.

If your work appears on a website or a social networking site links to your work on an authorized site, neither case is necessarily an infringement. Your publisher might have the right to grant sublicenses to post your work online and might have done so. Refer to your contract or ask your publisher. If the work is an excerpt from a book that is still in print and the contract was signed later than the mid-1990s, your publisher probably has some electronic rights and may have sublicensed them. A contract for a freelance article published after 1995 also probably grants digital rights to the publisher. But if your contract does not explicitly set forth a grant of digital rights or there is no written contract, then you probably own them.

If you find your work posted online and you granted the right to publish online to your publisher, notify the publisher and inquire whether permission was granted. If the publisher has the rights but did not grant permission, ask them to have the work removed by taking the steps described below. If the publisher has properly granted permission, your contract might entitle you to a share of any license fees. If you kept the electronic or digital rights, you have the right to notify the online service provider or website that you own the work and to demand that it remove your work from the site. Under the DMCA, the service provider must "expeditiously" remove the work on receipt of your notice and take down demand.

Tracking down the service provider can sometime be fairly easy; other times they are underground, hidden behind many layers of false and anonymous registrations. If the infringement appears on a website, including a social media site, review the site's terms and conditions or copyright policy to find the contact for copyright notices. If the site does not post this information, go to www.internic.net/whois.html, the site of the organization that registers virtually every site on the Internet. Enter the infringing site's URL to find its contact information and, more important, the name of the host service provider that has the ability and the obligation to take down the infringing work.

To qualify for immunity, a service provider also must drop repeat infringers from its service, publish its policy of terminating repeat infringers, and accommodate "standard technical measures" used to protect copyrighted works. You can easily check on whether it has published its anti-infringement policy. Service providers also must assign a designated agent to receive notice of infringement claims on their behalf. The identity and address of the agent should appear on the service provider's site and/or with the Copyright Office.

Once you have the correct agent's address or other method of contact specified by the service provider, you or your representative must send written notification of the infringement and demand that it be removed. Frequently, you may do this by email, but be sure to keep copies of your correspondence. Many providers post their copyright policy prominently via their home pages specifying the information they need from you. At a minimum, your notice should identify the copyrighted work being infringed, identify the material that contains the infringement, provide sufficient information to allow the service provider to locate the material (for example, the specific URL of the page where the infringement occurs), and provide your contact information. You also must certify that you are the copyright owner, or authorized to act on the owner's behalf, and believe that the appearance of your work on the site is unauthorized and is not a fair use.

When its agent receives this notice, the service provider must "expeditiously" remove the infringed work or interrupt access to it. If you want to go further and sue the infringer, the law makes it fairly easy to subpoena the provider for the infringer's identity. After the service provider has removed or disabled the offending material, it must promptly inform the alleged infringer of the change. If the alleged infringer claims in writing that a mistake has been made, the service provider, after informing you, must replace or permit access to the material within ten days, unless you bring a lawsuit to prevent restoration of the material. A true infringer is unlikely to respond in this way because the counter-notice must include its full contact information and agreement to submit to the jurisdiction of a court if sued.

If an online service provider has met all these legal requirements, you cannot recover damages from it regardless of how much damage the infringement caused. You may only sue for contributory liability if you can show that a service provider actually knew a subscriber was infringing your copyright, or that it supervised the content and received a specific benefit from its subscriber's infringement. (One exception to this exception: nonprofit institutions of higher education as long as they stop the piracy after learning of it.)

If a site actively encourages subscribers to upload others' published work, you should document that fact. Note any way in which the service provider might financially benefit from copying your work—charging a per-download fee, or using it to help sell merchandise or advertising. If it has done so, or has failed to comply with any of the DMCA safe harbor requirements described here, it could lose its immunity, leaving you able to seek recourse directly against this potentially deep pocket.

FAIR USE, THE PUBLIC DOMAIN, AND SECURING PERMISSION

Virtually every cultural creation borrows from and is built on works that came before it. If copyright's grant of a long-term monopoly over the use of original works were absolute, it would cripple, not promote, the development of culture, and it would violate the right of free expression. In fact, the copyright owner's rights are not absolute. Sections 107 through 120 of the Copyright Act exempt several specific activities from the prohibition on copying.[26] The most important exception to the owner's exclusive rights is the right of others to make fair use of a work, a centuries-old principle of

---

[26] Some of the exempted activities are library and archival copying to preserve works in danger of deterioration; use of sound recordings and instructional materials in long-distance teaching; and the "first sale doctrine" described in Chapter 2.

common law that courts devised based on the values underlying the First Amendment.

Congress wrote the fair use doctrine into the 1976 Copyright Act. Section 107 states: "the fair use of a copyrighted work . . . for purposes such as criticism, comment, news reporting, teaching (including multiple copies for classroom use), scholarship or research, is not an infringement of copyright." Technically, fair use is an affirmative defense to an infringement claim, meaning that an owner must prove infringement before the defendant must prove its use was fair. Note that the list of permissible fair use purposes in the Act is illustrative, not exclusive. Other purposes for which a user might copy an original work can and frequently are ruled fair uses. In theory at least, fair use is supposed to offer significant breathing space for all kinds of uses of copyrighted works.

Every fair use claim is decided on its particular facts in a four-part test set forth in the Act that is simple to state but challenging to apply and therefore requires some work to predict with confidence. One court complained that fair use is "so flexible as virtually to defy definition." But one thing is certain: simply quantifying the amount of an original work copied does not end the inquiry. The Supreme Court famously rejected a fair use claim when approximately 300 words were copied from a 200,000 word manuscript. By contrast, fair use has been repeatedly credited as a defense even when works were copied in their entirety, for purposes such as parody, criticism, archival preservation, online search facilitation, and illustration of a historical analysis.

The Copyright Act instructs courts to weigh each of the following four factors to determine whether an unauthorized appropriation of a copyrighted work is fair use and therefore noninfringing:

The purpose and character of the use, including whether the use is of a commercial nature or for nonprofit educational purposes;

The nature and character of the copyrighted work;

The amount and substantiality of the portion used in relation to the copyrighted work as a whole; and

The effect of the unauthorized use on the market for or value of the copyrighted work.

Courts may also consider other factors they deem relevant, but they must analyze all four statutory factors in any given case and weigh the results together, in light of the purposes of copyright.

Under common law and through the mid-1990s, courts followed the lead of the Supreme Court and tended to give the most weight to the fourth factor, "the degree in which the use may prejudice the sale, or diminish the profits, or supersede the objects, of the original work." In the same vein, the Supreme Court once opined that any commercial use was "presumptively unfair." Today, although the analysis in any given case can be complex, the inquiry into the economic effect on existing or realistically potential markets for the original work if the use were to become widespread remains an important factor. But beginning in 1990, with the publication of a seminal law review article by now-Second Circuit Appellate Judge Pierre Leval, the "transformative" nature of the use (i.e., whether it "transforms" the original by building upon it rather than simply taking its place) began to weigh more heavily relative to the effect on the original work's market. The Supreme Court soon adopted Judge Leval's argument that allowing the creation of transformative works, even when the use is commercial, advances the goal of copyright. In 1994, the Court defined "transformative" fair use to mean "add[ing] something new, with a further purpose or different character, altering the first with new expression, meaning or message" as opposed to "merely supersed[ing] the objects of the original creation." The weight given to any particular factor in the endless variety of factual situations presented is in the courts' discretion, but they must follow Supreme Court precedent. Thus, although the four factors interrelate in most cases and no one factor automatically trumps the others, recent fair use decisions tend to focus on whether a use was transformative. Even then, in every fair use analysis, courts will necessarily consider whether the user copied more of a work than necessary to realize the claimed objective.

Fair use questions arise for writers in a number of situations: use of historical works as background and reference for one's own work; quotations of passages from a work to illustrate its style, comment on its content, or compare it to another; parody; enhancement of a novel or essay with song lyrics or other quotations; inclusion of photos, drawings, maps and other images to illustrate text; downloading or copying articles and other materials to keep for easy reference, and others. Significantly, there are no hard and fast rules (i.e., not exceeding a specified word count) that can reliably apply to determine whether a given use is a fair use. Whether or not any particular copying is fair use must be determined through common sense application of the four factors, keeping in mind the nonexclusive list of statutory purposes.

The following descriptions of leading judicial decisions are intended to illustrate the permissible parameters around specific kinds of uses.

QUOTING OTHER WORKS

For a review or scholarly article analyzing a particular work or body of work, one generally has leeway to reproduce much of the subject work verbatim without infringing it. On the other hand, copying the "heart" of a work, even when it amounts to a small part of the whole, could fail the fair use test if it appropriates the original's intended audience or market. A landmark case involved the memoirs of Gerald Ford published by Harper & Row. The publisher had licensed the exclusive right to publish a 7500-word excerpt before book publication to *Time* magazine. Prior to *Time's* intended publication date, the *Nation* magazine got an embargoed copy and published an article paraphrasing a key passage and also containing about three hundred words copied verbatim from the memoirs—about .015 percent of the whole. The effect of this scoop was to preempt the *Time* excerpt, leading *Time* to cancel its deal with Harper & Row. The Supreme Court rejected the *Nation's* fair use defense. As required under the Act, the Court analyzed the four fair use factors:

1. *Purpose and Character of the Use:* Although its work arguably was for purposes of news reporting, scholarship or research, the *Nation* profited from exploiting the copyright without paying the customary license fee for serial rights.
2. *Nature of the Copyrighted Work:* Courts logically give greater protection to more creative works than to factual compilations or historical nonfiction. But even if not highly creative, if the copied work is unpublished, this factor will weigh against the user.
3. *Amount and Substantiality of Use:* Remarkably, the Court found 300 words from a 200,000 word manuscript to be the "heart of the book," i.e., Ford's internal deliberations about pardoning Richard Nixon. The Court also took the unusual step of comparing the 300 copied words in relation to the whole of the defendant's article of 2200 words.
4. *Effect on Potential Market or Value:* This factor weighed most heavily against the *Nation*. The negative effect on the market

for the work was manifest when *Time* withdrew from its licensing deal.

The moral for authors who want to quote from another work is that one simply cannot rely solely on the relative amount of the material to be copied. To be sure, if you are quoting a work, even extensively, to advance your analysis, illustrate a point, or comment on the quoted work or its ideas, you are more likely to be making fair use, particularly if you attribute the quote to its author. Purposes such as scholarship, criticism, and comment are at the core of what fair use supports, and they require incorporation of original source material for proper treatment of the subject. Quoting copyrighted material in historical works such as biographies is also likely to be fair use. On the other hand, if you use more than you need for such purposes, or cross the line into copying another author's expression to enliven your own writing (rather than to discuss something about the original) or avoid generating your own work, or if your copying is not otherwise serving one of the fair use purposes, you should seriously rethink your course of action. Either create your own expression of the ideas or facts found in the other work, seek permission from the owner, or consult a knowledgeable lawyer for an opinion on whether the copying is unfairly encroaching on the first work's value or audience.

USING IMAGES IN YOUR WORK

Where an established market exists for licensing photographs, drawings, maps or other images, incorporating them in a book, article, or website without permission is less likely to be fair use. But more important are the purposes for and the ways in which the images are used. To illustrate, an important 2006 decision by Second Circuit held that a publisher's reproduction of seven highly original concert posters, reduced to thumbnail size and placed on a timeline with other images and text to illustrate the history of The Grateful Dead, was fair use. The court reasoned that the publisher's purpose in using the images was "plainly different" from the posters' original purposes, which were "artistic expression" and concert promotion. The inclusion of the images had the beneficial purposes of enhancing the reader's understanding of the text and of serving as historical artifacts, both of which fulfilled a transformative purpose. Therefore, even though the copyright owner had a business in licensing images of the posters, the publisher's use did not impact the owner's potential to develop "traditional, reasonable or likely to be developed markets." The fact that the images were so reduced in size that the publisher did not usurp an existing market for reproduced posters was a key factor in the analysis.

A later case deemed the use of twenty-four magazine covers in a biography of the artist who created the cover art to be fair use. The images were used for a completely different purpose than the original purpose and only the covers, not the entirety of the magazines, had been copied. In the same vein, commenting on or reporting about images requires the reproduction of those images, and this practice is generally considered fair use. Note that the images themselves should be the topic on which the report comments, not the subject of the images. In other words, if the fact that the image exists is somehow newsworthy, using it is more likely to be fair than if the image simply illustrates the subject of the report. The latter use would generally require permission.

To illustrate this fine distinction, a few years before The Grateful Dead book case, the Ninth Circuit affirmed a ruling that the producers of a 16-hour film biography of Elvis Presley had used too much unauthorized copyrighted material for fair use. The film repeated numerous video and audio clips of Elvis's performances and appearances. The court held the purpose of the defendants' use was not only to illustrate historical references, which would have been fair use, but instead to "serve the same intrinsic entertainment value that is protected by plaintiffs' copyright." In particular, by showing 30-60 second clips of performances with minimal voiceover commentary, the filmmakers were found to have used more than they needed to make permissible transformative use.

PARODY

Whether a parody, which copies parts of a work in order to make fun of it, is fair use depends on whether it derives its value from what it copied of the original or from the new material added that makes it a parody. If the value comes mostly from the original work, applying the four factors is likely to result in infringement liability. The claimed parody must actually comment to a significant degree on the original, not use the original to comment on a different topic.[27] Below are the leading cases that illustrate this point.

---

[27] A leading copyright litigator offers this practical advice: a parody has a better chance in court if it makes the judge laugh.

In 1994, in *Campbell v. Acuff-Rose Music, Inc.,* the Supreme Court examined the rap group 2 Live Crew's takeoff on Roy Orbison's "Oh, Pretty Woman." 2 Live Crew called its song "Big Hairy Woman" and based it substantially on Orbison's work. In contrast to the original, "Big Hairy Woman" was blatantly comic and misogynistic. The album containing the song sold 250,000 copies. Refining its view of the "market effect" factor from the *Nation* case, the Court held that a parody of a copyrighted work can constitute fair use, even if purely commercial. In doing so, the Court redefined and increased the impact of the first fair use factor (the purpose and character of the defendant's use) to include the transformative nature of the use. The decision formally adopted Judge Leval's academic analysis and decreed that "the more transformative the new work, the less will be the significance of the other factors, like commercialism, that weigh against fair use." The Court defined parody as "the use of some elements of a prior author's composition to create a new one that, at least in part, comments on that author's work." Crucially, the Court distinguished a permissible parody from a work that has "no critical bearing on the substance or style of the original composition, [but is merely used] to get attention or avoid the drudgery in working up something fresh." It explained that in a true parody, the copyrighted work is the *object* of the parody, and not merely a vehicle with which to poke fun at a different target.

Following *Campbell,* the Second Circuit found fair use in the advertisement for the comedy film *Naked Gun 3*, which largely copied Annie Leibovitz's famous photo portrait of a pregnant and nude Demi Moore and superimposed actor Leslie Nielson's head on a pregnant model's body. The court observed with approval that at least one major purpose of the ad was to comment on the arguable "pretentiousness" of the original photo. By contrast, the Ninth Circuit held that a novelty book commenting on the 1995 O. J. Simpson murder trial using the style, characters, and rhyme scheme of Theodore Geisel's *The Cat in the Hat* was not a comment on the first work, but rather on a current event—a notorious murder trial. Therefore, it was not a parody of the first book and not fair use.

Later cases repeat the importance of this distinction in the analysis of a claimed transformative use. In *The Wind Done Gone* case, the appeals court found the retelling of *Gone With The Wind* by a slave character to be a pure transformative use, a parody that fulfilled a primary purpose of fair use: criticism and commentary on the original. In contrast, the *Seinfeld Aptitude*

Test book did not comment on or critique the original series, but instead tried to free ride on its success by creating a derivative work that would appeal to the show's fans.[28]

ARCHIVAL COPYING

Archival copying might be fair use if the copying is neither systematic nor institutional.[29] The Supreme Court established long ago that the individual recording of copyrighted broadcasts for the purpose of "time shifting," i.e., private viewing after broadcast, is fair use. More recently, the Second Circuit found no infringement by a Cablevision service that copies every program it provides on its own remote servers and allows its customers to access them any time for private viewing.

In a 1995 case, eighty-three publishers of scientific and technical journals sued Texaco for unauthorized archival copying of their journals by the company's large research staff. The court focused its fair use analysis on one typical employee who had photocopied eight articles for easy reference. The Second Circuit affirmed a district court decision rejecting fair use but limited the application of the lower court's analysis.

1. *Purpose and Character of the Use*: The employee had copied the work for the same reason for which Texaco would otherwise typically purchase a copy or license the work through a commercial database—to have it conveniently available for reference.
2. *Nature of the Copyrighted Work*: The law gives less protection to factual works, even highly advanced scientific research results that are expensive to publish, because of the great public interest in their dissemination.
3. *Amount and Substantiality of the Portion Used*: The defendant copied the articles in their entirety, so this factor weighed against fair use.
4. *Effect on the Potential Market or Value of the Copyrighted Work*: The publishers demonstrated harm to the value of their journals

---

[28] The facts of *The Wind Done Gone* and *Seinfeld Aptitude Test* cases are described above.

[29] In the UK and Canada, "fair use" *per se* does not exist but their copyright laws allow "fair dealing," a list of permitted uses of protected works that includes making copies for personal use.

from the loss of subscription and photocopy licensing revenue in long-established markets.

Balancing the factors, and noting that Texaco could readily have used available blanket licensing schemes, the Second Circuit rejected the fair use defense. In an amendment to its opinion, the court clarified that it limited the holding to the specific facts of the case, emphasizing that the systematic, institutional nature of the copying factored largely in its holding. Many observers take the amended opinion and additional factors as signals from the court that occasional archival copying by individuals, or for noncommercial purposes, is likely to be fair use.

As of this writing, a court in New York is considering an important fair use question in the Google Books suit led by the Authors Guild, which is described in chapter 14. The fair use question presented: does scanning entire copyrighted books and storing the texts in a digital database constitute fair use if only "snippets" (i.e., a few words) of the books are presented, along with ads, to Google users in response to their searches? An important element of the suit is the fact that Google gave copies of these scans in their entirety to the providing libraries without prior permission from the copyright owners.

EDUCATIONAL FAIR USE

One of the favored fair use purposes in the statute includes making "multiple copies for classroom use." After the 1976 Act passed, the Copyright Office convened the Conference on New Technological Uses of copyrighted works, a group representing the interests of authors, publishers, educators, and librarians, to help devise guidance on what this means. CONTU was concerned with the effect and the potential of photocopy technology on copyright owners' and users' interests. The Conference devised guidelines for classroom and library photocopying by nonprofit educational institutions. These guidelines, known as the CONTU Guidelines (www.cni.org/docs/infopols/CONTU.html), set forth the safe harbor conditions—that is, the minimum amount of educational copying permitted under fair use—but do not purport to define the maximum amount and frequency of copying allowed.

Under the CONTU guidelines, an individual teacher may copy portions of copyrighted works for a class if the copyright notice in the owner's name appears on the class materials and the use is not systematic (for example, done throughout a school system or for an entire semester). Systemic copying, including unauthorized copying of excerpts from books to create coursepacks, is not fair use. For educators who do not know whether a planned use of a work falls within fair use, the University of Texas has created an excellent, clear, and comprehensive explanation and "Rules of Thumb" for all kinds of educational uses: library uses, performance and display in face-to-face and long distance instruction, coursepacks, digitization, and multimedia uses. It is available at http://copyright.lib.utexas.edu/copypol2.html.

BEST PRACTICES IN FAIR USE GUIDES

Acknowledging that a lack of clear guidance and the harsh penalties for infringement together have a detrimental chilling effect on fair users, at least eight interested groups have taken action. Supported by the Center for Social Media, these groups have painstakingly devised codes of best practices in fair use for their specific vocations. They include poets, cinema and media studies writers, documentary filmmakers, media literacy educators, online video makers, open courseware creators, research and academic libraries, and makers of dance-related materials. The Center for Social Media has aggregated these codes and is actively working to facilitate more such codes for professions that need to make fair use in order to function. www.centerforsocialmedia.org/fair-use.

HOW TO GET PERMISSION TO COPY

Almost every publishing contract requires the author to warrant and represent that she has all rights necessary to include third party content in the work. This guarantee means that if you want to include a third party's materials, such as photos, illustrations, or maps, in your book or article, you must do one of three things: make fair use (or rely on another exception to copyright), use public domain work, or obtain permission to include the work from the holder of the copyright. This section briefly examines public domain status and then describes how to get permission to use materials if you need to do so.

WHAT IS IN THE PUBLIC DOMAIN?

If a work is in the public domain, anyone can use it however they wish without permission. In the United States, works published before January 1, 1923, works published without notice before 1978 (or 1989 in some cases), and works published before 1964 for which registration was not renewed are all in the public domain.[30] But it is not easy to know with certainty whether a work published after 1922 remains in copyright.[31] The peculiar way US copyright law has evolved makes determining the public domain status of a work complicated. For example, legislation passed in 1994 restored copyright protection in the United States to virtually every foreign work younger than 75 years old that entered the public domain because the owner did not observe American formalities of notice, registration, or renewal. Works published between January 1, 1978, and February 28, 1989, without notice might have forfeited copyright, but some of them may have been spared (see chapter 3). Unfortunately, the registration status of material published or registered before 1978 is not searchable in the Copyright Office's database or any other authoritative site. If you want to search those older copyright records, you must contact the Copyright Office and pay for the search or do it yourself in person.

Unless a work is clearly in the public domain or your proposed use is fair use or otherwise exempted under the Act, you will need to obtain legal permission to copy protected elements of it. To obtain permission, follow these steps: determine who owns the rights, contact the owner, negotiate permission to use the work for the duration, territories, and formats you need, possibly pay a fee, and document the permission in writing. It can take several weeks to several months to secure permission in the best case, so plan ahead and start as early as you can. The last thing you want is to have included third party material and be on the verge of delivering your work, or of publishing it, before you begin negotiations.

FINDING THE OWNER

If the work you want to include is obscure or unpublished it could be difficult, if not impossible, to find the owner.[32] Copyright registrations and all recorded assignments and licenses from January 1, 1978, to the present are

---

[30] Contrary to myth, the fact that a work is available via the Internet does not mean it is in the public domain.

[31] Appendix C is a chart that outlines the public domain or copyright status of a literary work depending on its age, publication date (if any) and registration status (if any).

[32] For several years, Congress has introduced, and failed to pass, so called "orphan works" legislation that would make it easier for users who make a diligent but fruitless search for an owner to use the work without facing harsh infringement liability.

searchable at the Copyright Office website, www.loc.gov/copyright/. (Of course, many copyrighted works are not registered and therefore will not appear in the Copyright Office's database.)

If the work in question is part of a published book that is in print, the publisher probably owns the exclusive right to grant permission; if the book is out of print, the publisher might direct you to the owner or her agent. Be aware that many publishers are notoriously slow to respond to permission requests. If you have trouble getting a response, your own publisher might be able to help you. The Authors Registry, a clearinghouse for payments to authors, has a database containing the contact information of more than thirty thousand authors and dozens of literary agencies. ((212) 563-6920 or staff@authorsregistry.org).

For song lyrics, you are less likely to prevail on a fair use claim even if you use only a couplet (although song titles are not protected by copyright). The music publisher probably owns the rights to a song's lyrics. If the Copyright Office's database does not reveal the claimant, try searching the databases offered by the major music performance rights associations: ASCAP, the American Society of Composers, Authors and Publishers, at www.ascap.com/ace/index.aspx; BMI, Broadcast Music, Inc., at www.bmi.com/search/; or SESAC, at www.sesac.com/Repertory/Terms.aspx. These groups do not grant permission to quote lyrics, but the databases provide contact information for the publisher or other claimants for the millions of songs in their repertoires.

Once you have found the owner, you can secure permission with a letter or email describing the project (including your publisher and the estimated print run), the material you want to use, the extent of the rights you need (that is, territory, formats, duration—which must at least mirror the rights you have granted to your publisher), whether exclusive or, more commonly, nonexclusive, the proposed credit line, and the permission fees, if any. Permission fees are negotiable and will vary depending on the amount and nature of the material you intend to use. Some publishers provide permissions kits to their authors, which include its preferred permission form and instructions. Once the owner indicates that it will grant permission, you should secure the license in writing.

The sample form below can be adapted to meet your particular situation by describing your proposed use clearly.

SAMPLE PERMISSION FORM

[Your name] (the "Licensee") is composing [your work, e.g., a book, play, article, etc.] tentatively entitled [Title] (the "Work") to be published [or produced] by [Publisher or producer]

For valuable consideration of [describe fee or other valuable exchange, if necessary], the receipt and adequacy of which is acknowledged, [Owner's name] (the "Licensor") hereby grants to the Licensee the [non-]exclusive right to reproduce [or translate or adapt] the following material (the "Material") in the Work in [specify media or formats, language(s), territory, time period, if any]:

Title: _____

Author: _____

Publisher: _____

Pages and/or lines: _____

Licensee shall not [or "may"] alter the Material without the prior written permission of the Licensor, and the Licensee shall include proper copyright notice and the following credit line in all versions of the Work:

_____.

Licensor warrants and represents that [she/he/it] has the sole and unrestricted right to make the grant contained in this agreement.

_____   _____
Licensor   Date

_____   _____
Licensee   Date

CREATIVE COMMONS LICENSES

Creative Commons (www.creativecommons.org) is a nonprofit service that makes it easy for copyright owners to license the right to use their works to the public without requiring any fee, subject to certain conditions. If you expect license to your own work to a paying publisher, including works licensed with a Creative Commons license might not be a feasible solution. If you include a Creative Commons work in yours, you must also "share alike," that is, subject your work to a similar free public license. It is unlikely that a commercial publisher would agree to that condition, but if you are self-publishing and want to disseminate your work widely for others to access and copy for no charge, a Creative Commons license is a convenient way to allow that.

CHAPTER 6

COPYRIGHT'S HISTORY

AND ITS FUTURE

Copyright protection is one of the most controversial issues of our time. Copyright creates tension between the interests of the public and those of creators and the industries that rely on it. The temporary monopoly given to creators denies the rest of society free access to literary resources, even as technological advances have made widespread dissemination and new ways to use works easier to accomplish every day. In recent years, that tension has escalated as the scope of works covered and the duration of the monopoly have grown dramatically. The music and film industries have grown more aggressive in prosecuting infringement and lobbying Congress for more tools by which to do so, and advocates for more access to knowledge have gotten more potent in mobilizing individuals and vocalizing their opposition to new copyright restrictions.

The Copyright Act in force today seems ill equipped to balance these competing interests effectively. It was passed when copyright owners' highest anxiety concerned photocopying technology—before personal computers became widespread and long before the Internet connected society across borders. Today, new and evolving methods to create, store, copy and deliver information are still governed by a law passed almost forty years ago and last amended significantly in 1998. While virtually any creative work can be digitally copied and transmitted in unlimited numbers or posted online instantly, these acts are subject to the same rules and penalties designed to remedy blatant plagiarism or the misappropriation of a manuscript by an unscrupulous publisher. As the term and scope of copyright protection have grown in the face of these new technologies, a groundswell of commentators and members of the public have argued, vehemently, that the purpose of copyright requires more, not less, access to creative works. At the same time, the copyright industry, including film, music, software producers and publishers, continues to lobby hard, often successfully, for stronger and longer protection. Would ending copyright as a monopoly and allowing more dissemination of literature, art, and other products of the mind better serve the public interest? Can the interests of the public and of creators be reconciled more effectively than the law currently allows? As owners and users of cultural works, writers have much at stake in the outcome of these issues. To put these questions into perspective, the following brief history of copyright attempts to describe some of the underlying forces that have shaped the law that governs our society today.

THE HISTORICAL UNDERPINNINGS

The ancient civilizations had no concept of copyright; the ownership of words was not distinct from the ownership of the papyrus or parchment containing the words. The Roman poet Martial complained that he received nothing when copies of his work were sold and coined the term *plagiarius* (which is Latin for "kidnapper") to describe a rival who had copied his work without attribution. Still, plagiarism was the norm, and even encouraged, for most of history. People did not consider literature as property, and had no trouble with the concept of borrowing from others. Many of Shakespeare's plays were openly based on previous works. A collective view of the products of creativity existed throughout the Middle Ages, when religious literature predominated; individual creativity was not rewarded and the reproduction of manuscripts rested in the dominion of the Church. It was only with the rise of the great universities in the twelfth and thirteenth centuries that lay writers began producing works on secular subjects. Extensive copying by trained scribes became the norm, but only the publishers could realize a profit by selling manuscripts to the wealthy.

Even before the introduction of movable type to the West in the fifteenth century, English publishers had formed a Brotherhood of Manuscript Producers in 1357 and received a charter from the Lord Mayor of London. Gutenberg's introduction of the printing press to the Western world in 1437 gave individual authors more opportunities for self-expression and the rise of printing techniques in England led to a growing demand for books. In 1483, Richard III lifted legal restrictions against foreigners if they happened to be printers, but within fifty years, the supply of books had so far exceeded demand for them that Henry VIII decreed that no person in England could legally purchase a book bound in a foreign nation. Henry's successor, Queen Mary, gave the Brotherhood of Manuscript Producers, now called the Stationers' Company, a charter—that is, a monopoly—over all book publishing in England. No writer could publish a book unless it was with a member of the Stationers' Company. The restriction served the Queen's purpose of preventing writings seditious to the Crown and heretical to the Church.

Under the Stationers' charter, the right of ownership in a literary work did not reside in the writer's creation, but solely in the printer's right to make copies of that creation. The Stationers' Company maintained its monopoly by clamping down on secret presses with the aid of repressive decrees from the Crown. Out of this monopoly, the recognition arose of a right to make copies of literary works as distinct from the ownership of the physical manuscript. This right was based in common law and had no expiration date as long as the Stationers' charter lasted.

Given its exclusive grip on the right to control the exploitation of printed works—even works of long-dead authors—the Stationers' Company objected vehemently when its charter and powers expired in 1694 and Scottish "pirates" began reprinting their titles and undercutting their prices. They lobbied the Crown for a new law, and eventually the Statute of Anne was enacted in 1710. Happily for individual creators, the law was largely crafted and promoted by writers, including Joseph Addison, Jonathan Swift, and Daniel Defoe. The Statute of Anne recognized authors' as well as publishers' interests and replaced the Stationers' perpetual common law monopoly with a statutory copyright for writers, who were permitted to sell their rights to publishers for a limited time, after which the rights expired. The goal of the Statute of Anne was to encourage "learned men to compose and write useful books." Booksellers and publishers objected to the term limits in the Statute and argued that their exclusive common law right to publish the books on their lists lasted forever. English jurists eventually ruled that the limited statutory copyright superseded the perpetual common law rights of printers.

Another effect of the Statute of Anne was to eliminate the use of copyright as a means of censorship. Any author could now legally sell his copyright to any publisher willing to invest in printing and distributing his work.

COPYRIGHT COMES TO AMERICA

The copyright law of the United States grew out of the Statute of Anne. Between 1783 and 1789, Noah Webster successfully helped lobby twelve of the original thirteen states to recognize copyright, but complained about having to travel to each state to register, because there was no legislative reciprocity among the Confederation of States. He urged the new Republic in 1789 to pass federal copyright protection. The US Constitution provided that "The Congress shall have the power . . . To promote the Progress of Science and the useful Arts, by securing for limited Times to Authors and Inventors the exclusive Right to their respective Writings and Discoveries." In crafting the Constitution, Thomas Jefferson and James Madison expressed ambivalence about the concept of a private monopoly over ideas and inventions. Their decision to include copyright rested on the "limited time" and private, as opposed to government, ownership of such monopolies.

In 1790, Congress enacted the first federal copyright statute, providing protection for books, maps, and charts for an initial term of fourteen years plus a renewal term of fourteen years, mirroring the term in the Statute of Anne. The renewal term only arose if the copyright owner took affirmative steps to file a renewal registration. Because most works did not retain economic value after their first term, they were not renewed and therefore entered the public domain. In 1831, Congress increased the initial term of copyright to twenty-eight years, plus a fourteen-year renewal term. In 1865, the law was amended to cover photographs and negatives. In 1870, it added coverage for paintings, drawings, sculptures, and models or designs of works of fine arts. In 1909, Congress completely revised the copyright law and expanded the exclusive rights granted to authors. The initial term of copyright remained twenty-eight years, but the renewal term was increased to twenty-eight years. For the first time, the right to make derivative works such as translations and abridgements was recognized as an exclusive right of the author.[33]

The 1909 Act as interpreted by the courts favored publishers' interests over those of authors. For example, the various rights to exploit a copyright were deemed indivisible, so an author's grant of publication rights had the effect of transferring the entire copyright to the publisher.[34] The courts also thwarted Congress's intent to allow the original author to enjoy the longer renewal term by enforcing agreements made during the original term to license away the renewal term, if one arose.[35]

The inventions of radio, television, motion pictures, satellites, software, and other innovations eventually required a complete revision of the 1909 Act, and the new Copyright Act of 1976 was passed as of January 1, 1978. Although subsequent amendments, such as the Digital Millennium Copyright Act of 1998, have tried to address the pressures of globalization and the development of new ways to make, copy, and deliver creative works, technology continues to outrun the law. Judicial interpretations of the Act, especially from the Second and Ninth Circuits and the Supreme Court, have had to try to fill the gaps in the law that fail to address the realities of the Information Age, with varying degrees of success.

INTERNATIONAL COPYRIGHT PROTECTION

Historically, copyright protection extended only within the nation of origin, that is, the country of first publication of the work. In the twentieth century, protection began to expand across national borders through treaties and bilateral agreements. Today, most countries, including almost all developed countries, offer some measure of copyright recognition of foreign works.

---

[33] In a notable judicial ruling from 1853, a court denied Harriet Beecher Stowe's infringement claim against an unauthorized publisher of a German translation of "Uncle Tom's Cabin," because derivative works were not recognized as part of a copyright.

[34] The 1976 Act specified that the "bundle of rights" bestowed on the author is severable and that the rights may be individually licensed. See chapter 2.

[35] The 1976 Act gave authors an expressly inalienable right to terminate grants of rights after 35 (for post-1977 works) or 56 (for pre-1978 work) years. The termination right is explained in chapter 2.

The US industries dependent on copyright consider international coverage to be acutely important. The export of copyrighted works is big business and remains a growing sector of the economy, one that faces widespread piracy abroad. But the stance of strong international protection was not always the prevailing view of the United States. In fact, from its founding, the United States was considered a "copyright island," even the "Barbary coast" of copyright. This attitude lasted until, after refusing to join for a hundred years, the United States signed the Berne Convention for the Protection of Literary and Artistic Works in 1989.[36] The United States had resisted joining Berne for several reasons: rivalries between American and British publishing houses; Berne's minimum standards requiring (at the time) at least a fifty-year term of protection and banning the formalities of notice, registration, recordation, and deposit; moral rights (the right to freedom from false attribution, improper editing or alterations, and mutilation, which has a long history in Europe and remains largely nonexistent in the United States); and so-called "national treatment" (the rule that member nations must protect foreign works to the same extent they protect domestic works). But the primary reason international copyright protection was not a high priority to US lawmakers was because until the late twentieth century, the United States was a net importer of copyrighted works.

The United States refused to join Berne in part because of its reliance on the cultural wealth of Europe. Through the nineteenth century, there was virtually no international market for American works, and between 1790 and 1891, foreign writers had no copyright protection in the United States. American publishers freely pirated the works of Dickens, Trollope, Hugo and many others. Dickens wrote of the "monstrous injustice" of foreign writers denied any royalties from brisk United States sales of their works. Adding to the injustice, American publishers could secure full international protection through the "back door" by simultaneously publishing a work in a Berne signatory, such as Canada, making the "country of origin" a Berne nation.

UNITED STATES PROTECTION FOR FOREIGN WORKS

As economics change, political accommodation is usually not far behind. As cheap British knockoffs, distributed without advances or royalties, began

---

[36] Chapter 2 describes the terms of Berne and other copyright treaties.

to undermine publishers and writers trying to market American literature abroad, Congress began to show interest in international copyright protection. After bearing the reputation as a copyright scofflaw for a hundred years, the United States finally passed the Chace Act in 1891, which allowed foreign writers to copyright their published works in the United States (and unpublished works of foreign origin to be protected in perpetuity under common law). But the Chace Act had a catch that essentially made US copyright recognition of foreign works illusory—the notorious "manufacturing clause." The manufacturing clause required that, to be eligible for copyright protection, foreign works must be printed from type set, negatives, or stone drawings made within the borders of the United States.

The 1909 Copyright Act treated foreign writers and publishers only slightly better. A foreign citizen could copyright a book in the United States as long as the writer actually lived in the United States when the book was first published and adhered to the unique American formalities of notice, registration, renewal, and deposit. The 1909 Act left the United States fundamentally at odds with both the specific tenets of the Berne Convention and the more liberal copyright protection offered by most Western European nations. Still unwilling to join Berne by 1952, the United States helped create the Universal Copyright Convention ("UCC"), which is still in force today. In most ways, the UCC merely codified existing American law. The only significant concession to foreign member countries was the abolition of the manufacturing clause with respect to UCC member nations. Under the UCC, works created by American nationals, regardless of where published, enjoy the same protection in any UCC member country that its local works receive. The United States retained its notice, registration, recordation, and deposit requirements, even though the few signatories that had such provisions had already abolished them. Despite its shortfalls, the UCC finally opened copyright relations between the United States and more than eighty countries.

In the mid–1980s, the United States attitude toward international recognition of copyright began to change more dramatically. Government research and the strong lobbies of the entertainment and publishing industries showed that American enterprises were suffering major losses from foreign piracy. As a result, the US finally joined the Berne Convention on March 1, 1989, accepting the (then) term of life-plus-fifty years and, significantly, abolishing most formalities.

Today, more copyrightable works are produced in the United States than in any other country, and they represent a substantial portion of United States exports. The US Chamber of Commerce estimates that approximately 19 million jobs in the United States are in the intellectual property industries. In the developing world, the piracy of US software and entertainment industry products is big business. The affected industries—film, music, software, book and periodical producers—are politically powerful. Because a substantial and growing portion of their profits come from foreign sales (a bright spot in the US economy's otherwise dismal balance of trade), they have vigorously demanded stronger worldwide protection, and the government has largely complied. The old US policy that encouraged American publishers to disseminate foreign works without paying the authors is long dead; combating the worldwide misappropriation of American intellectual property is now an urgent task for the government and the private sector. In addition to joining most of the world in the Universal Copyright and Berne Conventions, the United States has used other arenas to push aggressively for protection of its nationals' intellectual property interests, including trade sanctions, the World Trade Organization, and bilateral agreements.

The United States has promised to use trade sanctions and other economic weapons available under the General Agreement on Tariffs and Trade ("GATT") against nations that fail to protect United States intellectual property rights. Section 301, an amendment to the Trade Act of 1974, authorized the President to impose trade sanctions against any country that fails to protect American copyrights adequately or engages in unreasonable or unjustifiable trade practices. The World Trade Organization ("WTO"), which evolved from the Uruguay Round of GATT negotiations, came into force on January 1, 1995. One of its important elements is the standard that dictates the minimum levels of protection member countries must incorporate into their national intellectual property laws. In December 1994, the United States enacted a law to approve and implement the Uruguay Round agreements, including conforming amendments to United States copyright law.

In exchange for agreement on the minimum protection and enforcement provisions that nations, including Russia and China, were obligated to meet for membership in the WTO, the United States had to agree to restore copyright in foreign works that had fallen into the public domain because the owners had not observed the formalities of notice, registration, deposit or renewal prior to the passage of the 1976 Act. The United States restored copyright in these works on January 1, 1996. Restoration of formerly public domain works raised an outcry among many in the United States, including businesses that rely on exploiting such works. They sued the government on the theory that taking works out of the public domain violates both the "limited times" requirement of the copyright provision of the Constitution and the First Amendment. Remarkably, the case lasted twelve years, reached the Ninth Circuit twice, and the restoration of copyright to these works was finally upheld as constitutional by the Supreme Court in 2012.

RECENT EXPANSIONS OF COPYRIGHT: THE DMCA

With the rise of the Internet in everyday life, scholars and commentators have argued that the current copyright regime is both unfairly weighted in favor of owners and against the public interest, and ill-equipped to meet current and future technological challenges. Congress passed the Digital Millennium Copyright Act in 1998 in response to the reality that digital technology and the Internet makes it simple and free to obtain, copy, and widely redistribute copyrighted works. Copyright owners face a significant threat of having their works copied and distributed to a large audience instantly and without authorization. At the same time, digital, networked communication is an enormously valuable innovation for sharing information and entertainment to anyone with access to the web. It has tremendously enriched society and has the potential to build and distribute knowledge at ever increasing rates.

Many commentators have made the case that authors and societies benefit more if a large audience can enjoy copyrighted works with no barriers.[37] But for writers who need a publisher to distribute their works and to earn income from their writing, copyright is the only real mechanism by which to do so. The copyright lobby regards technological protections, such as encryption, "watermarking," and digital rights management systems, as necessary to control online distribution. Although these systems are far from foolproof and anyone determined to can defeat most technological

---

[37] Indeed, creators who choose these terms of dissemination can easily do so. For example, they can use a Creative Commons license to give the public free access to their works under certain simple conditions. See Chapter 5 for more about Creative Commons.

protections, they can significantly reduce infringement among most of the public and give publishers and distributors greater control over how their works are disseminated.

Thus, in addition to its "notice and take down" measures described in chapter 5, the DMCA made it a crime to circumvent encryption, digital rights management techniques, and other technical anticopying measures protecting copyrighted works. Circumvention of a digital "lock" is a crime even if done for noninfringing uses, such as to make fair use or to review a work in order to decide whether to purchase it, or to defeat malfunctioning encryption on a legally purchased copy. Understandably, many people, especially educators and librarians, bitterly protested the anticircumvention provision. They pointed out that it would give copyright owners, whose products are increasingly distributed in encrypted digital formats, a simple way to eliminate fair use with the force of criminal law.[38] Responding to the backlash, Congress devised a compromise. It delayed the effective date of the anticircumvention provisions for two years, during which time the Librarian of Congress was to exempt any classes of users that were, or were likely to be, adversely affected in their ability to make noninfringing uses. In October 2000, the Librarian exempted two categories of works from the prohibition: compilations of lists of websites blocked by filtering software applications, and literary works protected by access control technologies that fail to permit access because of malfunction or damage. Citizens may apply to the Librarian of Congress for an exemption from the circumvention prohibition every three years. The Librarian has since exempted several classes of users that demonstrated a legitimate need to circumvent encryption: anyone needing to access files in obsolete formats; film scholars needing to create clips from DVDs to teach more effectively; and later, documentarians, college teachers, film and media studies students, and noncommercial video creators needing to make fair use purposes.

THE BATTLE OVER TERM EXTENSION

In 1998, Congress added twenty years to the term of copyright protection for all works covered by the 1976 Act when it passed the Sonny

---

[38] In response to a First Amendment challenge, the Second Circuit ruled in 2001 that the anticircumvention provisions of the DMCA are not unconstitutional restraints on free speech to the extent they criminalize the publication of de-encrypting code.

Bono Copyright Term Extension Act.[39] Part of the rationale for extending the term was that it would equal those of many of the Berne countries, including the entire European Union and the United Kingdom. The EU had instructed members to deny the longer terms of protection to the works of nations that did not observe the same term. Congress wanted to secure the same term of protection for US copyright proprietors that their European counterparts have. Another justification Congress cited was that extending the term accounted for the increased life expectancies of the heirs of an author.

In *Eldred v. Ashcroft*, a group of public domain works publishers immediately challenged the constitutionality of the CTEA, arguing that it violated both the "limited times" requirement of copyright and the First Amendment by locking up for another twenty years millions of works that would have entered the public domain. The case reached the Supreme Court, which ruled in 2003 that although Congress had perhaps acted injudiciously, it had properly exercised its discretion to extend copyright because the term was literally "limited" in time. The Court opined that the Copyright Act complies with the First Amendment by not covering ideas and facts and by allowing fair use. Two separate dissenting opinions indicated that Court would not automatically accept future extensions of the term.

SOPA AND PIPA VERSUS THE INTERNET

In recent years, US intellectual property industries, including copyright owners and the makers of products with distinctive trademarks, have become worried about international websites that openly sell pirated films, software, games, music, books, and "knockoff" trademarked goods such as watches and handbags. Legally speaking, little can be done from here to prosecute or block the many foreign purveyors of pirated US goods. The industry came up short in court when it tried to go after the credit card companies that process sales of pirated goods and the search engines that

---

[39] Sonny Bono, a composer, producer, and recording artist, famously said the "limited times" of copyright should be "forever minus one day." He was elected to Congress in 1994 and sponsored term extension legislation. After he died in an accident in 1998, Congress thought to honor his memory by naming the CTEA after him.

help buyers find them. In 2012, the copyright lobby came close to convincing Congress to pass even more aggressive means by which to stop infringement on international websites by allowing the industry to target legitimate organizations that, through their normal operations, "facilitate" infringement by other websites.[40]

The Stop Online Piracy Act (SOPA) introduced in the House of Representatives and the Protect IP Act (PIPA) in the Senate would have given the Justice Department and private interests powerful new enforcement tools against international sites by targeting service providers and websites that associate with them. PIPA would have given corporations and the government the right to sue any website or service they alleged were "enabling" others' copyright infringement, whether in the United States or internationally. These "enabling" sites and services could have included search engines, blog sites, servers, DNS providers, directories, advertisers, payment processors or any other site that linked or pointed to an alleged pirate site. The copyright owners would have been empowered to devise a list of websites considered to be infringers, and the rest of the Internet community would have been legally required, on pain of injunction or lawsuit, to block them.

Shortly before Congress indicated it would enact these bills into law, the online community raised a sharp protest that went viral and grew rapidly. Big players such as Google and Wikipedia, and millions of individuals through online petitions, argued that SOPA and PIPA would lead to Internet censorship, security gaps, and stifle the creation of new websites and services that could face legal action if accused of enabling infringement by others. Wikipedia went "dark" on January 17, 2012, to protest the bills, bringing the controversy to the attention of the mainstream press and even more members of the public. Soon after, the White House signaled it would not sign the bills unless they were significantly amended to alleviate the censorship, security, and innovation concerns expressed by the public. Congress ultimately dropped the bills from consideration.

The demise of SOPA and PIPA seems to be a watershed event in the history of copyright expansion and enforcement. New bills have been

---

[40] Notably, the members of the Business Software Alliance, including Microsoft, Apple, and others, did not join their usual allies in the entertainment industry to support this legislation.

introduced to alleviate online piracy, though they do not have the teeth that SOPA and PIPA had, but the point is larger than specific bills. Many members of the public have made it clear to policymakers that they believe copyright has become unbalanced in protecting ownership interests to the detriment of the public, and that they are willing to challenge, with all the technology at their disposal, new attempts to expand the reach and enforcement of copyright. How the struggle will play out at this new level will affect writers' interests in unknowable ways.

CHAPTER 7

IDEA THEFT, MISATTRIBUTION,

REPUTATIONAL HARM: OTHER

PROTECTIONS FOR WRITERS

Most writers are sellers in a buyer's market. This reality puts any writer trying to shop her work and stay in favor with her publishers in a vulnerable position. It is well known in the publishing and entertainment industries that copyright does not protect the ideas embodied in a pitch or a query letter, and they may legally be taken and used by a recipient with impunity. Although doing so would be considered highly unethical in the trade book industry, it is not necessarily the same in the periodical, film, and game industries. As well, other kinds of unfair treatment are too often imposed on writers. For example, a manuscript might be edited beyond recognition and published under the writer's name, to the detriment of her reputation. A publisher might attribute one's work to a different, better-selling author, or assign a pseudonym to an author and then refuse to let her take it to another publisher for subsequent books. In the United States, legal protection against such abuses is limited. Not only does copyright law explicitly make ideas free for the taking, but it also prohibits claims under any other legal theory that deal with the same subject matter as copyright.

Nevertheless, aside from copyright, there are a few causes of legal action that can protect writers against some of these abuses. This chapter will describe laws dealing with the misappropriation of ideas and the legal doctrine of "unfair competition," which prohibits, among other things, the false designation of origin of a product, including a literary work. It will cover claims a writer might be able to bring for damage caused to her reputation, including defamation and invasion of the rights of privacy and publicity, and also describe the procedure by which a well-known writer can retrieve an Internet domain name identical (or very similar) to her name.

PROTECTION OF IDEAS

When Jeff Grosso finished film school, he had an idea for a script. He wrote *The Shell Game* based on his experiences working his way through school as a professional gambler. Seeking a buyer, Grosso saw the following listing in a 1997 Writer's Market Guide: "Gotham Entertainment Group . . . Buys 5/10 scripts a year . . . Query with completed script . . . Makes outright purchase . . . We have a deal with Miramax films . . ." He sent his script to Gotham (and to many others), got no response, and was surprised more than a year later to see that Miramax had released *Rounders,* the story of a professional gambler starring Matt Damon. Believing that Gotham and Miramax had "mined" his script for their film, Grosso sued for both copyright infringement and on another legal theory: breach of an "implied contract" to compensate him if his ideas were used.

The case was transferred from state to federal court, which has exclusive jurisdiction over copyright claims, and that court ruled that the script and the film were not substantially similar. The dismissal of his copyright claim left Grosso with only the argument that the producers had misappropriated his ideas. The court therefore had to examine his claim under the doctrine of copyright preemption.

COPYRIGHT PREEMPTION

When Congress passed the 1976 Copyright Act, it intended the scope of the law to be comprehensive and to eliminate all other laws regulating in the same arena. Not only did the 1976 Act establish the precept that nobody has the exclusive right to ideas, but it also explicitly preempted, that is, superseded, any claims in which a work at issue "come[s] within the subject matter of copyright" and in which state law recognizes "legal or equitable rights that are equivalent to any of the exclusive rights within the general scope of copyright." (Copyright Act, Section 107(a)) In practice, these tenets mean that the law does not recognize any claim, federal or state, alleging only that the defendant stole the plaintiff's idea. Ideas fall "within the subject matter of copyright" and are, to quote one court, "as free as the air," and a claim of idea theft is based on a right that is "equivalent to" a right "within the general scope of copyright." Thus, copyright preempts claims—notably, idea theft—for which it explicitly does not offer redress.

Preemption does not, however, give publishers and producers carte blanche to appropriate ideas offered to them without permission. It does mean that a claim involving idea theft must assert a right that is qualitatively different from the rights recognized by copyright. The claim must contain at least one element in addition to the bare assertion that a proprietary idea was used without permission. The additional element that courts credit most often is the allegation that the publisher agreed, either implicitly or explicitly, to compensate the writer for the use of her idea, and the claim is therefore for breach of contract. Courts also recognize a claim of "breach of confidence," which alleges that the defendant promised not to disclose an original idea conveyed in confidence in exchange for being privy to the idea.

These legal theories (which Grosso was permitted to allege but could not ultimately prove) require that a writer take steps so that she can prove a bilateral agreement actually exists either to pay for the use of, or not to disclose, her idea.

BREACH OF EXPRESS OR IMPLIED CONTRACT

An *express* agreement to pay for an idea, whether or not in writing, is relatively easy to prove. It must evidence that each side agrees that if the recipient of the idea uses it, the purveyor will be compensated. The more details provided in the contract about the payment offered and the uses that may be made, the more likely it is that a court will recognize an enforceable contract.

An *implied* contract is necessarily more difficult to prove. It requires proof of an expectation by both parties that the use of the idea will be compensated. To prove an implied contract, the circumstances surrounding the interaction must show that the writer disclosed the idea in order to sell it, that she expected to be compensated for the idea if it was used, and that the defendant knew the writer's conditions, had the opportunity to decline to receive the idea, and nonetheless accepted disclosure. As with any contract, a basic meeting of the minds is the sine qua non; thus, both parties must understand that the writer is disclosing the idea on the condition that she will be compensated if it is used. Whether those circumstances in fact exist depends on factors such as the particular industry's custom and practice, whether the pitch was solicited by the party receiving it, and the substance of the parties' communications around the conveyance of the idea.

If a publisher has affirmatively asked a writer to disclose her idea, courts are more likely to find an implied promise to pay if it is used. Some courts actually require that the recipient solicited the idea to find an implied contract. Others courts are more lenient and will recognize an implied contract if the writer gave advance notice that she expected compensation and gave the recipient the opportunity to decline receipt of the idea, such as by placing it in a sealed envelope with an explanatory cover letter. An implied contract might also arise if a publisher agrees to an author's verbal request not to use her idea without compensating or retaining her.

Even in the absence of a solicitation, request for payment in exchange for disclosure, or advance notice and an opportunity to decline, some claimants have argued that a promise to pay should be implied if industry custom dictates. Although no court has yet reportedly accepted this argument explicitly, some have implicitly adopted it, and California courts are increasingly giving the film and television industry practices a hard look in appropriate circumstances.[41]

In some states, including New York, courts require that the idea disclosed be "novel," that is, not formerly known. In 1988, the idea of portraying a close-knit, upper middle class African American family at the center of a situation comedy was held not to be novel, and so a writer who claimed that his idea was appropriated to create *The Cosby Show* was not able to show an implied contract to pay by the producer. But other states' courts eschew the novelty requirement if the idea disclosed was new to the recipient and the other factors show an agreement, or when a fiduciary relationship, such as that between author and agent, has led to the disclosure.

---

[41] Jeff Grosso could not prove the Writers Guide listing was a promise to pay, or even a solicitation to submit ideas. He had not included a request for payment with his submission and had had no further contact with any of the defendants. Although his case established that an implied promise to pay for an idea is not preempted by copyright under California law, his claims were ultimately dismissed without a trial for lack of proof.

BREACH OF CONFIDENCE

A breach of confidence alleges that the plaintiff disclosed truly novel and confidential information, that the defendant knew this and agreed to keep it confidential, and that the defendant disclosed that information in breach of the parties' understanding. As with an implied contract, showing a breach of confidence depends on the circumstances leading up to the disclosure and evidence of the parties' understanding.

PROTECTING YOUR IDEAS

If you simply send out an unsolicited proposal, screenplay treatment, or a detailed query letter, you are not likely to have any protection beyond what copyright provides. The recipient might like your ideas conveyed, but choose to retain a different person to express those ideas in a fully realized work. Although this practice is rare among reputable agents and book publishers, Hollywood and Silicon Valley have different industry standards and practices. To be fair, producers, publishers, and agents receive multitudes of ideas, many of them similar both to one another and to projects already in development. Therefore, except when dealing with reputable literary agents,[42] try to protect your interests with a contract when possible, or with a paper trail if a contract is not feasible.

The ideal contract is in writing and expressly provides for compensation if the recipient uses your idea. Such an agreement can be simple. For example, the following brief letter might do:

> Dear Sir/Madam,
> I understand it is your practice to entertain or receive program materials, ideas, or suggestions for [specify the market]. I have developed such a [indicate what will be submitted] for submission and would like to disclose this to you. I understand that if you use it, you will pay reasonable compensation and give appropriate credit to me based on current industry standards. If this understanding is correct, please advise me if I should send this submission to you.
>
> Yours, etc.

---

[42] See Chapter 15. Once you have engaged an agent, she has a fiduciary duty of loyalty to you and may not misappropriate your idea or otherwise break your confidence.

Although an express contract is the best way to protect your idea, it is unrealistic to expect most producers and publishers to agree to it for unsolicited works. In fact, after *Grosso v. Miramax*, many purchasers of literary property began to require writers submitting ideas, proposals, treatments, and manuscripts to sign releases before they will consider the submission. The typical release bars the writer from bringing any claim over the recipient's subsequent use of similar material and expressly acknowledges that the writer is aware that similar ideas may come from other sources. It usually stipulates the (small) maximum value of the material and the total recovery possible should the author sue and win despite the release. Naturally, you should exercise caution before signing such a release in order to submit your work. The risk might be worth taking, but due diligence is a must. Research the organization to determine its reputation in this area, and look for different entities to query that might accept your submission agreement.

If you cannot get an express agreement to compensate you for your idea or you must sign a release, consider writing some of the work before submitting it. The more complete your rendering of the idea when submitted, the more copyright protection the work will enjoy and the less incentive a publisher might have to use somebody else to flesh out your idea. It is also more likely to be protected under the implied contract theory.

As mentioned, one way to show an implied contract to pay for your idea is to give the recipient advance notice and an opportunity to decline your proposal. Place the proposal in a sealed envelope, and place that in a larger envelope with a cover letter informing the recipient that by opening the smaller envelope, it thereby agrees to compensate and/or retain you if it uses your idea. If you are meeting with a representative of the publisher or producer, bring a third party with you, and verbally set forth your conditions for disclosure and use of your ideas.[43] If the recipient agrees, your companion is a witness to the agreement. In this case, you should also create a paper trail by setting forth terms of agreement in a follow-up letter.

To demonstrate the date on which you created a film or television-related idea, register it with the Writers Guild of America, East or West

---

[43] It is the custom and practice in the entertainment and game industries to stop a verbal pitch or to quickly indicate no interest if the producer has a similar project already in development.

(described in Appendix A to chapter 1). These unions register film and television scripts, synopses, outlines, ideas, treatments, and scenarios in order to document the completion date and identity. The Writers Guild rules governing the treatment and use of writers' ideas govern the many film and TV producers that have collective bargaining agreements with the Writers Guild. You do not need to join the Writers Guild to register your work.

UNFAIR COMPETITION

The objective of federal and state trademark and unfair competition laws is to prevent a party from confusing the public in order to benefit from another's reputation. Misappropriation is a category of unfair competition used to prevent the unauthorized use of unique characteristics of a product. The Lanham Act, the federal trademark protection law, defines unfair competition as "any false designation of origin, false or misleading description [or representation] of fact" that is "likely to cause confusion . . . or to deceive as to affiliation, connection or association." State unfair competition laws are similar, but somewhat broader: "The essence of an unfair competition claim is that the defendant assembled a product which bears so striking a resemblance to the plaintiff's product that the public will be confused as to the identity of the products," according to New York's highest court.[44] Unfair competition claims can prevent the unauthorized use of a writer's character in a new work if it would cause confusion as to the source of the second work, prevent the false attribution of a work to someone other than the writer who created it, and allow a writer to prevent attribution to her for another's work or for a distorted version of her own work.

MISAPPROPRIATION OF CHARACTERS, TITLES, AND AUTHORS' NAMES

In the 1950s, the title of Ernest Hemingway's play *The Fifth Column* had acquired such a strong association with the author among the general public that a court forbade a producer from using the title *Fifth Column Squad* for an unrelated film. Hemingway's winning case was based on trademark misappropriation. The doctrine of misappropriation protects against the

---

[44] *Shaw v. Time-Life Records* (New York Court of Appeals, 1975).

unauthorized use of almost any mark imaginable that the public associates with a specific source of a product.[45] Marks protected by federal and/or common law trademark include specific phrases (e.g., "E.T. phone home"), logos, packaging, sounds (e.g., "Doh!" as uttered by Homer Simpson), even smells. Registration of a trademark is not necessary for full protection. A mark earns protection through its use in commerce in connection with a product sufficient to create an association in the minds of consumers. Protected marks can include property related to literature that copyright does not cover, such as the name, appearance, dress, and unique traits of literary characters, titles of series, and well-known authors' names.

Unfair competition laws exist to protect the public, not the creator of the mark. In a case from the 1930s that is still considered a good explanation of the doctrine, the proposed title of a motion picture was the same as the name of the main character in a well-known book series. A court enjoined the film's producer from using the proposed title:

> The plaintiff's copyrights do not cover the titles to the stories. . . . But a name that has become descriptive, and is closely identified in the public mind with the work of a particular author, may not, during the life of the copyright, be used *so as to mislead*. . . . Nor may such a name be used even after the expiration of the copyright, unless adequate explanation is given *to guard against mistake*. . . . In the present case, the name has become associated in the public mind solely and exclusively with the plaintiff's authorship; it is a name which is highly descriptive of his work; and ordinary principles of unfair competition are peculiarly applicable. (emphasis added).[46]

The key to proving misappropriation of a mark is to show that it has acquired secondary meaning and is associated by the public with a single source, and that the unauthorized use raises a likelihood of public confusion about the identity of the source. "Secondary meaning" means that the mark has become a resonant symbol of the source of a product. Marks that are not widely known, unique, or well established enough to have acquired secondary meaning are not protected. The strength of the mark depends on a combination of its uniqueness and the extent of its use in the marketplace. The more unique the mark, the less it needs to be used in

---

[45] For simplicity, the property covered by unfair competition is referred to here as "marks."
[46] *Patten v. Superior Talking Pictures* (S.D.N.Y. 1934).

commerce to acquire secondary meaning, and vice versa. The stronger the mark, the easier it is to prove the second element, a likelihood of confusion among the public. For example, the estate of Edgar Rice Burroughs successfully enjoined advertisements for a pornographic film called Tarz & Jane & Boy & Cheeta. Rightly or wrongly, the court saw the characters from Burroughs's works as having such strong secondary meaning that the public was likely to think the estate might have authorized the film. Here, as in many such cases, a prominent disclaimer on the second work might have alleviated the likelihood of confusion and thereby eliminated the claim.

Even marks that are well known might not be protectable if the public associates them with more than one source. For example, the longtime publisher of the Peter Rabbit books by Beatrix Potter could not legally prevent another writer from using some of Potter's original illustrations in his book. (The copyright had expired in Potter's works.) The court found that although the illustrations were identified with Beatrix Potter as the author, they were not sufficiently identified with the publisher of the books to justify an injunction.

FALSE ATTRIBUTION

False attribution, also known as "passing off" or "palming off," means the wrongful attribution to an author for a work that she did not write, essentially misappropriating her name. The doctrine has existed in common law for many decades; in 1816, representatives of Lord Byron successfully sued to prevent the publication of poems falsely attributed to him. As in other unfair competition cases, the wrongful use must be likely to cause public confusion as to the source of the product. For example, in the 1970s, the author Ken Follett wrote a series of bestsellers. A publisher for whom he had edited a book years earlier decided to capitalize on his newfound fame and reprint the early work with Follett's name given top billing, even though other writers had written most of the book. Follett sued to stop this misuse of his name. The court ruled that the publisher could not give greater billing to Follett than to the writers who had contributed more, because to do so would mislead the public and harm the author through the false attribution of others' work to him.

As in Follett's case, false attribution can involve material that was partially written by the person to whom authorship is attributed. This often happens with textbooks that are repeatedly revised over the years. In an extreme case, wrongful attribution might even be libelous. One such case involved Joseph Clevenger, a lawyer who wrote and edited *Clevenger's Annual Practice of New York* for more than thirty years. In 1956, he ended the association with his publisher and revoked the right to use his name as editor of subsequent editions. The publisher nonetheless put out a later edition trading on the established "Clevenger's" mark; the edition also stated that it was "Annually Revised" without revealing that the publisher's staff had made the revisions. Clevenger sued for libel, arguing that the public would attribute numerous mistakes in the text to his errors, harming his professional reputation. The court concluded that a jury might reasonably find that the wording and arrangement of the title page defamed him. Had Clevenger brought an unfair competition claim, he might not have prevailed if the cover had correctly stated that others had revised the book.

Passing off claims cannot be used to enlarge the proper scope of copyright protection, such as through the use of pen names. Samuel Clemens published some literary sketches but did not register the copyrights, and they therefore entered the public domain. Years later, they were published without his permission under the name Mark Twain. Although Clemens objected to the use of his pseudonym, arguing that it had become a trademark that could not be used without his permission, a federal court disagreed, holding that a pen name cannot give a writer more rights than he would have under his real name, and that there was no likelihood of confusion as to the source of the works.

NONATTRIBUTION OR "REVERSE PASSING OFF"

"Reverse passing off"—identifying a product with the wrong source—can apply in cases when a writer's work is not appropriately credited. As with other forms of unfair competition, the remedies for reverse passing off can include money damages and an injunction to prevent distribution of a mistakenly identified product. However, unfair competition law does not, by itself, entitle a writer to authorship credit if her publishing contract states otherwise. Various arrangements exist in the industry in which a writer agrees to work under a pseudonym or not to receive credit; these agreements are enforceable. One mass-market romance publisher is known to "assign" pseudonyms to its authors and then to reassign them at will to other authors. According to its contract, the first author may use her pseudonym with a different publisher only with permission. Although it seems intended to cause consumer confusion, this practice has not yet been tested in court.

Nor is it clear that a publishing contract that is silent about giving the writer credit requires attribution. Although the custom in trade book publishing is to attribute books to their authors, it has been held that a disclaimer or acknowledgment of a person's contributions to a work instead of authorship credit might be sufficient if it eliminates the likelihood of consumer confusion. The best practice is to make sure your contracts provide that your book or article will be published under your name. Doing so protects your interests in two ways; first, of course, is to ensure you receive appropriate credit. But attribution is also necessary to win recourse in an unfair competition case involving the unacceptable distortion of your work.

DISTORTION

The hallmark of unfair competition, misrepresenting the source of a particular product, includes attributing such a distorted version of an original that the attribution itself misleads the public. An infamous example of literary distortion was ABC's editing of episodes of *Monty Python's Flying Circus* for broadcast. In their original agreements with the BBC, the members of Monty Python had approval rights over changes to their scripts. When ABC bought the right to broadcast the episodes from the BBC, it cut twenty-four minutes from each ninety-minute program to make time for commercials. The result was a "gross distortion" of the sketches, according to the Second Circuit Court of Appeals. When the creators sued under the federal unfair competition act, the court wrote:

> The Lanham Act . . . has been invoked to prevent misrepresentations that may injure plaintiff's business or personal reputation. . . . It is sufficient to violate the Act that a representation of a product, although technically true, creates a false impression of the product's origin. . . . [When] a television network broadcasts a program properly designated as having been written and performed by a group, but which has been edited, without the writer's consent, into a form that departs substantially from the original work . . . [it] present[s] him to the public as the creator of a work not his own and thus makes him subject to criticism for work he has not done. . . . In such a case, it is the writer . . . rather than the network, who suffers the consequences of the mutilation. . . . Thus, an allegation that a defendant has presented to

the public a "garbled," distorted version of plaintiff's work seeks to redress the very rights sought to be protected by the Lanham Act.[47]

In this case, the Court held that even a prebroadcast disclaimer that the network had edited the works would not have protected the writers sufficiently because not all the viewers would have tuned in to the disclaimer. To be sure, the extent of ABC's distortion of the series was more profound than a garden variety disappointing editing job on a book or article. ABC had eliminated story lines and climactic moments in the drastically shortened episodes. A writer would face a high bar to legally challenge editorial changes in her work. As is usually the case, writers are better off preserving the right to approve of editorial revisions in their publishing contracts.

MORAL RIGHTS

Unlike France and other European countries, the United States does not recognize moral rights of writers.[48] The unfair competition claims described above are the closest thing to moral rights provided to writers in this country. Moral rights are derived from French civil law and are neither economic nor based on the ownership of intellectual property. Instead, they embody the belief that, regardless of who own the property rights in a creation, the creator should have control over its exploitation in order to protect her reputation and honor. The Berne Convention defines moral rights as:

> the right to claim authorship of the work and to object to any distortion, mutilation or other modification of, or other derogatory action in relation to, said work, which would be prejudicial to his honor or reputation.

In France, *droit moral* is perpetual and inalienable, meaning it cannot be lost or sold by the author. Moral rights give only the author the right to

---

[47] *Gilliam, et al. v. American Broadcast Company*, (2d Cir. 1976).

[48] In order to join the Berne Convention providing for reciprocal international recognition of copyright (described in Chapter 2), the United States had to recognize a minimal level of moral rights for visual artists, but not for writers. The US adopted this optional provision of the Berne Convention with respect to certain works of visual art under the Visual Artists Rights Act enacted in 1990.

decide when a work is completed and should be made public. The author even has the right to reconsider and retract the work from public distribution after publication, although she must pay in advance for the losses such a withdrawal will cause the party that has the distribution rights. The right of paternity, a variety of moral rights, also guarantees that the writer's name and authorship will be acknowledged in any exploitation of her work. An agreement requiring the author to use a pseudonym would not hold up in France because it would violate the right of paternity. By the same token, the right allows an author to prevent the use of her name in association with a work created by someone else. Another variety, the right of integrity, prohibits any alteration or distortion of a work without the writer's consent.

RETRIEVING INTERNET DOMAIN NAMES

Well-known people, including writers, might be able to retrieve Internet domain names containing their names from unrelated parties who do not have a legitimate right to them. Although federal trademark law provides a remedy, it is burdensome to bring a federal lawsuit to retrieve a domain name. The Internet Corporation for Assigned Names and Numbers (ICANN), the body that assigns and regulates the use of domain names, established an arbitration procedure and standards by which owners can quickly retrieve domain names to which they own the trademark. The arbitration panel has the authority to order the transfer of a contested domain name. To retrieve the name, the owner must show three things: that the name is confusingly similar to her mark (registered or common law), the party who registered the domain name has no rights or legitimate interests in the name, and the registrant registered and used the name in bad faith.

The Authors Guild helped set a precedent in this area years ago when it brought an ICANN proceeding against an individual who had registered numerous domains matching famous authors' names. The registrant did not use the names to point to a website. He simply demanded large fees to transfer the names to the authors. The arbitration panel found that authors have common-law trademark rights in their names and that warehousing and offering the names to the highest bidder do not give the early registrant a legitimate right to the names. In fact, the warehousing in itself demonstrated bad faith in light of the other facts, and the authors won the right to the domain names.

HARM TO AN AUTHOR'S REPUTATION

On occasion, some public treatment of a writer or her work might be a defamation,[49] but a critical review of a writer's work, no matter how vicious, cannot in itself be defamatory. Under the "fair comment" rule, a writer who places work before the public invites criticism of the work. But if untrue, disparaging statements of fact about the work or the author are made in a review, the critic might have crossed the line into defamation. It is also possible to claim that publication of a badly distorted work defames the author, as in the *Clevenger* case described above. Because work in the public domain can be freely copied by anyone, an author is unlikely to succeed in claiming a defamatory implication that she consented to distort her work in a derivative rendering. For example, the use of the Russian composer Shostakovich's public domain works in an anti-Russia film was held not defamatory.

RIGHTS OF PRIVACY

Rights of privacy encompass several somewhat different personal interests, including the right to be free from unwanted and unnecessary publicity, the right to shield one's most private and intimate moments from publicity, and protection from being shown in a false light before the public. A writer might make out a case of invasion of privacy in particular situations. For example, a professor's privacy was held invaded when he was shown in a false light by the use of his name on the unauthorized publication of his course lecture notes. The court found that using his name implied the plaintiff consented to the publication when, in fact, he reasonably believed publication would harm his professional standing. In the same vein, false attribution might be ruled a false light invasion of privacy, although courts are not all in agreement. Some courts have held that the right of privacy only protects a writer's real name, not her pen name, although this seems to make little sense. As described in more detail in chapter 8, the right of

---

[49] Defamation and invasion of privacy as the bases for a lawsuit are described in Chapter 8.

privacy diminishes as the subject gains stature as a public figure, particularly with respect to areas of her life that are matters of legitimate public interest.

RIGHT OF PUBLICITY

The right of publicity recognizes that individuals have the exclusive right to benefit from commercial exploitation of their names, likenesses, and personae. By definition, the right of publicity is of less value to a person who is not famous. The right of publicity also does not overcome the First Amendment right to use a famous person's name and likeness commercially if the use is incidental to legitimate reporting. For example, Ayn Rand's review of *Chaos Below Heaven* by Eugene Vale was accurately quoted on the book's jacket without her permission. She sued over what she termed a "blatant commercial exploitation of her personality," but the court concluded the quotation was a legitimate use of a comment by a public figure on a matter of current interest.

Most personal rights, including the right to privacy and the right to redress for defamation, die with the person. In 1984, however, California enacted a "celebrity rights" law that gave publicity rights to deceased celebrities' estates. Other states, notably Tennessee (the home state of Elvis Presley's estate), have followed suit. The basic approach of these laws is to protect the publicity rights of deceased people for up to fifty years after their death. The right applies to people whose names, voices, signatures, or likenesses had commercial value at the time of death, whether or not that commercial value was exploited during their life. Unlike defamation and invasion of privacy claims, the right of publicity can be assigned to and sold by the heirs. New York, the media capital of the country, has so far resisted passing a "dead celebrities" restriction on commercial speech.

On the other hand, valuable as the right of publicity might be to well-known writers, it does not protect a writer from receiving accurate credit for a work to which he contributed. Stephen King objected to the use of his name in the credits and advertising for a film based on a short story he had written and optioned years earlier. The court agreed with him that calling the film "Stephen King's *The Lawnmower Man*" violated the Lanham Act because he had not written the screenplay or had any other involvement with the film. But the court permitted the producers to bill the film as "based on a story by Stephen King," because it was accurate to do so.

CHAPTER 8

FREE EXPRESSION

AND ITS LIMITS

One of the unique hallmarks of US society is the right to freedom of expression, enshrined in the First Amendment to the Constitution: "Congress shall make no law . . . abridging the freedom of speech, or the press . . ." Our courts have determined that the word "speech" includes both spoken and written expression, and "the press" includes not just newspapers, but books, magazines, broadcast media, the Internet, and motion pictures—virtually any means of conveying information. The right belongs not just to the speaker, but also to the audience. The theory on which freedom of expression rests was famously explained by Supreme Court Justice Oliver Wendell Holmes, Jr.: " The ultimate good desired is better reached by free trade in ideas . . . the best test of truth is the power of the thought to get itself accepted in the competition of the market . . ." Thus, the marketplace of ideas is a social good to be encouraged and the appropriate response to offensive or untrue speech is not punishment or restraint by the state, it is more speech. The prohibition against government restricting its citizens' speech extends to the fifty states by virtue of the Fourteenth Amendment.

But this freedom is far from absolute. First, only the government (including the courts) is prohibited from abridging free expression; private enterprises may restrict or punish speech by employees and other parties.

Copyright, trademark, and unfair competition laws may penalize expressive activity that infringes the rights of others. Some kinds of speech can harm individuals, and all states offer remedies against the publishers of defamation and for invasion of privacy. Laws criminalizing obscenity exist in all fifty states, and schools and libraries routinely censor literature, usually within their legal rights to do so.

A full treatment of any one of these topics and the many hundreds of judicial interpretations of the related laws would fill volumes; an in-depth study is not possible here. But this chapter will attempt to explain the definitions and parameters of defamation, invasion of privacy, newsgathering risks, obscenity laws, and censorship in schools and libraries. It will also examine the legal risks of defamation and privacy violations that professional writers must navigate, whether or not they are members of the press, and offer practical advice for self-protection.

State and federal courts have interpreted laws governing defamation and privacy over many decades, and the legal definitions and standards vary, sometimes considerably, from state to state. In fact, it is not always clear which state's laws apply to a work distributed nationwide, and this uncertainty can work against a writer's freedom of expression if a potential plaintiff lives in a state with particularly unfavorable laws. But one set of standards applies to all works published in the United States, and those are the parameters outlined by the Supreme Court interpreting the First Amendment. For that reason, this chapter focuses on the limits the Supreme Court has drawn around every state's defamation and privacy laws. If your work meets constitutional standards, it should be safe from liability in any state.

DEFAMATION AND "FALSE LIGHT" INVASION OF PRIVACY

Common law or legislation in every state has long recognized that damage to a person's reputation deserves redress, and every state provides a civil remedy to a defamed person.[50] In most states, defamation is defined as the publication of a false statement of fact about a person or entity that is derogatory and tends to injure the subject's reputation, and which was published with some degree of fault. "False light" is a variety of invasion

---

[50] There is no federal cause of action for defamation. Only states, through legislation and judicially crafted standards, provide a remedy for defamation.

of privacy akin to defamation; it is defined as the widespread publication of facts that show the subject in a misleading light in a way that would be highly offensive to a reasonable person.

Reporting about public officials, public figures, and matters of public concern is highly valued in the United States, and plaintiffs in such cases must meet higher standards of proof and show more fault by the publisher of a false statement. As well, the press enjoys certain privileges that exempt it from liability for merely repeating defamatory statements made in public proceedings, such as indictments, legislative hearings, and lawsuits.

Every one of the elements of defamation, examined below, must be proven to give rise to liability.

PUBLICATION

"Publication" means that the offending statement was uttered to and reached at least one person other than the subject of the statement. The size of the audience does not matter, and if a statement appears in a published book, blog post, or article, "publication" is assumed. The statement may be spoken (slander), or expressed through fixed or written words or images, including motion pictures (libel). In many states, injury to reputation is easier for a plaintiff to prove when the claim is for libel rather than slander.

Under the "republication rule," every party who participates in publishing or who republishes another's defamatory statement can also be liable for defamation. This means that both the publisher of a writer's defamatory statement and the writer are individually responsible for their own publications of the statement. A writer who simply quotes another person's defamatory statement can be liable herself for a new instance of defamation, even if she names the original source, or indicates doubt that the statement is true, or uses the customary phrase "it is alleged," or discloses that the story is based on rumors. By contrast, a mere distributor of a defamatory statement, such as a bookseller or newsstand, is not liable unless it receives notice of the defamation and continues to distribute the publication.

The press enjoys certain exceptions to the republication rule, such as the "fair report privilege," which exempts it from liability for repeating defamatory statements made in judicial and other public proceedings. Section 230 of the federal Communications Decency Act gives Internet service providers and website operators that publish user-generated content immunity from liability for defamatory statements that users make through their services. (This immunity does not, however, extend to online publications' own published statements.)

STATEMENT OF FACT

Whether a statement is "factual" depends on whether it can be objectively verified. Courts have found humor, ridicule, sarcasm, questions, alterations of quotes, and insinuations to be potentially defamatory statements of fact. By contrast, a genuine statement of opinion cannot be verified as true or false, so it cannot be defamatory. This distinction does not, however, give writers carte blanche to make or imply a defamatory statement in the guise of an opinion. The Supreme Court has held that "expressions of opinion may often imply an assertion of objective fact," which, if false and defamatory, can lead to liability. If a writer asserts facts on which she bases an opinion, the opinion might be defamatory if the facts are incorrect or incomplete.

In examining a statement's meaning, a court must interpret the words as they were "reasonably understood in view of all the circumstances," including the context in which they were published. If the contested statement is "reasonably susceptible of a defamatory connotation," a claim is likely to survive a motion to dismiss the case. To make this determination, the court must give the disputed language a fair reading in the context of the publication as a whole. For example, in 1994, a writer named Dan Moldea sued the *New York Times* over a negative review of his book. Among other things, the review said his book contained "too much sloppy journalism." Moldea claimed that this statement injured his reputation as an investigative reporter. After first ruling that Moldea had stated a valid claim, a federal appellate court took the unusual step of reversing itself and dismissed the case. It ruled that a book review is "a genre in which readers expect to find spirited critiques of literary works that they understand to be the review's description and assessment of texts that are capable of a number of possible rational interpretations," and that the "sloppy journalism" statement was the reviewer's "supportable interpretation of" the book. Only if no reasonable person could conclude that a statement in a review is a "supportable interpretation" of the reviewed work could it be deemed a false factual assertion.

Some states recognize defamation by implication, similar to "false light" invasion of privacy, where the claim is premised not on false assertions but on false impressions and implications arising from otherwise truthful statements. For example, a news account was found to have implicitly defamed a woman when it reported that a wife had shot her "upon finding her husband" at the victim's home, because it failed to explain that the assault happened during a social gathering that included both parties' husbands. The concern that substantially truthful speech must be protected has led courts to embrace high standards through which to find defamation by implication. For example, one court has held that a defamatory implication must arise from a material omission of information. Federal courts have ruled the defamatory implication must have been a "reasonable interpretation" and the author must have intended to convey the implication. Other courts have rejected the concept of libel by implication altogether, as contrary to free speech values.

"OF AND CONCERNING" THE INJURED PARTY

The offending statement must actually be understood to be about an identifiable person. Accusing all members of a particular ethnic group of being criminals, though offensive, is not "of and concerning" any single member of that group so as to give that person a claim for defamation. Although a person need not be identified by name, the statement and the context must reveal enough identifying information about a subject that those who know her would recognize the statement as being about her. A statement about an unnamed member of a group might be deemed "of and concerning" a particular person if the group is small enough, or if other information describing her is given that leads to the reasonable inference that she is the subject.

A legal entity, including a corporation, can be the subject of a defamatory statement and has the same rights to relief as an individual.

FALSITY

Defamation liability requires that the statement be false. The truth or substantial truth of the statement is considered an absolute defense. "Substantial truth" means that immaterial details are wrong but the offending statement is accurate in substance. Unauthorized biographies and unflattering portraits are legally acceptable if they do not include false and defamatory statements about their subjects. Where the statement made concerns a public official or a public figure or relates to a matter of public concern, the plaintiff bears the burden of proving the statement false. Where the statement involves a private matter and nonpublic figures, some states require the defendant to prove the statement was true or substantially true, but only if the plaintiff has proven all other elements of the claim.

DAMAGE TO REPUTATION

The published statement at issue must in fact harm the plaintiff's reputation. Merely being offensive or insulting does not suffice. The kinds of statements that can injure a person's reputation vary as much as people do. Any assertion can injure a person's reputation if it exposes her to hatred, ridicule, or contempt, or reduces esteem or respect for her among her peers, causes her to be shunned, or injures her professionally. For the most part, the plaintiff must prove that a published statement actually injured her reputation in specific ways. Some kinds of statements, however, are considered so universally injurious that they are considered defamatory *per se* and do not require that the plaintiff prove actual damage to her reputation.[51] *Per se* defamation includes statements that impugn a person's honesty, ethics, or mental health, or that claim the subject has a dreaded disease, is an alcoholic or drug abuser, is sexually promiscuous or impotent, or is a criminal.

Only living people may sue for defamation because the dead cannot suffer personally from injury to their reputations. Some states make defamation of the dead a crime, but they do not give surviving relatives a right to sue for civil damages.

FAULT: ACTUAL MALICE, GROSS IRRESPONSIBILITY OR NEGLIGENCE

Under the First Amendment, liability for publishing an injurious falsehood requires some degree of fault by the defendant. If writers and publishers faced liability to every person about whom they published an incorrect statement, they would necessarily self-censor their reporting and writing to unacceptable levels of timidity. This tendency to self-censor is known as the "chilling effect" on speech, and it is quite relevant in First Amendment jurisprudence. The Supreme Court has recognized the important role of the media: "acting as the 'eyes and ears' of the public, [the press] can be a

---

[51] One possible exception: a person with a notoriously bad reputation is less likely to prove reputational injury even when a falsehood published about her is *per se* defamatory.

powerful and constructive force, contributing to remedial action in the conduct of public business." Given the need for the "marketplace of ideas" and the watchdog role of the press in a free society, in 1964, the Supreme Court held that the First Amendment requires significant levels of fault by the speaker, depending on the newsworthiness of the story.

In the 1964 landmark case of *New York Times v. Sullivan*, the Court held that under the First Amendment, the press may make inaccurate statements based on honest error without liability. *Sullivan* provided that public officials may not claim defamation for false statements relating to their official conduct unless they can show the defendant published the statement with "actual malice," i.e., knowledge of falsity or reckless disregard of the truth. The aggrieved public official must prove actual malice "with convincing clarity," a higher level of proof than for most civil lawsuits. Subsequent cases have fleshed out the definition of actual malice. The Court has ruled that even deliberately altering a plaintiff's quoted words does not amount to knowledge of falsity unless the changes result "in a material change in the statement's meaning." "Reckless disregard" for a statement's truth means something worse than just failing to fact-check a news story. Instead, there "must be sufficient evidence to permit the conclusion that the defendant in fact entertained serious doubts as to the truth of his publication." This standard obviously does not excuse a publisher from skipping the fact-checking process. To a jury, it might be a short step from that omission to "entertaining serious doubt about the truth."

Since *Sullivan*, the Court has extended the "actual malice" standard of fault to apply to "public figures" as well. Public figures include individuals who, by their accomplishments or positions in life, have given the public a legitimate interest in their affairs. They can include politicians, sports figures, media personalities, and other celebrities, but not necessarily their family members. Private individuals can become "limited purpose public figures," and therefore must meet the actual malice standard, when they actively, voluntarily, or willfully seek the public eye or inject themselves into a matter of public concern. For example, when Richard Jewell, the heroic security guard who granted interviews following the bombing at the 2000 Olympic Games, was later wrongly reported to be a suspect, he was found to have placed himself into the center of a public debate about park safety and thus considered a limited purpose public figure. In contrast, if a person has no public role in society and did not voluntarily join in a public debate intending to influence its outcome, she is much less likely to be deemed a "public figure" for defamation purposes.

In defamation claims brought by private figures, Supreme Court precedent still requires fault, but allows states to impose a lower standard, such as negligence, which is defined as falling below the standard of care that a reasonable person would employ in a similar situation. Where a public official or public figure is defamed as to private aspects of her life, she is treated as a private person. But if a statement made about a private party is in the context of reporting a matter of public concern, the publisher must have acted in at least a "grossly irresponsible" matter to be liable, and no *per se* or punitive damages are allowed unless the defendant acted with actual malice. Celebrity gossip writers should take care: celebrity breakups have been held to be private matters, even in media-friendly New York.

FALSE LIGHT

False light is a variety of invasion of privacy that some, but not all, states recognize (California does; New York does not). In substance, false light overlaps with the definition of defamation and the same constitutional limitations, described above, apply. The states that recognize the claim define it in different ways, but in general it means the wide dissemination of a statement that identifies the plaintiff and presents her to the public in a misleading way that would be "highly offensive to a reasonable person." The statements made do not have to be false, but they do have to create untrue implications. Unlike defamation, the publication must reach a large number of people, and the implication made must reach a high level of offensiveness on an objective basis. Some states require plaintiffs in false light claims to show a higher level of fault by the defendant than for defamation.

One example of false light is the use of an identifiable person's photo to illustrate a story about nefarious activity. Other cases have involved fictionalized accounts of events of public interest. If substantially true, the account is protected under the First Amendment. If false, the Supreme Court has held that the publisher must have acted with knowledge of its falsity or reckless disregard of the truth to be held liable.

DEFAMATION IN FICTION

While most defamation lawsuits against writers involve nonfiction, defamation can occur in a work of fiction, even if it does not refer to a real person by name. Court rulings in the 1970s and 1980s have suggested an alarmingly easy test for proving that the depiction of a fictional character constituted a defamatory statement of fact about a real person. Two federal courts allowed the question of whether "the libel [in fiction] designates the plaintiff in such a way as to let those who knew him understand he was the person meant" to be decided by a jury. The Illinois Supreme Court has held that defamation is possible if it is reasonable for objective readers of a work who know both the author and the subject of the statement to have discerned the reference to the plaintiff. New York courts have articulated a stricter test, acknowledging that writers, of necessity, base fictional characters on their own experiences, and that identification alone is not sufficient to overcome a presumption that a character in a work of fiction is imaginary. Rather, the reader must be "totally convinced that the book in all its aspects as far as the plaintiff is concerned is not fiction at all." Another New York court has held that "the description of the fictional character must be so closely akin to the real person . . . that a reader of the book, knowing the real person, would have no difficulty linking the two."

If you are using some traits of people you know in your fictional characters, you can protect yourself by changing identifiable features—their names, physical traits, familial situations, professions, locations—as much as you can. The more unflattering your character, the more distinct you should make him or her from any person you know.

Novels and motion pictures often include disclaimers, such as, "This is a work of fiction. The people, events, and circumstances depicted in this novel are fictitious and the product of the author's imagination, and any resemblance of any character to any actual person, whether living or dead, is purely coincidental." Although a disclaimer might not protect your work if the depiction of a character defames a real person, it can decrease your risk or the potential amount of money damages.

OTHER LIMITS TO LIABILITY: PRIOR RESTRAINTS

In 1971, the Supreme Court refused to issue a prepublication injunction against the publication of the Pentagon Papers, a classified report on US policy in Vietnam that had been leaked to the press. After the *New York Times* and the *Washington Post* jointly began publishing parts of the report, the Nixon Administration sued to enjoin continued publication. In a watershed victory for freedom of the press, the Supreme Court ruled against the government. It held that any prior restraint on publication is heavily presumed to be unconstitutional, and that the government must prove that a prior restraint is justified. In the *Pentagon Papers* case, the government failed to prove its claim of harm to national security.

A court-ordered restraint on the publication of a work—whether it is deemed defamatory, infringing, or invasive of a person's privacy—is presumptively unconstitutional. The Supreme Court has held that, illegal or not, virtually no work of authorship should be judicially silenced before it is published. Although a work might cause damage to others and liability to its author, the courts generally may not prohibit it from being published and read. Only exceptional circumstances justify a prior restraint on expression. For example, in wartime, publication of the number, location, or sailing dates of troops might be legitimately prohibited.

OTHER LIMITS TO LIABILITY: RETRACTIONS

In many states, damages for defamation against the media will be limited if the publisher retracts the defamatory statement or if the plaintiff fails to demand a retraction before suing. The relevant state laws generally hold that the retraction must be a complete and unequivocal attempt to repair the injury caused to a reputation. The retraction must receive the same prominence and publicity as the defamation and appear as soon after the defamation as possible. Even where the state of jurisdiction does not have a retraction statute, a retraction can help show that the plaintiff suffered less damage and that there was an absence of the malice necessary for liability (for public figures) or punitive damages.

INVASION OF PRIVACY

The doctrine of invasion of privacy gives people the right to redress for the publication of certain true statements and the use of certain intrusive newsgathering methods. The right to privacy is defined as the right to be free from unwanted and unnecessary publicity or interference that could injure one's personal feelings or present a person in a false light. Recognized in varying forms in almost every state, invasion of privacy claims generally protect against four distinct types of injury:

The appropriation of a person's name or likeness for advertising or commercial uses; or

The disclosure to the public of embarrassing private facts; or

The placing of a person in a false light before the public (as described above); or

Intrusion into a person's seclusion or private life.

In every privacy suit, the plaintiff must demonstrate that she had a reasonable expectation of privacy. Therefore, a person's statements made and actions taken in public may be recorded and published without violating her privacy rights.

RIGHT OF PUBLICITY

New York recognizes only the first of the privacy categories, also called invasion of the right of publicity. New York's statute is a good example of this right as it is recognized by most other states. It provides:

> Any person whose name, portrait or picture is used within this state for advertising purposes or for the purposes of trade without . . . consent . . . may . . . sue and recover damages for any injuries sustained by reason of such use and if the defendant shall have knowingly used such person's name, portrait or picture in such manner as is forbidden or declared to be unlawful . . . the jury, in its discretion, may award [punitive] damages.

Most other states recognize the right of publicity either by statute or in common law. This right is limited to the commercial exploitation of a person's name or likeness, that is, in connection with advertising or marketing products or services. Therefore, the use in a work of fiction of the name and physical traits of a real person does not infringe her right of publicity (though it could be defamation, as described above). The press may freely use the names and likenesses of people, famous or not, for newsworthy purposes and even for advertising the newsworthy qualities of the publication.

DISCLOSURE OF PRIVATE FACTS

The public disclosure of embarrassing private facts could constitute an invasion of privacy if the disclosure would be highly offensive to a reasonable person and is not of legitimate concern to the public. Courts use a liberal definition of newsworthiness or legitimate public interest. For example, they have ruled that a statement that a person committed a crime is newsworthy, even if the statement is later shown to be false and defamatory. Where the disclosure is about a public figure, it is less likely to be deemed an invasion of privacy; this allows unauthorized biographers of famous subjects some breathing room to disclose private facts they discover about public figures.

INTRUSION

The final category of invasion of privacy involves intrusion into another's seclusion or private life, where the claimant had a reasonable expectation that the activities or information obtained would be private. "The First Amendment has never been construed to accord newsmen immunity from torts or crimes committed during the course of newsgathering. The First Amendment is not a license to trespass, to steal, or to intrude by electronic means into the precincts of another's home or office." *Dietemann v. Time Inc.* (NY, 1971). The intrusion could be physical, such as trespass into someone's home, but it often relates to unauthorized electronic access or surveillance, such as a wiretap, snooping through windows, and overzealous shadowing, whether or not accompanied by trespass to property. Intrusion and defamation are separate claims. Publication of the information obtained is not required to make a case for intrusion, and the fact that information was obtained through intrusion is irrelevant to whether publishing it is wrongful. "[W]here the claim is that private information concerning the plaintiff has been published, the question of whether that information is genuinely private or is of public interest should not turn on the manner in which it has been obtained." *Pearson v. Dodd,* 1969. However, the money damages awarded for intrusion might be larger if the information obtained was subsequently published.

Given the complexity of the doctrines relating to invasion of privacy, you should seek legal advice if you anticipate difficulties.

AVOIDING DEFAMATION AND INVASION OF PRIVACY CLAIMS

Virtually all book publishers, and a fair number of periodical publishers, require their writers to indemnify them for all costs associated with defending defamation and privacy claims (and obscenity claims, for that matter) based on the authors' work. If an aggrieved party sues your publisher, even if the claim is not valid, you could be held financially responsible for all your publisher's costs, including its attorneys' fees. Most publishers have media liability insurance that covers their costs and liability, but these policies typically have very large deductibles. If you have not been diligent enough, your publisher might require you to cover its out-of-pocket costs if it is sued, or it might charge its costs against your work's earnings.

To protect yourself against libel claims, you should document your fact-finding thoroughly and methodically to show you have not negligently made a false statement about anyone. Be careful throughout the process—while researching, writing, working through the editing process, fact-checking, even approving jacket copy. You should be able to cite the specific source of the statements of fact in your manuscript. Keep copies of all documents you use, including printouts of online material, and make sure they clearly show their sources and identity. If a source has provided a confidential document, clearly indicate the conditions for its publication, if any, on all copies. Mark your notes and tapes to indicate the identity of their sources or interview subjects and the date, time, and place of the interview or research. When taking notes, identify the words that are direct quotes. Tape recordings or even handwritten contemporaneous notes of interviews carry more weight than word-processed versions.

When conducting an interview, consider tape-recording it (the subject's permission is usually advisable).[52] Always begin each segment of a taped interview with a statement identifying the date, time, and subject. Within your time limits, you should always make the best possible effort to confirm sensitive statements. Consider the reliability of your sources, and try to evaluate whether your subject constitutes a public figure or the matter is newsworthy. Keep in mind that many libel claims come from figures who are minor players in a story and are often not public figures. In *Kirsch's Handbook of Publishing Law*, attorney Jonathan Kirsch advises that while preparing your manuscript you should cross-reference the manuscript to the source materials as much as possible. As you write, create two versions of your work—one with and one without footnotes giving the source for each statement and quote. The version with footnotes will be much easier to fact-check and legally review.

Most publishers have attorneys on staff who will review manuscripts that contain risky content. If the publisher does not supply a legal vetting, and your work contains statements that could be considered defamatory, consider con-

---

[52] Many states require all parties to a conversation to consent to its recording; some require only one party to consent. Unless you have a very good reason and clearance from a lawyer to record an interview without the subject's consent, it is best to get permission.

sulting your own publishing lawyer. Defamation and privacy law, like all laws, are subject to change without warning, and only an attorney who knows the current law can vet a manuscript effectively. The self-help steps described here will make the vetting lawyer's job easier and faster, and therefore less expensive.

PROTECTING CONFIDENTIAL SOURCES

Journalists need sources to reveal information, often confidentially, in order to investigate the behavior of public officials and of the government. In the era of civil unrest during the Vietnam War, prosecutors commonly sought to subpoena journalists' notes and files, and government agents made unannounced newsroom searches. These circumstances would understandably deter sources from revealing confidential information to the media. After Vietnam, the government reformed many of its own abusive practices. For example, the Privacy Protection Act of 1980 required law enforcement agents seeking information about crime from the media to give reporters advance notice and an opportunity to contest a subpoena in court.

If journalists can routinely be compelled to reveal their sources, people will be less likely to talk to them.[53] Occasionally, courts have ordered journalists to disclose the sources of relevant information, but virtually every reporter would willingly serve jail time for contempt of such court orders, rather than reveal the identity of a source who was promised confidentiality. Courts and legislatures recognize the larger importance to the public of allowing a reporter to keep sources confidential. The majority of states have so-called "reporter's privilege" or "press shield" laws that give journalists the right to refuse to disclose identities of confidential sources, although there is no federal counterpart. Under both the First Amendment and state press shield laws, reporters may have grounds to resist demands by the government that they reveal their sources and notes.

The reporter's privilege, like most others, is not absolute. Under most states' laws and judicial interpretations of the First Amendment, journalists

---

[53] Beyond the intangible harm to a journalist's ability to investigate, other harms can arise from revealing the identity of a confidential source. In 1991, the Supreme Court upheld a breach of contract claim against reporters who voluntarily revealed a confidential source's identity. The Court observed that the law of contracts applies as much to confidentiality agreements with news sources as to other contracts, largely because imposing contract damages on the reporters does not interfere with the newsgathering process.

can be ordered in some circumstances to disclose their sources. Some interests, in particular a criminal defendant's right to a fair trial, are considered more important than the reporter's privilege. Thus, courts will usually order disclosure if it is shown that the reporter likely has information relevant to the commission of an unlawful act, the prosecution or defense has tried and failed to get the information elsewhere, and the prosecution or defense requires the information to prepare its case.

NEWSGATHERING CLAIMS

Disgruntled subjects of media scrutiny sometimes rely on what media lawyers call "trash torts," such as trespass claims, to circumvent First Amendment accommodations for the press. Trespass is defined as intruding on private property after being told to leave or advised not to enter. Courts generally do not give journalists special treatment under trespass laws. In one New York case, a reporter went onto a person's property with law enforcement investigators who had a search warrant. The plaintiff objected to the reporter coming onto the property, and a court upheld his subsequent trespass suit against the reporter. Some courts award the plaintiff damages flowing from both the trespass itself and the resulting publication, even if not defamatory. Other courts, including those in New York, allow damages only for the trespass itself.

Wiretapping and recording interviews without the subject's permission are risky endeavors. Some states do not require that all parties to a conversation consent to being recorded, but a number of them do; it can be a crime to record a person without their consent in a "two party consent" state. If you are recording an interview or conversation, it is the better course to get all parties' consent, unless you have a good reason not to do so and you know it is legal to do so in the state(s) in which the recording is done.

CENSORSHIP

Under the First Amendment, the only types of expression that may be censored absolutely are obscenity and speech that creates "a clear and present danger that it will bring about the substantive evils that Congress [or the state] has a right to prevent." Even if objectionable material does not fall into either category it may, however, lawfully be kept from minors.

OBSCENITY

Material containing sexual content has existed for millennia, and has been prosecuted since at least Victorian times. Prior to 1973, the test for banning erotic expression, as developed in Britain and substantially followed in the United States, was whether the material "tended . . . to deprave and corrupt those whose minds are open to such immoral influences." In the United States, this led to bans on such works as Giovanni Boccaccio's *Decameron*, John Cleland's *Fanny Hill*, Gustave Flaubert's *November*, Henry Miller's *Tropic of Cancer*, James Joyce's *Ulysses*, D. H. Lawrence's *Lady Chatterley's Lover*, Eugene O'Neill's *Strange Interlude*, and Edmund Wilson's *Memoirs of Hecate County*. The law applied equally to works of obvious literary merit and to hard-core pornography. Obscenity prosecutions became a common way for government officials and private citizens to prevent the public from having access to sexually explicit and violent works. Until the mid-twentieth century, prosecutors commonly went after authors, publishers, and distributors, and the post office, customs, and police routinely seized books and other materials. In 1957, the Supreme Court ruled that obscenity does not warrant the protection of the First Amendment and that obscenity prohibitions and censorship are constitutional. The Court reasoned that "implicit in the history of the First Amendment is the rejection of obscenity as utterly without social importance."

Although this ruling remains the law, the tide in favor of free expression began to turn decades earlier, in 1934, when the Second Circuit Court of Appeals held that Joyce's *Ulysses* was not obscene and could freely pass through US customs. The court ruled that the use of "dirty words" in "a sincere and honest book" did not make the book as a whole "dirty." This distinction made in the case called *United States v. One Book Entitled "Ulysses"* became the precursor to the most crucial part of the current legal definition of obscenity.

In 1973, the Supreme Court formulated the test that remains the law for assessing whether a particular work is obscene. In *Miller v. California*, the Court allowed states and local governments to exercise autonomous, but limited, authority to restrict obscenity in their communities. In assessing whether material is obscene, a jury must determine:

(a) whether "the average person, applying contemporary community standards" would find that the work, taken as a whole, appeals to the prurient interest; (b) whether the work depicts or describes, in a patently offensive way, sexual conduct specifically defined by the applicable state law; and (c) whether the work, taken as a whole, lacks serious literary, artistic, political, or scientific value.

If the answer to all three questions is affirmative, then the work is obscene, and local authorities may remove it from circulation and prosecute the author, publisher, and even the distributor.

To what extent does this definition endanger sexually oriented works that might be valued by only a minority of readers or viewers? Henry Miller eloquently illustrated the importance of the "merit" requirement in his essay "Defense of the Freedom to Read," which he wrote in response to Sweden's attempt to suppress his book *Sexus*: "But it is not something evil, not something poisonous, which this book offers. . . . It is a dose of life which I administered to myself first, and which I not only survived but thrived on. Certainly I would not recommend it to infants, but then neither would I offer a child a bottle of *aqua vitae*. I can only say one thing for it unblushingly—compared to the atom bomb, it is full of life-giving qualities."

The Court subsequently clarified that in fact, "contemporary community standards" may not be applied to assess a work's literary, artistic, political or scientific merit. The "merit" prong of the definition must be determined by a national "reasonable person" standard. Thus, if a work is intended to convey "serious literary, artistic, political or scientific value" to any material degree, it cannot be deemed obscene. Under this standard, most pornography is considered to convey some value, so it is not legally obscene.

Under the First Amendment, procedural safeguards must be given to a writer and publisher whose work is challenged as obscene. Law enforcement officials may not seize the work simply because they think it is obscene. They must file for and serve notice of a judicial hearing to make the determination so that the court rules based on all relevant evidence.

SCHOOL AND LIBRARY CENSORSHIP

Most states give school boards the authority to dictate curricula, course books, and library holdings free from outside interference. Although the discretion of school boards is somewhat limited under the First Amendment, book censorship in schools is rampant. Works by such writers as Alice Walker, Toni Morrison, J. D. Salinger, James Baldwin, Mark Twain, Kurt Vonnegut, Joseph Heller and many others are routinely banned from class curricula and school libraries. Censorship campaigns led by parents, advocacy groups, school boards, or community leaders demand that schools refuse to purchase certain books, remove books from libraries, place them in restricted or infrequently used areas, or remove them from a class curriculum. Most often, these campaigns target the placement of books in public school libraries.

In 1982, the Supreme Court analyzed the constitutionality of book removal from school libraries and curricula in a case involving a school district's board of education removal of nine books from school library shelves, including Kurt Vonnegut's *Slaughterhouse-Five* and Richard Wright's *Black Boy*. A parents' advocacy group had pushed to have its list of "questionable" books banned; they characterized the books as "anti-American, anti-Christian, anti-Semitic and just plain filthy." The Court sought to balance the First Amendment right of students to read freely and the right of public school authorities to exercise discretion over student access to materials. It recognized that both groups have constitutional rights, but they are not absolute. Although it did not hold the board of education's actions unconstitutional, the Court set a standard for subsequent book removal cases. A school board may maintain wide authority concerning removal of books, but it may not institute such actions because the works contain "partisan or political views [the board does] not share." It acknowledged a student's right to access information when engaged in "voluntary inquiry" and the library's role as a place of inquiry essential to the student's understanding and maturation. Thus, the Court distinguished an educator's selection of books for the curriculum from the banning of books in the library system. School boards have greater discretion to select and reject books for the curriculum, so long as they do not ban works based on partisan or political views, than in choosing library books.

Although the Court did not provide guidelines for how school authorities may choose books for libraries, it acknowledged that they may remove books if they are deemed vulgar or of questionable "educational suitability." In cases following this decision, lower courts have given greater protection to students' rights. A 1989 California appellate court found library book removal to be an invalid use of a school board's authority because "[if] school boards are granted such authority, every library book bears the imprimatur of the present board."

Other courts have ruled that the removal of library books curtails freedom of speech and thought, particularly where the school board does so because they find the books personally distasteful. Although neither a state nor the board is constitutionally required to provide a library or to choose any particular books, once they create such a privilege for the benefit of its students, a court is loath to allow the authorities to condition the use of the library based solely on the social or political tastes of school board members.

School systems maintain formal procedures for the approval of books for libraries and curricula. Those who want to censor books in schools have learned these procedures and use them to their advantage. Opponents of censorship can obtain copies of this information through "Government in the Sunshine" and Freedom of Information Act requests to learn the administrators' policies and to determine whether they are following proper procedures in censorship cases. The active participation of writers and anticensorship groups in school administrative proceedings has helped to defeat many attempts to censor unreasonably what students may read.

CHAPTER 9

HOW TO USE OPEN

GOVERNMENT LAWS

If you are a journalist, you are probably already aware of the rich source of data and other research material available from government agencies at every level. Any writer, not only journalists, can take advantage of various open government laws to expose the work of public agencies, corroborate other sources, identify leads and story lines, and otherwise use the enormous amounts of data compiled by federal, state, and local government agencies. The right of the public to obtain information from and about the federal government is embodied in the Freedom of Information Act ("FOIA"); the Government in the Sunshine Act and the Federal Advisory Committee Act ("FACA"). FOIA requires all federal agencies promptly to make most of their records available on request to any member of the public. The Sunshine Act allows the public to attend most meetings held by federal agencies. FACA gives the public the right to attend most meetings of federal advisory committees (defined below). Every state also has its own versions of each these laws, which apply to state and local government agencies.

The dozens of agencies of the executive branch of the federal government affect the public every day in countless ways. Open government laws apply to virtually all of them.[54,55] Congress passed FOIA, FACA, and the Sunshine Act in order to ensure an informed citizenry, which is necessary for a functioning democracy. The laws were intended to check official corruption and waste and to hold the government accountable to the governed. As a federal appellate court described it: "the Act's basic purpose 'was to protect the people's right to obtain information about their government, to know what their government is doing and to obtain information about government activities and policies' and to remedy the 'mischief' of 'arbitrary and self-serving' withholding, by agencies which are not directly responsible to the people, of official information on how the government is operating . . . ," *Westinghouse, et al. v. Schlesinger* (4th Cir. 1976).

For similar reasons, criminal and civil litigation proceedings involving adults and related court records are also generally open to the public unless a defendant's right to a fair trial is threatened by open access or another compelling interest favors a closed proceeding. Juvenile court proceedings and records are generally closed to the public to protect minors.

If you are considering using any of these open government laws, visit the invaluable website of the Reporters Committee for Freedom of the Press (www.rcfp.org" www.rcfp.org). It provides access to every state's current open meetings and freedom of information laws, a comprehensive Federal Open Government Guide, sample request letters, a FOIA request letter and appeal generator, and writer-friendly legal advice.

THE FREEDOM OF INFORMATION ACT

The federal Freedom of Information Act ("FOIA") offers public access to records relating to the structure, operation, and decision-making of government agencies, their final opinions and orders, information and statistics they have compiled, indices, most staff manuals and instructions, statements of policy, and interpretations of those policies. Its scope is wide. FOIA applies to all executive branch cabinets (for example, the Departments of State, Justice, Commerce, Education, Defense, the Treasury), the Executive

---

[54] The Privacy Act limits the force of FOIA and other laws by preventing the disclosure of certain information about individuals to other people.

[55] Congress exempted certain government entities completely from the requirements of FOIA—Congress itself, the federal courts, and the President and Vice President and their advisors.

Office of the President, the Office of Management and Budget, all branches of the military, the Central Intelligence Agency and National Security Agency, the Federal Bureau of Investigation, NASA, the Environmental Protection Agency, government corporations such as the Postal Service, government-controlled corporations such as Amtrak, and other agencies in the executive branch, including presidential commissions, and those agencies' numerous offices and subagencies. It applies equally to all independent regulatory agencies, such as the Federal Communications Commission and the Federal Trade Commission.

The government's FOIA website, www.foia.gov, maintained by the Department of Justice, lists every agency to which FOIA applies and has direct links to each agency's individual FOIA office and procedures.

Under FOIA, any member of the public who requests and "reasonably describes" documents in the possession of an agency has the right to receive them. The person requesting the information need give no reason for the request, and in fact, need not even reveal her identity to the agency. The law requires that agencies respond substantively to FOIA requests within twenty days and disclose the data requested "promptly." If the agency claims an exemption from disclosure, it has the burden of showing the exemption is valid. Some agencies meet the deadlines, but many others have backlogs and take much longer to respond. The Justice Department's FOIA website tracks the number of requests made, rejected, appealed, pending, and the length of time for responses and disclosures of every agency by year, sorted according to "complex" and "simple" requests. Your target agency's track record can help you plan your project and prepare to follow up and to appeal, depending on the complexity of your request and the nature of the documents you seek.

Every requester has the right to appeal a denial of disclosure to a specified official of the agency and then to a federal court. Each agency has established and published on its website its own procedure for requesting documents and for appealing denials. The law requires that if a court reverses an agency's denial of a disclosure request, the government must pay the requester's attorneys' fees.

THE PRESUMPTION IN FAVOR OF DISCLOSURE

Every open government law, both federal and state, contains categories of information that are exempted from the disclosure requirements for various policy reasons. FOIA exempts nine specific categories of data, and some of the exempt categories are broad enough to give an agency great leeway to refuse disclosure.[56] Even though FOIA imposes the burden of justifying an exemption on the agency, the experience of the past two decades shows that an agency's tendency to exploit an exemption to avoid disclosure depends largely on the current Administration's stance. The Clinton Administration's Attorney General instructed federal agencies in 1993 to lean in favor of disclosing requested documents and that even if requested information could arguably fall into an exempt category, the agency should not invoke it unless a specific foreseeable harm would arise from disclosure. The Bush Administration took the converse position. It encouraged federal agencies to carefully consider and use any reason to deny disclosure. In 2001, the Bush Administration's Attorney General assured agencies that the Justice Department would aggressively support denials and delays of disclosure if they were "legally defensible." One of President Obama's first acts as president was to reverse the Bush Administration's directive on FOIA disclosure. President Obama directed his Attorney General to reestablish the presumption in favor of disclosure and urged agencies to disclose information on a timely basis. Obama's directive essentially revived the presumption in favor of agency disclosure that the Clinton Administration had instituted. In addition, it encouraged more "proactive disclosure" of agency records (i.e., without specific FOIA requests) and many agencies have posted a wealth of information on their websites since 2009.

Federal agencies are required to disclose certain categories of records on a continuous basis. These records include final opinions and orders from the adjudication of administrative cases; specific agency policy statements; certain administrative staff manuals; and records disclosed in response to FOIA

---

[56] The nine exempt categories are:

1. Records properly classified in the national defense or for foreign policy.
2. Internal personnel rules and agency practices.
3. Records required to be kept secret by other federal laws.
4. Confidential trade secrets belonging to private entities.
5. Internal agency memos that would normally be privileged from discovery in litigation in a lawsuit involving the agency.
6. Records with sensitive, medical or personnel information that would invade a person's privacy if disclosed.
7. Certain law enforcement records (where secrecy is needed to protect public or personal safety or privacy).
8. Bank examination reports prepared by agencies.
9. Oil and gas well geological and geophysical data.

requests since March 31, 1997, that the agency determines will be the subject of subsequent requests for substantially the same records. Moreover, all such records created since November 1, 1996, must be available online. Most agencies accomplish this through "electronic reading rooms" on or through their websites. If you are seeking documents of a federal agency, review what the agency has already published before formulating a FOIA request.

HOW TO MAKE A FOIA REQUEST

You can access the request and appeal procedures and the office dealing with FOIA requests for every federal agency at its website, in the Federal Register (www.gpoaccess.gov/fr/), or by calling the FOIA or public affairs department of the agency. If you are not sure which agency has the records you are seeking, these sources or your local congressional representative's office might be able to help you navigate the executive branch to pinpoint the right agency or agencies.

Some agencies will accept an oral request, but your rights under FOIA do not arise unless you make a written request for documents. To obtain access to specific records, you must submit a written request to the agency that "reasonably describes" the records sought. Beyond that, each agency has its own, often detailed, procedures. Some agencies allow you to submit the request through an electronic request form. If you use regular mail, you should clearly label your letter and the envelope as a "Freedom of Information Request," address the request to a particular FOIA officer, and send it to the specified location. In most cases, you will want to describe what you are looking for as specifically as possible. Although you do not need to explain the reasons for your request, doing so might help the agency find responsive documents more quickly. Nor do you have to disclosure your identity, but if you identify yourself as a journalist, scholar, or as a person seeking information in order to contribute significantly to public understanding of government operations and activities, you are entitled to fee waivers and expedited processing.

A sample generic FOIA request appears at the end of this chapter.

DEADLINES TO RESPOND

Once you have filed a FOIA request, the burden is on the government to respond and to release the documents promptly or show that they are covered by one or more of the nine exemptions. Under amendments to FOIA made in 2007, all requests are given a tracking number, which allows you to check the status of your request online or by calling, and the agency website should also disclose the estimated date by which the request will be processed.

Depending on the scope and complexity of your request, you might need to spend more time and effort than you planned to obtain the desired information. The agency is required by statute to respond to a written FOIA request within twenty working days, but agencies often do not respond within that time, and they are not penalized, except to the extent your fees might be waived for late responses. The required agency response is an actual grant or denial of the records sought; an acknowledgment that the agency has received your request is not the timely response that FOIA requires. The agency may also respond that it is extending its deadline to produce or deny the information by up to ten additional working days if they must search through voluminous records, retrieve files from various offices, or consult other agencies. If you do not follow all the procedural requirements in your initial request letter, such as setting forth the amount in fees you are willing to pay (beyond any fee exemptions) or adequately explaining your entitlement to a fee waiver, or if the agency seeks to clarify the scope of your request, then it might send you a request for this information, and that request effectively stops the clock on its response deadline.

Once your request is properly filed, the agency must make responsive records "promptly available" to you. The amount of time any given agency really takes to disclose records depends on the situation, and an agency is entitled to an extension if it has made a good faith, diligent effort to comply. The agency should advise you that it is taking the extension and its reasons. It might ask you to narrow your request in order to respond more quickly. Should the agency fail to issue a response or to produce the records within the twenty-day deadline, it is legally allowed more time if it claims "unusual or exceptional circumstances," although a backlog of requests does not count.

In short, if you are making a FOIA request, you should plan ahead as much as possible for delays, because there is little you can do about them until they become unreasonable.

EXPEDITED PROCESSING

If you have an urgent need for the information, you may ask for "expedited processing." You are entitled to expedited processing if you can show a "compelling need" to the agency. Most often, an agency will expedite processing if someone's health and safety are at issue or if you are a journalist or author primarily engaged in disseminating information and there is an urgent need to inform the public about an actual or alleged governmental activity. Agencies may also decide to grant expedited processing in certain other specific situations. For instance, the Justice Department will grant expedited processing for requests concerning issues of government integrity that are already the subject of widespread national media interest. The Justice Department (including its components such as US Attorneys' offices and the FBI) also grants expedited processing if a delay might cause the substantial loss of somebody's due process rights.

FEES

Agencies may use their discretion to charge "reasonable" fees to search for, review, and duplicate documents for requesters. Fee schedules for each of these categories are typically available on agency websites and in the Federal Register. In deference to freedom of the press, FOIA exempts representatives of the news media (including book authors who cull and use information from agency documents, established freelancers, and journalistic bloggers) and noncommercial requesters from academic institutions from paying hourly search fees and for the first 100 pages of duplication. All other noncommercial requesters receive two hours of search time and the first 100 pages of duplication free. But fees can fluctuate dramatically among agencies and in many cases can be prohibitive. Some agencies will ask a requester to pay in advance if they anticipate that fees will exceed $250. Review the agency's fee schedule and be sure to state in your request letter how much you are willing to spend (many agencies require this) and request an estimate of the costs to satisfy your request. If costs will be too high, reconsider whether you have the right to a fee exemption or reduction, or, if possible, ask the agency to make them available for review in its offices instead of making copies for you. Also, consider asking your publisher for a research budget if you anticipate high costs for FOIA requests.

No matter what category of requester you are in, FOIA might entitle you to further fee waivers or reductions if you can show that the disclosure of the information you seek is "in the public interest because it is likely to contribute significantly to public understanding of the operations or activities of the government and is not primarily in the commercial interest of the requester." If you are making the request for commercial purposes, it might be difficult to meet this standard. You may appeal the denial of a fee waiver request in the same way you appeal the denial of disclosure (described below).

In 2007, Congress amended FOIA to prod agencies to meet their statutory deadlines to produce documents. Now, if an agency fails to comply with any time limit, it may not charge search fees, even if the requester is not a journalist, writer, or scholar. For requesters already exempt from paying search fees, agencies that miss deadlines may not charge duplication fees, no matter how much copying is required.

APPEALING A DENIAL

If an agency refuses to disclose all or part of the information, or does not respond within twenty working days to your proper FOIA request, you may appeal to the agency's FOIA Appeals Officer. You may avoid the agency appeal process and sue directly in federal court only if the agency does not respond at all within the required time period. If you file an agency appeal that is denied or not addressed within twenty working days, you may then file a lawsuit in federal court. (The Reporters Committee's website has a sample complaint.) If you can demonstrate the need for prompt consideration, the court might expedite your case. If you win in court, a judge will order the agency to release the records and may award you attorney's fees and court costs.

EXCEPTIONS TO THE DISCLOSURE REQUIREMENT

Congress recognized that legitimate government interests, such as national security, the right to privacy, and the needs of law-enforcement agencies to maintain secrecy in investigating crime might override the strong disclosure policy of FOIA. In such cases, the agency involved might decide to disclose responsive information, but it is not legally required, and therefore cannot be compelled, to do so. If it refuses disclosure on the basis of an exemption, it must explain that on its response to your request. It is also possible for the agency to redact (i.e., black out) information it considers exempt on documents it discloses.

SAMPLE REQUEST

This sample letter is illustrative. You should always review and follow the agency's specific instructions and procedures.

FREEDOM OF INFORMATION ACT REQUEST
SAMPLE REQUEST FOR DISCLOSURE OF INFORMATION

Date:

Agency Headquarters [specify FOIA officer and address]

Agency Field Office (if applicable) [specify FOIA officer and address]

Dear FOIA Officer:

This letter is a non-commercial request under the Freedom of Information Act, 5 USC. Sec. 552.

I request a complete and thorough search of all filing systems and locations for all records maintained by your agency pertaining to and/or captioned:

[clearly specify and describe the information you are seeking, including names, dates, places, etc. Be as thorough and specific as possible]

If possible, I would like to receive the information in electronic [or other] format [if applicable].

I am required to pay fees only for the cost of duplication beyond the first 100 pages because I [am a representative of the news media affiliated with [name of organization] and am compiling this information for dissemination to the general public; or I am a freelance author under a publication contract writing about [name subject][57].]

However, I request a waiver of all fees because I am compiling information that is in the current public interest because it will contribute significantly to public understanding of government operations and activities. [Explain].

If I am not entitled to a waiver of fees beyond two hours of search time and 100 pages of duplication, I agree to pay fees for the fulfillment of this request in an amount not exceeding [fill in your maximum]. Please advise me of the estimated cost to fulfill my request prior to incurring fees, and please advise me before incurring fees in excess of [your maximum].

If my request for disclosure of any of these documents is denied in whole or in part, please specify which exemption(s) is (are) claimed for each passage or whole document denied. Give the number of pages in each document and the total number of pages pertaining to this request and the dates of documents withheld. I request that excised materials be "blacked out" rather than "whited out" or cut out

---

[57] If you are a freelancer but do not yet have a publishing contract, you must convince the FOIA officer that you expect to have your piece published by setting forth your publishing history or describing the interest expressed in your work by publishers.

and that the remaining nonexempt portions of documents be released as provided under the Freedom of Information Act.

Please send a memo (with a copy or copies to me) to the appropriate unit(s) in your office to assure that no records related to this request are destroyed. Please advise of any destruction of records and include the date of and authority for such destruction.

I can be reached at the phone number and email address listed below. Please call rather than write if there are any questions or if you need additional information from me. I expect a response to this request within twenty (20) working days, as provided in the Freedom of Information Act.

Sincerely,

(Signed) _____

Name: (print or type) _____

Address: _____

Telephone: _____

[for access to files related to a person]

Date of Birth: _____

Place of Birth: _____

Social Security number: [optional] _____

[for access to files related to an organization]

Date of founding: _____

Place of founding: _____

Address of organization _____

To obtain documents pertaining to an individual, give the individual's full name and include all other names used by that individual. To obtain documents about an organization, state the full name of the organization and any other name used to describe the organization. To obtain files about a specific subject or event, give the full name of the subject or event, including any relevant dates, locations, news coverage or other helpful identifying data.

CASE STUDY—*THE NATION MAGAZINE V. DEPARTMENT OF STATE*

Just before the presidential election of 1992, author Max Holland, a contributing editor to the *Nation*, attempted to obtain information from the CIA and other federal agencies about the prominent independent presidential candidate H. Ross Perot. In his FOIA requests, the writer stated he hoped to "contribute to the ongoing public debate about [Perot's] qualifications to become President of the United States." He and his publisher noted that a FOIA request for information about candidate Bill Clinton made by another had been filed after Holland's requests and that the CIA had expedited it. In response to Holland's request, the CIA directed him, for privacy reasons, to first obtain the written consent of Mr. Perot. Holland replied that he could not obtain consent and therefore requested all documents that were not protected by Perot's privacy rights, and also suggested that his privacy rights should be circumscribed due to Perot's national prominence. When he received no response, he hand-delivered a request for expedited processing to the CIA, claiming an urgent need for the documents on the grounds that the election was less than a month away. In denying his request, the CIA stated that it granted requests for expedition "only in the rare instances where health and humanitarian considerations create circumstances of exceptional urgency and extraordinary need" and that his request did not satisfy those criteria. The other government agencies involved, including the Department of Defense, the FBI, and the Department of State, also denied Holland's requests either explicitly on privacy grounds, or implicitly through silence.

Holland and the *Nation* sued and sought a court order from a federal district court that would compel the government to disclose the requested documents on an expedited basis. The court refused to grant the writer's motion because it found he had not shown a "substantial likelihood" that the agencies were violating FOIA by refusing to expedite his requests. The court ruled that even though they had exceeded the deadlines given by FOIA, the deadlines were "not mandatory but directory" if the agencies could establish exceptional circumstances and were processing his requests with due diligence. The agencies demonstrated that they were "deluged with FOIA requests" and that the plaintiffs had failed to show requisite urgency, such as a deportation proceeding, a murder trial, or other felony criminal proceeding. The court did not find the dual purposes of selling magazines and adding to the political debate sufficiently urgent to warrant moving the writer's FOIA request to the front of the line.

When the plaintiffs pointed out that the CIA had expedited a similar request for documents about Bill Clinton, the court responded that it would have ordered the Perot documents expedited had the Clinton documents actually been released on an expedited basis. But the agency had admitted it was wrong to expedite the Clinton-related requests, had curtailed the processing mid-stream, and had sworn that it had "returned the requests to their proper places in the queue, and not disclosed them." The court also opined that two wrongs do not make a right: no law requires an agency to extend the erroneous treatment of one party to other parties, "thereby turning an isolated error into a uniform misapplication of the law."

OPEN MEETINGS AND PROCEEDINGS

Along the same lines as FOIA, the Government in the Sunshine Act gives anyone the right to attend meetings of the governing boards of dozens of federal agencies. The Sunshine Act applies to the same agencies as are subject to FOIA. It requires that every part of every meeting conducted by a federal agency be open to the public, unless the meeting is exempt, as determined by a vote of the membership of the agency that is confirmed by the agency's chief legal officer. Agencies must publicize the time, place, and subject matter of their meetings at least a week in advance and publish the notice in the Federal Register (www.gpoaccess.gov/fr/), but the Act does not dictate how the agency must announce the meeting. Some leave an outgoing message on a special phone line; others send messages to parties on its mailing list. Others only list the meeting in the Federal Register. Transcripts of meetings must be kept and made available to the public. If the meeting is closed, detailed minutes must be kept and made available.

The Federal Advisory Committee Act allows the public to attend federal advisory committee meetings. A federal advisory committee is a body of individuals, generally in the private sector, that an executive branch agency establishes or uses to obtain advice or recommendations about government policy. The records and materials of such advisory committees must be publicly available, subject to the FOIA exemptions, and their meetings must be open to the public and publicized in the Federal Register in advance.

CHAPTER 10

CONTRACTS: INTRODUCTION

AND NEGOTIATING BASICS

Y ou are going to be signing contracts. All your business relationships with publishers, with your agent, with third parties who want to re-use your work, with interview subjects from whom you get releases, and more, are governed by contracts. A contract is an agreement that creates legally enforceable obligations between two or more parties. In the event that one party does not fulfill its obligations under a contract, a court can order that it pay money damages or perform its obligations. In the publishing industry, a contract provides the framework in which the rights and obligations of the author and the other party are set forth. With a few exceptions, contracts generally do not have to be in writing to be fully valid and enforceable, although any lawyer will advise her client that the better practice is to use written and signed (i.e., "executed") contracts for all but the simplest transactions.

This chapter explains the elements of a contract and the general law of contract interpretation as a foundation for later chapters covering specific kinds of publishing agreements. It also gives some advice about negotiating contracts. Negotiating intelligently is essential for contract parties in the "weaker" position, and in a publishing transaction, the party with the weaker hand is more often the writer.

OFFER AND ACCEPTANCE

An offer invites the recipient to enter into a contract. It is a promise to give something of value to the offeree in exchange for something of value from the offeror. It may be accepted by a return promise or sometimes by performance based on the terms of the offer. When you receive a communication from a publisher indicating interest in publishing your work, it should contain basic terms, such as a description of the work, the scope of the rights the publisher wishes to license, payment terms, and the approximate delivery and publication dates. If the inquiry does not outline these fundamental terms, then it is not legally an offer.

For example, if a publisher conveys to a writer, "I will pay you $1,000 for first North American serial rights in your story, 'The Doves of Peace,' for my September issue," it has made an offer. The publisher has promised to purchase in definite terms and the author may accept by agreeing to sell the rights to the story on those terms. By contrast, if the publisher says, "Your story, 'The Doves of Peace,' would be a great addition to my September issue," or "'The Doves of Peace' is worth $1,000," or "I'm going to keep this story for a few weeks," it has not yet made an offer, because there is no binding promise that the author can accept. If the publisher says, "You write a story about X, and we'll agree later about the price," or "You write this story and I'll pay you as I see fit," it has not made an offer because at least one essential term—the price—has been omitted. If the publisher says, "Write a story for my forthcoming anthology, and I will pay you $1,000 for it if I decide to include it," it has made a valid offer.[58]

Acceptance of an offer creates a legally binding agreement; rejection terminates the offer. Generally, a party making an offer is free to revoke or revise it any time before it is accepted. The offeror may also legitimately limit the time for acceptance—"I will purchase your story for publication for $1,000 if you will agree to sell it to me within the next ten days." The offer will expire if not accepted at the end of ten days. If no time limit is

---

[58] You should generally avoid accepting such an offer. As a rule, courts allow a dissatisfied commissioning party to reject a work even if a reasonable person would have been satisfied. In other words, you would be working on speculation, an arrangement that you should try to avoid. When you take an assignment to write a piece for a periodical, be sure to include a "kill fee" if the publisher decides not to publish. Chapter 12 covers freelance contribution contracts.

given, the offer expires if not accepted after a reasonable period of time has passed. Importantly, an offer is deemed rejected by a counteroffer. For example, if a publisher offers $1,000 to publish a story and the writer counters for $1,250, the original offer of $1,000 is no longer effective. If the publisher rejects the writer's counteroffer, the writer cannot then accept and enforce the terms of the original offer. Of course, in negotiating the terms of an agreement, the process of offer and counteroffer can happen many times as the parties seek a deal they can each live with.

Acceptance occurs when the offeree agrees to the offer. If the publisher offers $1,000 to a writer to deliver a story on a given topic, the writer may accept by responding: "I agree to write and deliver the story for that amount." The end result of the process of offer and acceptance is a meeting of the minds, a mutual understanding of the parties' intentions as manifested in the contract (whether written or verbal). The courts in every state use the same basic rules to interpret contracts. In all jurisdictions, public policy favors enforcing what the parties have agreed to in their negotiations. When interpreting contracts about which the parties later disagree, courts seek first and foremost to determine the parties' intentions at the time of contracting and will examine primarily the language of the contract, often called the "four corners of the agreement." A court will not rewrite the contract, consider industry custom or prior dealings between the parties, renegotiate a bad deal on one side's behalf, or interpret the conduct of the parties with respect to the particular contract, unless the language of the contract is truly ambiguous about the parties' intentions.

For writers, as for any contracting party, these rules mean that you will be held to the bargain you have struck with the other party, whether or not it is standard in the industry or fair and reasonable or if unforeseen events make performance less profitable or more burdensome.

CONSIDERATION

To be valid, every contract requires the exchange of consideration, which is defined as something of value from each party that is given or promised to the other. Consideration is understood to be the inducement to enter into the contract. When the publisher promises to pay $1,000 for a story that the writer promises to write, each party has exchanged consideration with the other in the form of their promises. The consideration must have been bargained for and agreed upon at the time of entering into the contract. If the parties agree to $1,000 for a story that the author delivers and the publisher says, "Your story is so good that I'm going to pay you an extra $500," the author cannot enforce the second promise, unless some additional bargained for consideration from the author is given.

The only case in which consideration is not required for a contractual obligation to arise occurs when a party relies to her detriment on a promise made. For example, if a patron promises to give money to a writer to buy a computer, and should reasonably know that the writer will rely upon the promise, she cannot refuse to pay the money after the writer has in fact relied on the promise by purchasing the computer. Even though the writer gave or promised nothing of value to the promisor, a court is likely to enforce the promise. This concept is known as "detrimental reliance."

COMPETENCY OF THE PARTIES AND LEGALITY OF PURPOSE

The law will not enforce a contract if both parties are not legally competent to enter it, because in that case there can be no meeting of the minds or mutual understanding. This means that a contract entered into by a person of unsound mind or a legal minor is not enforceable, or is "voidable." A contract made for a purpose that is illegal or against public policy is "void," meaning that it is considered nonexistent in the law.

WRITTEN AND ORAL CONTRACTS

Most contracts need not be written to be fully enforceable by a court.[59] Even when not required, it is usually best to render your agreements in writing to avoid disputes over the terms after you have begun performing your obligations. Reliance on the parties' memories to substantiate

---

[59] Under the Copyright Act, an exclusive license of a copyright or a right under copyright—which encompasses virtually every book and freelance contribution agreement with traditional publishers—must be in writing signed by the licensor. Nonexclusive licenses, on the other hand, may be granted verbally. In addition, oral contracts for services are enforceable in New York if the services can be performed within one year. If the services cannot be completed in one year, the agreement must be made in a writing containing all essential terms of the contract. Other states might require certain kinds of contracts to be in writing.

the terms of a verbal agreement can leave much to chance, unless there are witnesses to the agreement. A written contract need not be a formal document. An exchange of letters or emails constituting the offer and its acceptance can suffice. Often one party proffers a signed letter agreement, and the other party executes the contract by signing at the bottom of the letter beneath the words ACCEPTED AND AGREED. A check can create or be evidence of a contract. For example, a check from a magazine to a writer that states in the memo line: "Payment in full for first North American serial rights to publish 'Doves of Peace'" could be enforced as such.[60] If both parties have not signed an agreement, then a letter, memo, or email from the party against whom enforcement is sought might be enough evidence of a valid contract. As well, if the parties show from their conduct that they believe a binding contract exists, a court might infer an enforceable agreement. But as previously mentioned, when a court has to interpret a written contract, it will not allow evidence of the parties' subsequent oral promises to vary the terms of the writing. Nor will courts accept evidence of promises made before the contract was signed if these promises do not appear in the written contract. These rules apply unless the written contract was procured by fraud or mistake or cannot be understood without the additional oral statements.

AMENDMENTS

Any contract can be changed subsequent to execution if both parties agree to do so. Amendments are routinely made to extend deadlines or change the subject matter or length of the work to be delivered. Even when the contract is oral, amendments should be made in writing; if the contract is written, amendments to it must be in writing to be enforceable.

WARRANTIES

Caveat emptor—"let the buyer beware"—is the long-standing view of the courts toward agreements to purchase property. Unless specifically agreed otherwise, most property is still considered sold "as is." Warranties reverse

---

[60] If the check conflicts with your agreement, return it to the publisher and ask for a check that accurately states that the agreed terms.

this presumption. Warranties are express or implied promises on which the purchaser of property, including the publisher of your book or article, may legally rely and therefore may legally enforce. Even if the contract is in writing, some warranties can be given orally. They can be created during negotiations, at the time of making the contract, or, in certain transactions not normally relevant to writers, after entry into the contract.

An express warranty is created when the seller makes a promise relating to the character of or title to the work, if the purchaser relies on them in deciding to purchase. In most book publishing contracts, the author must expressly warrant to the publisher that the work is original to the writer and that it does not infringe any copyright or trademark rights, violate other personal or property rights, or contain any defamatory or unlawful matter. If any of these express warranties prove untrue, the author will be in breach of the contract and legally obligated to the publisher for the losses that result. But sales talk or opinions by a party about the value or merit of the work do not create a warranty. For example, if an author convinces an agent or publisher that her work is "the next Harry Potter," or "is sure to lead to a movie deal," the agent or publisher cannot logically rely on that opinion, so no warranty arises.

An implied warranty is created by operation of law, rather than express representations of the parties, based on the circumstances of the transaction or the relationship of the parties. In some sales (though not in publishing licenses), there is an implied warranty that the seller has title or the right to convey title in the goods being sold. In other sales of complex products or services, courts might find an implied warranty of fitness for a particular purpose. As a result, savvy sellers will make sure their contracts specifically disclaim any such implied warranties, and such disclaimers are enforced.

ASSIGNMENTS OF CONTRACTS

Sometimes one party to a contract may, without permission of the other party, substitute a third party to assume its obligations and/or reap the benefits of the contract. Assignments are not generally enforceable when the contract is based upon the unique skills or persona of one of the parties. For example, in a publishing contract the author may not delegate her obligation to write the manuscript to another author, but she may assign to a third party her right to receive the royalties. On the other hand, a publisher that is acquired by or merges with another publisher might be allowed, without the author's permission, to assign her contract to the acquiring publisher. A well-drafted contract will set forth the understanding of the parties as to the right to delegate duties or assign rights under the contract.

SUBSTANTIAL PERFORMANCE

Unless the contract specifies that performance obligations must be strictly followed, courts accept substantial performance as adequate and therefore not a breach. For example, if a book contract requires delivery of a manuscript by January 15, delivery by January 20 will constitute substantial performance unless the contract says that "time of delivery is of the essence."[61] On the other hand, in most states, a party who only partially (as opposed to substantially) performs is not entitled to partial payment of the consideration, unless the partial performance substantially benefits the other party who accepts and retains those benefits. If the performance obligations in a contract can be neatly segregated, such as when certain payments are intended for each of a number of specified articles, the author might be able to recover the payment agreed for each partial performance. Otherwise, delivery of only some of a promised work will not entitle a writer to payment under a contract, and in fact will constitute a breach.

NONPERFORMANCE EXCUSED

There are a few situations in which a party's failure to perform her contractual obligations will be excused. The death of an author prior to delivery of a manuscript, for example, does not amount to a breach of contract, so the publisher could not recover the advance from the author's estate. Similarly, because the author's work is personal to her, a disabling physical or mental illness must excuse performance, although some contracts expressly extend the author's time for performance in the event of ill health. If one party to a contract takes action or refuses to act and thereby prevents the other from performing, the aggrieved party's obligation is excused and she has a case

---

[61] For periodical contracts, strictly meeting delivery deadlines might be essential for the publisher; this is virtually never the case for book contracts.

for breach of contract. Similarly, impossibility might excuse performance, as in the case of an interviewer who cannot conduct the interview because the subject becomes unavailable. Finally, performance is excused if it would be illegal under a law passed after the contract was made.

REMEDIES FOR BREACH OF CONTRACT

If either party fails to perform her obligations under a contract, she could be held liable for the financial loss suffered by the other party that arises from the breach (unless performance is excused). But, unless it is specifically written into the contract, termination (or "rescission") of the agreement is not ordinarily a remedy for a breach. For example, if a publisher accepts an author's manuscript but fails to pay the advance due or to publish as promised, the author could sue for her financial losses, but she could not walk away from the contract and sell her work elsewhere, unless the remedy of rescission for such a breach is expressly provided. Also, contracts often give the nonperforming party a chance to perform her obligations within a certain period of time after notice from the other party before she is liable for breach.

Courts generally award damages only if the nonbreaching party demonstrates its actual loss or measurable detriment because of the breach. The amount of damages awarded typically equals the reasonably foreseeable losses, including out-of-pocket costs and lost profits, actually caused by the breach. Usually, the injured party must take steps to minimize (or "mitigate") the damages. Some contracts specify the measure of damages in advance to avoid the necessity of having to prove them at trial. Courts will enforce these provisions, known as "liquidated damages," if actual damages would be difficult or impossible to establish and the amount specified is not unreasonable or punitive. Many book contracts provide for liquidated damages equal to the amount of the advance paid or due under the contract if the publisher breaches the obligation to publish the manuscript. Some contracts provide that if the author fails to deliver, she must repay the amount of the advance received; whether or not such a term is considered a liquidated damage provision depends on the language used.

SPECIFIC PERFORMANCE

In rare situations, money damages will not adequately compensate for the loss caused by a breach of contract. In those cases, courts might require the breaching party to actually perform its contractual obligations. Because involuntary servitude is, of course, illegal, contracts to provide personal services cannot be enforced by specific performance. Therefore, the obligation to create a written work cannot be forced on an author, and, for First Amendment reasons, a publisher cannot be forced to publish a work against its will, despite having contracted to do so. But if an author has written a story pursuant to a contract and refuses to deliver it to the contracting publisher, a court might well order specific performance of the author's promise to license the publishing rights to the work; whether it does might depend on whether the contract specifically provides for liquidated damages for such a breach.

When personal services promised under a contract are not performed, a court cannot order specific performance, but it might prohibit the breaching party from giving the promised services to another party. For example, if a famous author agrees to give a lecture series at a certain institution, her failure to honor the contract might be difficult to value in dollars, so a court could enjoin her from giving lectures at any other institution during the time period covered in the first contract.

STATUTES OF LIMITATIONS

The *statute of limitations* is the time period within which an injured party must bring suit to seek redress. After the statute of limitations has expired, an aggrieved party is forever barred from suing for the breach. In cases of breach of contract, the statute of limitations begins at the time of the breach, and varies from state to state. In New York, it is six years, and in California, it is four years for written agreements, two years for oral agreements.[62] The parties may agree in the contract to decrease the applicable limitations period, and such agreements will be enforced. In book publishing contracts, which are frequently based on New York law, the publisher often tries to limit the time in which an author may claim royalty underpayments to two years, in contrast to the six-year statute of limitations for breach of contract.

---

[62] Many states recognize a longer limitations period for written contracts than for oral or implied contracts.

BAILMENTS

A *bailment* is a situation in which one person gives her property to be held by another person. For example, an author or illustrator might leave a manuscript containing unique artwork at the office of her agent, publisher, or printer. In such cases, where both parties benefit from the bailment, the law requires the person who takes possession of the property to exercise reasonable care in safeguarding it. If that person is negligent and the work is damaged or lost, the other party may recover for the loss. Even if the work has no easily ascertainable market value, damages might still be awarded based on the intrinsic value of the work.

BASIC RULES OF CONTRACT NEGOTIATION

The short-term end product of a negotiation is the written contract embodying your agreement. The long-term result, of course, is your ongoing relationship with the other party over the course of the agreement—which, in a book publishing deal could last a lifetime, or even longer.[63] When it comes to licensing the rights to your work, therefore, the stakes are high.

First, and foremost, remember that you must live with the contract you sign. Many written contracts state outright that the terms expressed in the agreement set forth the entirety of the parties' intentions with respect to the subject matter of the agreement, and that no promises made during the negotiations will be enforced unless they appear in the final contract. Even if a contract does not contain such a "merger clause," courts will interpret most contracts to provide the same thing. Keep in mind, therefore, that if any of your publisher's promises are not set forth in your contract, they are worthless.

Most established book authors have literary agents who will negotiate the terms of book and other licenses on their clients' behalf, but that does not make you a passive participant in the negotiation. Whether or not you have an agent, you should learn some basic negotiation rules. There is much literature covering the art and science of negotiating avail-

---

[63] Your copyrights last for seventy years after you die; your publishing contracts could stay in force through the entire term of copyright.

able, free online and in many books and journals. Take the time to review some of this advice before engaging in direct negotiations; it will prove a very good investment of your time. Although the advice below refers to book publishing contracts, it applies to any other deal you might negotiate, including with a literary agent, periodical publisher, self-publishing entity, or a collaborator.

To negotiate effectively, you must plan. The more you plan, gather information, and strategize, the better your chances of getting the best possible deal. Negotiation consists of trading concessions with the other side on the various terms of a transaction, and the better you understand and can rank both your own and the other side's priorities, the better you will understand how to make and receive concessions that effectively satisfy both sides' desires—the ideal outcome.

WHAT DOES YOUR PUBLISHER WANT?

Book publishing is a business. Of course your publisher wants to make a profit from publishing your work; in today's industry, that is usually a given. As well, every publisher, even among the "Big Six" North American tradebook publishers,[64] has unique priorities and needs. And importantly, although you are legally dealing with a corporate entity, you are in fact dealing with people, primarily one person—usually the acquisitions editor who has initiated the offer. Perhaps she does not envision your work as a big money maker, but is instead looking for prestige and awards. Or, as with Amazon in its new direct publishing venture, a new publisher or imprint might be willing initially to publish at a loss in order to increase its market presence. Your job, prior to beginning direct negotiations, is to find out what your publisher likely wants to gain from offering to publish your work. If you assume it wants to profit both from publishing your book and from investing in you as an author with a future, you are probably correct.

Beyond these assumptions, it is perfectly acceptable to ask questions during the negotiation to assess the publisher's priorities, although you will

---

[64] As of this writing, they are Random House, Simon & Schuster, Penguin Group, Macmillan, HarperCollins, and Hachette Books Group, but they might soon become the Big Five—in a troubling sign about the weakness of the trade book industry, Random House and Penguin have announced plans to merge. Each of the big publishers has many imprints, some of which have their own standard form contracts.

probably want to corroborate the information you receive to the extent you can do so.

WHAT DOES THE PUBLISHER BRING TO THE TABLE?

In order to secure for yourself the things you want most from your deal, you should understand the extent to which your publisher can deliver those things, and what it will cost to do so. For example, if you think your work can sell well in the college market and you want to be in a position to earn steady royalties from the work, you should find out whether a publisher that wants your work has a presence in and invests in selling in that market, as well as whether or not it withholds significant amounts of royalties earned against returns. Or, if you have a significant public platform—a well-read blog or frequent appearances on TV or radio—and you want a publisher that is willing and able to leverage your platform by dedicating competent staff and other resources to work with you, discover whether it does so for other writers on its list. If a publisher making you an offer does not normally provide its authors with the things you want, you must take that into account when negotiating.

How do you discover your publisher's needs, strengths, and weaknesses? One easy way is to ask questions in a diplomatic way during the negotiations. Beyond that, if you join a writers organization and subscribe to some of the industry resources set forth in chapter 1, you can readily utilize those resources, which are among the best available. Call on your network of fellow writers and do a lot of research about the publisher and the editors with whom you will be working.

WHAT DO YOU WANT?

Beyond the satisfaction of having their creative work made widely available to the public, professional authors must consider other priorities. Earning a fair financial return from publication of your work is important, so you will need to understand and address the many terms of a book contract that deal with money—the advance, royalties for every territory, format and discount rate, subsidiary rights license fees and accounting. But there are other interests that can be equally or even more important. If you want to work with a particular editor, or to have the freedom to write and publish in a variety of genres with different publishers, or if you have established a reputation in a particular field and want to enhance it by giving copies of your book away at speaking engagements, you should keep these other priorities in mind as you review an offer and plan the negotiation.

Control over the final product. Editorial control over the final manuscript, the identity of the editor, publication format and pricing, and copyediting might be more or less important to secure, depending on your publisher's record in these areas. Having any measure of control over any of these elements of your work is not a given, unless stated in the contract.

Future projects. Standard book contracts often contain clauses that require the author to offer her next work to the publisher during an exclusive period and not to publish "competing works" with another publisher. Depending on your plans for future projects, these terms might be acceptable, or not. Even if you have a good experience with the publisher, you will want to limit its rights to option and restrict your future work to comport with your plans. In addition, if sometime after publication, the work is no longer selling, you will want the rights you granted to revert back to you. Dean Koons's first four books had modest sales and eventually went out of print. Before his agent brought him to another publishing house, the agent made sure to get the rights back to those titles. After Koons became a bestselling author, those early books had a very fruitful second life under terms that were much more favorable to him.

Reputation. The prestige and reputation for quality of your editor and publisher might trump short-term financial return for you. Or the converse might be the case; if you are publishing mass market genre fiction under a pseudonym to make some quick cash, the first thing on your list of priorities should be the largest advance you can get.

WHAT DO YOU BRING TO THE TABLE?

In agreeing to license your work for publication, you might think you have nothing more of value to trade. Any publisher or agent will tell you that this is not, and should not be, the case. Your publisher will want to know whether you can sell your book to the public and to other potential licensees, such as foreign publishers, Hollywood, or Broadway. Examine your strengths, your network of contacts, do your best to build a publicity platform, and determine what more you can bring to the table. Doing so will inform the concessions you might ask for, such as a higher discount for copies of the book that you buy from the publisher to sell during speaking engagements. It can also give you more concessions to trade for your priorities. For example, if you already have interest from an established film producer in your book but you need six months to finish it, you can advise the publisher and offer a share of film production license fees in exchange for a higher advance.

NEGOTIATION TIPS

Know your BATNA. The BATNA—the "best alternative to a negotiated agreement"—is a fundamental concept of negotiation, popularized by Roger Fisher and William Ury in their classic book *Getting to Yes*. It is a simple idea and essential to, even inherent in, any negotiation. If you have no or few other options to reach your ultimate objective, this knowledge will affect your strategy. But think hard about whether you have other options. For example, if your proposal has only recently reached other publishers and you are waiting for responses, or if you have received more than one offer, or if you believe you can self-publish and successfully market your work, then you have feasible alternatives. Knowing your BATNA will strongly inform your strategy and your bottom line, i.e., the point beyond which you will reject the deal.

It can also be tremendously useful to try to ascertain the publisher's BATNA. Perhaps it is obvious that, as buyers in a sellers' market, the publisher has many other choices of works to publish if you cannot come to an agreement. But remember: the fact that it has made you an offer means that it has already invested time and resources into acquiring your work and therefore values it. If the publisher walks away, it loses that particular investment and valuable work.

The more they invest, the more they will invest. It is a fact of human nature that the more a person invests in a product, service or potential return, the more she will be willing to continue investing in it. Watch people who spend a lot of time at particular slot machines at a casino. The longer they spend putting money into "their" machines, the harder it is for them to tear themselves away. It might seem counterintuitive, but if you take your time in a negotiation, causing the other party to invest time and effort toward a successful conclusion, the more that party is likely to continue to invest and the less likely it is to walk away.

Do not accept the first offer. If you posted an item for sale for $100 on Craigslist and received a full-price offer within seconds, would you be happy, or would you think you had sold yourself short? By contrast, what if a purchaser had offered you $80 and you negotiated to an agreed price of $90? Would you think you had offered the item for too little? That is less likely than in the first scenario, where you actually received more money. Similarly, if a publisher offers you a certain advance and royalty rates and your agent leaps to accept the deal, the publisher will probably think it offered too much.[65] There is no reason in the world why you should immediately accept the first offer, even if you end up at the original numbers offered after some rounds of discussion.

Be aspirational, even unreasonable. The fact that a party wants to make a deal with you means that it sees an opportunity to profit from doing so. That said, when it makes an offer, it is likely to be offering as little as it can without being unreasonable. The publisher knows that the first offer sets the tone and anchors the entire negotiation. Consider this when deciding on your counteroffer. That is not to say your counter should be outlandish, but understand that the publisher's first offer is not likely to be what it is willing to give in the end. A good way to determine your counteroffer is to ask for the basis on which the publisher is making its offer. If it offers a principled basis, your counter can take that into account.

Be creative. A negotiation does not have to end with a "winner" and a "loser" on every issue. If you reach what seems to be an impasse on a particular point, see if you can each gain what is really being sought by approaching the question creatively. Ask yourself, and the other side, what is each party's objective? Perhaps there are other ways, besides money, for each side to come away with at least a portion of what it is seeking.

Control the timing, and negotiate in rounds. Do not let yourself be rushed. You might be anxious for the deal to be signed, especially because you might be getting some compensation upon execution. But keep in mind the tried and true rule that negotiators tend to concede more to close a deal when they believe the window of opportunity is closing. Remember, the publisher has already invested in you and your agreement and no doubt wants to be finished as soon as possible as well. Find out when the publisher plans to publish your work. If it intends to list your book in its catalog soon, then it, too, has a short window to conclude the deal. By the same token,

---

[65] Do not worry that your agent will do this; even if the book has been rejected by two dozen other publishers, a good agent is savvy enough to understand this basic rule.

it is a mistake to think that one round of offer, counteroffer, and response is all you can expect in the negotiation. Consider the publisher's response to your counteroffer and send another round of comments and requests for changes on terms if you are not satisfied with the response. You are likely to achieve more than is offered in response to your first counteroffer if you ask.

CHAPTER 11

NEGOTIATING A BOOK

CONTRACT

Receiving a serious offer of any size from a publisher to pay you an advance and publish your book is cause for celebration. Publishing any book calls for a major investment. If it has made you an offer, the publisher has had professionals read and re-read your submission, analyzed its projected earnings and loss, and concluded either that it will profit from investing in your book, or that your work is so good that it must be published, even at a loss. Truly, congratulations are in order if you have reached this stage.

NEGOTIATION BASICS

The offer might be embodied verbally or in a letter or a "deal points memo" that contains the financial and other basic terms of the transaction and will be the basis of the first phase of negotiations. The terms at this stage typically include a description of the work, the scope of the rights to be granted—territories, formats, languages, and certain subsidiary rights, the advance and its payment schedule, base royalties and subsidiary rights fee splits, the manuscript delivery date, and possibly other features of publication, such as a publicity plan. These terms are the meat of the deal and tend to be the focus of the most intense part of the negotiations. The advice in this chapter applies both to the deal points and the formal contract.[66]

Once these basic terms have been settled, you will be given the publisher's standard form contract to sign. It should contain the basic terms you have agreed to, but it will also probably be long, detailed, and written in so-called legalese. If the document incorporates the agreed deal points, you might be tempted to sign it without trying to fully understand, much less negotiate, the boilerplate. Resist that urge. The contract will govern your relationship with the publisher for years to come. If you sign the standard form without requesting changes, you might someday regret having done so. Beyond the deal points, many other critical terms governing the business relationship appear, and they are drafted to favor the publisher's interests at the expense of yours. Your agreement to the deal points does not oblige you to accept these other terms. No matter how many or how few books you have previously published, you can successfully negotiate changes to the contract, but you must ask for them.

This is not to say the publisher will agree to all your requests. There will surely be a gap between your ideal terms and what the publisher will concede. You are more likely to encounter intransigence from genre fiction publishers, particularly, it seems, from category romance publishers (i.e., Harlequin, Kensington). Their boilerplate terms are generally stingier across the board, with lower royalties and subsidiary rights shares, a larger scope of rights demanded, and more onerous option and noncompetition clauses. No matter what kind of contract you are dealing with, the best way to help yourself is to choose the issues most important to you, rank them in order of importance, and concentrate on negotiating the corresponding terms. Achieving an acceptable compromise on your high priority clauses will be a significant accomplishment.

Most book contracts appear on forms referred to as "boilerplate" that your publisher supplies. The parties can amend the boilerplate by deleting, adding, and revising terms as agreed. If the publisher cannot process the changes into the document, they can be attached as an addendum incorpo-

---

[66] Every writer who is offered a book contract should read Mark L. Levine's book *Negotiating a Book Contract* (Asphodel Press, 2009). It explains the terms of a publishing contract clearly and gives invaluable negotiating advice.

rated by reference or added by hand or typed directly onto the document, in which case, both parties should initial all changes to the form.

If you have an agent, she should be practiced in successful negotiations. If she has previously sold other clients' work to your publisher, she should have her own, prenegotiated "agency version" of the publisher's form, which favors her clients' interests. Still, review the proposed contract and don't be afraid to suggest additional changes to suit your priorities, and remain engaged with your agent throughout the negotiation.[67]

The following explanation covers the typical provisions of most trade book publishing contracts in thematic sections corresponding to the business relationship: ownership and control of the work; acceptance and publication of the manuscript; financial matters; allocation of the legal risks of publishing; and the future of the book and the author/publisher relationship. Genre fiction and academic publishing contracts will differ somewhat in their terms (usually to the writer's detriment) and in what the publisher will agree to change, but the advice here does apply to these contracts.

Although a member of the editorial department will probably negotiate the deal points, many publishers have a contracts department that handles legal negotiations. For that reason, the best way to request changes might be in a letter to your agent (if you have one) or editor, who can forward it to the contracts department.

OWNERSHIP AND CONTROL

THE GRANT OF RIGHTS

The heart of the transaction is the author's grant to the publisher of some rights under copyright[68] to exploit commercially in exchange for a share of the proceeds. The "grant of rights" clause sets forth the rights you are licensing to the publisher. You can limit the grant according to the kind of

---

[67] Members of the Authors Guild receive a Model Trade Book Contract and Guide and may call on Guild attorneys to review, explain, and advise on their contracts at no charge. If you need help understanding or negotiating provisions, and especially if you do not have a literary agent, you should join the Guild and take advantage of these valuable tools.

[68] The rights under copyright include: reproduction; distribution of copies; public display; public performance; and the creation of derivative works. These rights can be further divided according to such specifics as territory, languages, and formats, and can be granted exclusively or nonexclusively. See chapter 2 for basics of copyright and licensing.

media or formats the publisher intends to exploit (e.g., "the right to print, publish and sell hardcover and/or paperback and/or mass market paperback editions"), the territory (e.g., "the right to sell copies in North America" and/or "world rights"), languages, and duration (e.g., "for the full term of copyright," or less). These rights are valuable to each party. The key tension in the negotiation will therefore involve the division of rights. As a rule, you should reserve rights the publisher cannot gainfully exploit and seek the highest possible revenue for the rights you do grant. The publisher, in turn, will seek the broadest scope of rights it can get for the lowest possible payment.

Read the grant of rights clause carefully. It should say that you are granting your publisher the right to print, publish, and sell your work in book formats (possibly including ebooks) in the United States and its territories. It might also include additional rights that the publisher will not directly exploit, but that it wishes to control ("subsidiary rights"). It might do this through extremely broad language, such as "The Author grants to the Publisher all rights in and to the Work," or " . . . grants the copyright in the Work," or " . . . grants all rights of whatever nature in and to the Work." You should reject such broad language and request that the contract delineate every right you are granting in words you can understand. A blanket grant of all rights or the entire copyright is not industry standard for a trade book contract, and you should not agree to it.[69]

If you grant more than the right to publish the work in various book formats, then the contract should contain a separate "Subsidiary Rights" clause, listing each ancillary right and the allocation of income earned from them to be shared by author and publisher. Beware of any "catchall" right (e.g. "all other rights to license the work in any format . . . ") in the subsidiary rights clause; you are more likely to see this in genre book contracts. If you cannot delete it, seek at least a 50 percent share and prior approval for exploitation of such rights.

SUBSIDIARY RIGHTS

Rights that your publisher takes but does not directly exploit, instead sublicensing them to third parties, are known as subsidiary rights, or "subrights."

---

[69] Some academic publishers request a grant of the copyright, but they are generally willing to limit the grant and to revert the rights when the work is out of print.

It can be helpful to think of subsidiary rights as falling into three general categories: print-related, non–print-related, and foreign. Each category is treated somewhat differently. Print-related subrights include reprints of the book in other formats (e.g., paperback) by another publisher, abridgments, book club versions, first (prepublication) and second (postpublication) serial rights (i.e., excerpts appearing in periodicals), the use of selections in anthologies, coursepacks, or other publications, and audio books. Non–print-related rights include syndication, merchandising uses, film, television, dramatizations, multimedia uses, and translations. Typically, the author grants exclusive print-related subrights to the publisher, but reserves nonprint and foreign rights if she has an agent. It is generally better to reserve rights that you or your agent can directly market, because the income from them goes directly to you instead of being applied against your publishing advance.

PRINT-RELATED SUBRIGHTS

Print-related subsidiary rights are typically granted to the publisher and the income from exploiting most of them are shared with the author 50-50. The exceptions are first serial and audio book rights: if you have an agent, she will try to reserve those rights for you; if you grant first serial rights to the publisher, your share of the income should approach 90 percent. Consider asking for the right to approve of how and to whom the publisher sublicenses the work in print-related formats, how much of the book may be used, and the fees charged. Otherwise, the publisher may sell these rights for any price it chooses without your knowledge, unless and until the sale appears on your royalty statement.

NON-PRINT-RELATED SUBSIDIARY RIGHTS

Although many boilerplate contracts include grants of non–print-related subrights, it is unusual to grant them. Because the publisher cannot directly use or market these rights, it should not control or receive a share of the proceeds from them. The publisher might argue that by publishing the book, it is making a large investment, without which third party filmmakers and others would not know the work has value. If you have an agent, that argument will hold no water and she will reserve these rights on your behalf. If you do not have an agent or the means to exploit the rights, you might be better served by granting dramatic (including film and television) and other rights. But if you grant any of these rights make sure to include appropriate safeguards and payment terms. The publisher should not receive more than 10 percent of the income as its share (or up to 25 percent for foreign sales of these rights). The rest should go to you.[70] For all such subrights, it is important that you retain the right to prior approval of any proposed sublicenses (especially for dramatic, film, and multimedia rights), to limit the number of years the publisher has these rights before they revert back to you (two to three years after the book is published is reasonable), to receive your share of advances paid for these rights immediately, without having it applied against your unearned book advance (this right is called "flow through"), and to obtain certain royalty accounting terms (such as those set forth at the end of this chapter) in the sublicenses. In any case, it is unwise to grant merchandising rights to the publisher. Doing so could interfere with your ability to write sequels or use certain characters or to exploit other reserved rights.

FOREIGN RIGHTS

The right to publish in countries outside of the United States and its territories and to publish in languages other than English might be listed as separate subsidiary rights or included in the main grant of rights (i.e., "worldwide rights in all languages"). If you have an agent, she will try to reserve foreign rights. Many of the largest publishers have international affiliates or operations, however, and might demand exclusive publishing rights in the foreign countries in which they operate, or even worldwide rights. Before you grant any foreign rights, scrutinize the royalties offered for foreign sales. They are usually lower than royalties for US sales and they could be significantly lower than an unrelated foreign publisher would be willing to pay if you contracted directly with it. If you grant your US publisher the right to publish in foreign countries, consider asking it to agree to match (or exceed) the best royalties available on the open market in each territory, or to allow you to bring in a better offer from a different publisher in a territory. You should also ask for a higher advance to reflect the extra value of what you are granting; remember, if you reserved and licensed those rights to foreign publishers, you would receive separate advances from them.

Your agent should reserve the rights to publish in countries where your publisher does not publish directly. If you do not have an agent, it makes

---

[70] Children's book publishers might ask for up to 50 percent of the income for these rights. Taking more than 50 percent in any context is unreasonable and unfair.

sense to grant foreign rights to your publisher. The income from foreign sublicenses is typically split 75 percent to 85 percent to the author and 15 percent to 25 percent to the publisher, corresponding to an agent's share (including a foreign agent's commission). Typical boilerplate contracts allow the publisher to subtract its expenses, including a foreign agent's commission, from this income before splitting it with you; this is double-dipping and unfair. If your agent reserves and sells the rights, she will typically take a 20 percent to 25 percent commission to cover both hers and the foreign agent's commission.

Whether you grant foreign publication rights directly or as subsidiary rights, consider asking the publisher to revert the rights back to you if they are not sold within two or three years after US publication. Another option is to grant foreign rights nonexclusively, which allows you to market them yourself whether or not the publisher does so.

ELECTRONIC RIGHTS

For almost twenty years, authors and agents have wrestled with publishers over electronic rights. The issues of contention included the kinds of digital formats to be granted, whether ebooks and multimedia uses were treated as subsidiary or direct publication rights, and the corresponding amount of royalties and/or subsidiary rights fees. But these arguments were largely theoretical until 2007. That was the year ebooks, defined as digital versions of a printed book without significant additional material (sometimes called "verbatim electronic rights" in contracts), became a substantial and growing component of the retail market, thanks to the reading public's embrace of eReaders such as the Kindle, the Nook, and the iPad. Growth in the number of sales of ebooks is rising rapidly, and this—along with Amazon's current dominance of that market—is wreaking big changes in the industry.

Negotiate the scope of electronic rights to be granted at the time you discuss the advance and other deal points. The contract should distinguish ebooks from multimedia uses, which add audio, animation, images, and other media to the text. Most publishers will ask for ebook rights and treat them as another book format, offering a royalty per sale, and will often agree to let the author reserve multimedia rights. If you grant ebook rights, include a clause stating that the publisher may exploit the book electronically only in its entirety and without changes, or ask for the right to approve in advance of hyperlinks, abridgments, anthologies, or the exploitation of excerpts. If you grant multimedia rights, reserve the right to approve of all formats and other media added to the work. Obtain assurance that the work will be protected from unauthorized copying using at least industry-standard technology and that sublicensees will be required to display a copyright notice prominently and also to use the best available means to prevent unauthorized copying. Ask for a reversion of rights to you of digital uses that the publisher fails to exploit for a specified period after first print publication. Multimedia rights are not directly exploited by publishers and are more akin to non–print-related subsidiary rights; this fact gives you a good argument that you should get more than a 50 percent share for these rights.

LENGTH OF THE GRANT

The duration of the grant of rights (and, therefore, the duration of the contract) is usually "the full term of copyright and any renewals and extensions thereof."[71] The publisher is likely to veto a request for a shorter term. However, as explained below, every contract should also provide that your rights will revert back to you and the contract will end when the work goes out of print. As mentioned, you might also request a reversion of non-print-related and foreign subsidiary rights if not exploited by the publisher within a short window of time—such as two or three years—from the date of first publication. As long as the reversion of rights clause appropriately defines "out of print," it is generally not worth arguing about the duration of the grant of rights.[72]

RESERVATION OF RIGHTS TO AUTHOR

Every contract should provide that "all rights not specifically granted in the contract" are reserved by you. If yours does not, add it. Above all, do not allow the reverse, that is, for the publisher to be the owner by default of any rights that you did not specifically grant. As well, make sure that any non-competition restriction in the contract (explained later in this chapter) does not defeat the purpose of your reservation of rights by prohibiting your use of a new, or newly popular, method of exploiting the work.

---

[71] The full term of copyright currently expires 70 years after the author's death.

[72] Even if your book never goes out of print, you have an inalienable right under the Copyright Act to terminate any license after thirty-five years. See chapter 2.

DELIVERY, ACCEPTANCE, AND PUBLICATION OF THE MANUSCRIPT

The clauses addressing this aspect of the relationship are the preamble to the contract, terms addressing what you must deliver and how the publisher must treat the manuscript, and the publisher's obligation to publish.

THE PREAMBLE

This clause typically introduces the contract and should identify the work by describing the proposed subject matter, format, length, and possibly the market (e.g., "young adult"). Make sure the description is consistent with your proposal and what you plan to deliver. Consider giving yourself some flexibility here. For example, you might avoid characterizing the point of view of the book or describe the length in terms of the "approximate number of book pages" (which can be adjusted) rather than the number of words or manuscript pages. Your book will be defined for purposes of the contract as the "Work."

DELIVERY OF THE MANUSCRIPT

The contract will give the deadline for your delivery of the complete, "satisfactory" manuscript. The publisher is planning to publish your book in a particular seasonal catalog and needs the finished manuscript within a certain time frame in order to do so. Still, its plans will not come to fruition for many months and are likely to be somewhat flexible. You should be realistic about how much time you need to deliver—and then add more time for unexpected delays. If your book depends on future events, the availability of information, or other contingencies, then add a clause that permits you to extend the deadline unilaterally with written notice if such contingencies prevent delivery on deadline. After the contract is signed, if you agree to extend the delivery deadline, make sure to formalize the extension in writing signed by the publisher.

Most importantly, delete any words to the effect that the deadline for delivery is "of the essence." Courts allow a reasonable grace period for late contract performance unless the contract says that "time is of the essence" regarding a deadline. If that language, which is not standard in the book industry, appears, then delivering even one day late is a breach that cannot be remedied.

Be careful of language requiring the author to deliver "all" or "any" additional materials deemed necessary by the publisher. This language makes you vulnerable to demands for work—an index, illustrations, appendices, for example—that you did not consider when you agreed to the advance and deadline. It is better to specify in the contract as precisely as possible the materials you have agreed to provide, or at least state that additional materials must be "mutually agreed" by author and publisher. The publisher might require that illustrations be delivered at the same time as the manuscript for art books, children's books, and similar works.[73] Otherwise, allow yourself a realistic time and grace period to prepare any other materials you have agreed to provide.

Most contracts make the author responsible for obtaining and paying for permissions to include others' work in the book. You might argue that the publisher is better able to pay for permissions, but the publisher might then want to reduce the advance. For anthologies, textbooks, and similar works, publishers often agree to provide a budget for permissions. For more information about obtaining permissions, see chapter 5.

SATISFACTORY MANUSCRIPT

Most book contracts are offered on the basis of a proposal and give the author several months or more to deliver the manuscript. Almost every contract further states that the author must deliver a "satisfactory" or "acceptable" manuscript. Be careful about the wording of this clause. If the manuscript must be "satisfactory [or acceptable] in the publisher's sole discretion," the publisher may legally reject the manuscript and terminate the contract even if the book is professionally competent and fits the contractual description. Should this occur, the publisher's obligation to publish vanishes and the author can be deemed in breach and obliged to repay the advance received. Events such as your editor's departure from the publisher, the publication of a competing work, a decrease in general interest in the subject matter, or a change in the publisher's financial outlook could all be deemed legitimate reasons to reject a publishable manuscript.

---

[73] If you are providing illustrations, consider inserting a clause requiring the publisher to provide insurance against loss or damage to the original artwork and to return it to you when no longer needed.

Authors' advocates recommend substituting "professionally competent and fit for publication" for "satisfactory." The publisher is more likely to agree to stipulate that the manuscript must be "acceptable in form and content to the publisher" or "satisfactory in the publisher's editorial judgment" or its "reasonable judgment." This additional language is the bare minimum you should negotiate for; and it should prevent the publisher from rejecting a competent manuscript because of countervailing events outside your control.

You can also protect yourself by requiring the publisher to give you written editorial comments and a realistic period, such as sixty days, to submit revisions before rejecting the manuscript, and by making sure the preamble and delivery clauses contain accurate descriptions of what you intend to deliver. If the publisher made the offer on the basis of an entire manuscript rather than a proposal, indicate that the satisfactory manuscript "has been delivered," or that it will be deemed satisfactory with minor edits. Consider asking whether you may submit portions of the work in progress and get the publisher's acceptance of each portion within a reasonable time of receipt.

Another protection is a stipulation that if the advance must be returned because the publisher rejects the manuscript for editorial reasons, it will be repaid out of the "first proceeds" of a subsequent contract with another publisher for the same book. Some publishers will agree to provide that repayment must be made from first proceeds or by a specified date, whichever occurs first.

Finally, negotiate for language that allows you to keep the entire advance and quickly terminate the contract if the publisher decides not to publish for other than editorial reasons. This would free you to sell the work elsewhere and keep your advance.

COPYEDITING, PROOFREADING, AND CORRECTION OF PROOFS

You should obtain a right to approve of any substantive changes your editor makes to the manuscript, although the publisher might insist that your approval not be "unreasonably withheld." Copyediting changes—punctuation, grammar, spelling, and capitalization, and corrections of errors of fact or manuscript inconsistencies—could affect the manuscript significantly, and so should be subject to your review. Most publishers will reasonably ask you to review page proofs and to pay the cost of your alterations to proofs that exceed 10 percent of the cost of their composition, unless caused by printer's errors.

PUBLICATION

Make certain that your contract gives the publisher a specific deadline to publish after acceptance of the manuscript, and that "publication" means the distribution of printed books in the United States. Most contracts require the publisher to publish the work within twelve to eighteen months after acceptance, or up to twenty-four months for smaller publishers or children's picture books. Except in special circumstances, any period longer than that is unreasonable.

If possible, provide that if the publisher fails to publish a US edition on time, you may terminate the contract, recover your rights, and keep the advance; some publishers will agree to this only after the author makes a written demand and gives the publisher an additional grace period of several months. Art books and children's picture books are especially vulnerable to open-ended publication clauses that depend on the selection of the artist and completion of the artwork, two details that fall outside the author's control. Negotiate deadlines for the publisher's completion of these events; otherwise you could wait many years for publication.

Most contracts allow the publisher to publish the work "in a style, manner, and price" that it determines unilaterally. A right to consult on retail price and print runs (i.e., the number of copies published) is probably out of the question for all but the most powerful authors. But title, design, and artwork can be crucial elements of the book, and you might want some input into them. Publishers will often agree not to change the title unless the author consents, and to consult with the author about the format and style of the text, graphic material, and cover design. If it allows you to approve of any of these elements, it will probably require that your approval not be "unreasonably withheld or delayed." Whether you should negotiate for these concessions depends on their importance to you, because the publisher will consider them to be significant.

MARKETING AND PROMOTION

Almost universally, authors are unhappy with their publishers' marketing and promotion efforts. Unless your contract specifically provides for promotion, book tours, and publicity, expect very little from the publisher beyond a listing in its catalog and possibly the mailing of review copies. If your advance is higher than $25,000, however, it is worth discussing an advertising budget and promotional plans. If the publisher offers you a book tour or advertising budget, it will nonetheless be reluctant to put that promise into the contract, so it will not be a legal obligation. In any case, plan on arranging most publicity efforts on your own.

COPYRIGHT REGISTRATION

The contract should require the publisher to register the copyright with the Copyright Office in your name within three months of publication.[74] Do not allow the publisher to take your copyright or to publish the copyright notice in any name other than yours. Except in the case of academic or textbooks, registering copyright in the publisher's name is not standard in the industry and could harm your economic interests.

FINANCIAL MATTERS

Many of the financial terms will be negotiated before you receive the contract. In order to negotiate the financial terms effectively, you should understand some basics underlying the transaction.

Money in hand is worth more than the promise of money in the future. Therefore, the publisher will not want to pay more in advance of publication than it can negotiate, and in any case, will not normally agree to advance more than it projects the author will earn in royalties over the life of the contract. On the other hand, the larger the publisher's initial outlay, the more likely it is to invest in making the book a commercial success.

There is a principled basis for calculating an advance and royalties, although that basis is not necessarily used in the publisher's first offer. For example, royalties, the author's share of the proceeds from the sale of each copy, should equal what remains after the costs of editing, designing, printing, storing, shipping, overhead, interest lost on the advance, and all other costs, as well as a profit margin for the publisher, are subtracted from the proceeds received by the publisher.[75] Subsidiary rights fees are shared in a higher proportion with the author because the publisher is not spending

---

[74] Copyright registration filed later than three months after publication (unless you previously registered the manuscript) could bar recovery of statutory damages and attorneys' fees in cases of infringement.

[75] The higher the number of sales, the lower the unit cost of each copy sold, which is why many contracts increase, or "escalate" the royalty rate after a certain number of sales. Also note that most of those costs are eliminated in the ebook format.

funds to produce and distribute the licensed product; it is granting the right to a third party, which itself incurs those costs and calculates them in the agreed license fee.

When negotiating royalties and subsidiary rights shares, you can help offset a weaker negotiating position by gathering as much information as you can about the publisher's practices and plans. For example, if you know the standard discount the publisher offers to retailers and distributors for each edition it publishes, you can readily calculate what your actual royalty will be for royalties based on "net receipts" from copies sold. If you know the planned size of the first printing of your work, and the format (that is, hardcover or paperback), you will know better which royalty category to try to increase and the highest realistic advance to aim for. If you know the markets in which your publisher is active, such as the library market for children's books or the university market for academic nonfiction, you can focus on increasing the royalties offered for those sales.

You will have an "account" with the publisher upon receipt of an advance payment. The advance is counted as a negative balance in your account. Your earnings from the book will be applied against the advance and all other amounts you owe the publisher (for such things as indexing costs and books you purchase) until it reaches zero, at which point your earnings will begin to accrue as a positive balance. The publisher will report to you (or your agent) on your earnings, and once you have "earned out" the advance, it will pay what it owes you on a periodic (usually semi-annual) basis. During at least the first year after publication, the publisher will withhold a portion of royalties due as a reserve against returned copies.

THE ADVANCE

The advance is the amount paid to the author before the book is published, which is deducted from the author's earnings. Advances vary considerably, depending on such factors as your reputation and platform, the success of your last book, the subject matter, potential audience, the illustrator's reputation (for children's books), and the publisher's likely income from subsidiary rights. The advance offered is usually a portion of the royalties the publisher calculates will be earned by the author on projected first year (or first print run) sales. Before you agree to the advance offered, try to ascertain (1) the publisher's projection of first year sales (or the size of the first print run); and (2) the expected retail price (or the format). Then, calculate what the publisher projects your earnings will be by multiplying the applicable royalty by the projected sales or print run. Aim for an advance in this amount.[76]

As a general rule, you should negotiate for as large an advance as you can get. The publisher's first offer is less, sometimes significantly, than what it ultimately is willing to pay. It does no harm during the deal points negotiation to ask the publisher for more, especially if you are granting non-print-related subrights. The advance is your hedge against the risk that your work might disappoint commercially, as most books do. Through the advance, the publisher shares this risk. Moreover, the higher the advance, the greater the publisher's incentive to make the book a success.

By the same reasoning, you should have no obligation to repay any part of an unearned advance unless you have failed to deliver an acceptable manuscript. The contract should clearly state that the advance is "nonrefundable." If your contract contains or implies any obligation to repay an unearned advance (or to have an unearned advance counted as indebtedness in another contract with the publisher), you should strike it.

Usually, the publisher agrees to pay one-half of the advance upon execution of the contract and the balance on acceptance of the manuscript. To avoid long payment delays, try to limit the publisher's time to accept the manuscript or to respond with specific comments within a specified time after you have delivered. Unless the advance is for six figures or more, it is unusual for any portion to be withheld until publication.

ROYALTIES: "LIST" VERSUS "NET"-BASED

The primary royalty rates in most trade book contracts are based on suggested retail (or "list") price of each book sold. Some publishers instead offer royalties based on "net" (or wholesale) price. Because it greatly affects your earnings, it is crucial to understand the difference. "Net receipts" or "net price" means the amount the retailer or wholesaler pays the publisher—at least 45 percent to 60 percent off the retail price. If your royalties

---

[76] Sometimes the author's share of projected first year subsidiary rights income is included in the advance. Frequently, the publisher determines the amount of the advance after assessing whether licenses can be sold, or even after agreeing on sales. It is worth asking whether your publisher is marketing or has completed any subsidiary rights sales before agreeing to an advance. If you grant reprint rights, this is the time to ask for "flow through" of the advance paid by the reprint publisher.

are based on "net price," "net proceeds," or "the amount received by the publisher," they will in fact be much lower than list-based royalties computed at the same rate. For example, where a book listed at $20 retail is sold to booksellers at a 45 percent discount (i.e., for $11), a 10 percent royalty based on list price is two dollars, but a 10 percent royalty based on "net" is one dollar ten cents. To approximate the list-based royalty would require a rate of 18.1 percent based on "net." In negotiations, you might not be able to learn the projected list price, but you can find out the publisher's standard discount to booksellers and the intended format (i.e., hardcover or paperback) for your book. If any of your royalties are based on net (and at least some of them are likely to be), you would be well served by finding out the standard discount to retailers and using it to calculate your actual royalty compared to the amounts recommended here.

The rates in the following sections are the standard rates offered by established, large and midsized publishers in the adult trade, children's, and text and academic markets. Standard royalties were established long ago on the principle that the author and publisher would equally share the profit from each copy sold. Thus, your royalty for printed books should roughly equal your publisher's profit. That said, your publisher's rates could differ from those presented here. If the publisher is small, they might be lower. Although publishers are unlikely to agree to higher percentages than the following, they might be willing to decrease the number of sales (i.e., "escalation points") at which the percentages increase.

ROYALTIES—HARDCOVER TRADE BOOKS

For adult trade hardcover books, publishers typically pay 10 percent of the retail price for the first 5,000 copies sold, 12.5 percent for the next 5,000 copies, and 15 percent for all copies sold in excess of 10,000. Established authors can often obtain better terms, such as 15 percent on all copies sold. If your publisher operates in the United Kingdom and you have granted rights to publish there, the royalty rates for all formats there should mirror those of the US rates (i.e., 10 percent of the UK retail price for hardcover, etc.), but the escalation points might be higher.

TRADE PAPERBACK ROYALTIES

The typical royalty rate for trade paperback editions (which are of higher quality and higher retail price than "mass market" paperbacks) is at least

7.5 percent of the retail price on all copies sold. Some authors can do better. For example, you might receive 7.5 percent up to 25,000 copies and 10 percent thereafter. The advantage of permitting your hardcover publisher to issue its own paperback edition, as opposed to sublicensing reprint rights, is that you do not share the royalties received from the paperback publisher; the disadvantage is that you do not receive a separate advance for the paperback rights. Take this into account when negotiating your advance.

MASS MARKET ROYALTIES

Mass market editions are the cheaper, smaller paperbacks you find for sale at newsstands, airports, and grocery stores. So-called genre fiction titles, such as category romances, westerns, and science fiction, are often published only in this format, and major fiction titles are often published in this format after hardcover publication. Most publishers offer an initial royalty of 8 percent of the retail price on sales of up to 150,000 copies and 10 percent to thereafter. Some authors can negotiate rates of 12.5 percent up to 15 percent or more, or receive a three-tiered escalation.

ROYALTIES—CHILDREN'S BOOKS

Royalty rates for children's books should be similar to those for adult trade books. Young adult book authors can expect the same royalties as are offered for adult titles. The royalty escalation points for books for younger children (up to about eight years old) are sometimes higher, for example 10 percent on the first 10,000 copies, 12.5 percent on the next 10,000 copies, and 15 percent on all copies in excess of 20,000. When artwork represents a significant portion of the work (in which case the book is referred to as a "picture book"), the illustrator typically receives a separate contract that is comparable to the text author's, and each contributor separately receives half of the royalties paid. Some children's book contracts provide that the royalty for library editions will be based on net receipts rather than on list price. Because a substantial part of a children's book's sales might be in this category, it is worth trying to aim for a list-based royalty for the library-bound edition that approaches or equals the rate offered for the trade edition.

ROYALTIES—TEXT AND ACADEMIC BOOKS

Royalties for professional, scientific, and technical books are customarily based on net receipts instead of list price. The discount to distributors and retailers for textbooks is in the range of 25 percent to 33-1/3 percent, so the effect of a net-based royalty is not as significant as for trade books. A typical royalty rate should approximate 15 percent based on net. A substantial part of sales are likely to be library and/or export sales, so try to increase the rates in these categories. For college textbooks, the royalties are also based on net price, and the standard discount to bookstores is 20 percent (although some publishers offer as much as 33 percent). For a hardcover textbook, try for 15 percent of net receipts on sales up to a specified number of copies (between 7,500 and 15,000), and 18 percent thereafter. An original paperback textbook will earn royalties in the range of 10 percent to 15 percent of the net price.

EBOOK ROYALTIES

Publishers sell ebooks to retailers based on two different models: the so-called "reseller model" and the "agency model."[77] Under the reseller model, the publisher sells to the retailer at its standard discounted price (typically a 50 percent discount) and the retailer decides what to charge consumers. Under the agency model, the publisher sets the retail price and the seller acts as its agent, earning a 30 percent "commission" for each sale, but the publisher commits to set the price of the book well below the price for hardcover sales. Each unit of an ebook sold is significantly cheaper for publishers to produce and distribute than are traditional printed books. It is therefore logical to expect a higher royalty than those offered for printed books, regardless of the sales model employed. Currently, however, most publishers are offering 25 percent of the "amount received" for each

---

[77] Five of the "Big Six" publishers agreed to let Apple sell ebooks for the iPad and other applications under the agency model in 2010, but the US Justice Department has sued all these parties for colluding to fix prices. All five publishers—Hachette Book Group, HarperCollins, Simon & Schuster, Penguin, and Macmillan—have settled the case against them by agreeing not to use the agency model for two years. (Random House made a deal with Apple the following year and is not a defendant.) Industry observers, citing Amazon's demand to use the reseller model coupled with its practice of pricing many ebook titles at a loss, believe the Justice Department's suit will help Amazon grow its market dominance into a monopoly, dramatically harming bookstores and publishers in the process.

sale of an ebook.[78] This rate is not considered fair, reasonable or rational by authors' advocates, because it skews the basic formula that author and publisher share the profits equally; publishers earn a higher rate of return, and writers a lower rate, for ebook based on these royalties. The result is a natural publisher's bias in favor of ebook over print sales, which is manifested in promotion and print-run decisions. The Authors Guild and other advocates argue that no less than a 50-50 share of net proceeds is the appropriate balance, and eventually this should become the norm. But there is a catch: most standard ebook royalty clauses contain a "most favored nation" clause, whereby the publisher promises automatically to increase the writer's ebook royalties if and when it agrees to a higher rate with any other writer. While including "most favored nation" protection is a must for you, its existence in most contracts makes publishers extremely reluctant to increase any writer's ebook royalties, because to do so could require an increase for all.[79]

"DEEP DISCOUNT" ROYALTIES

Most contracts provide that when the book is sold at discount of more than 55 percent (hardcover) or 60 percent (paperback) to a distributor or retailer, royalties on those copies are reduced to 10 percent of the publisher's net receipts. This "deep discount" rate could sharply decrease your royalties and puts too much control over your royalties in the publisher's hands. The publisher could theoretically increase its profit by selling at just enough of a discount to cut your royalties by more than half.

Powerful retailers can demand discounts of up to 55 percent or higher, so try to specify that the deep discount rate applies only when given "to

---

[78] Ironically, some of the genre publishers' contracts—which tend to be far less favorable to writers than trade book contracts—have long required writers to grant them "all other rights not listed [in the contract]," in exchange for 50 percent of the net proceeds from these rights. Apparently upon realizing that this "catchall" clause could be read to include ebooks, and that 50 percent is twice what most trade book publishers are paying for them, Harlequin began to send letters their backlist authors attempting unilaterally to change the royalty for series ebooks to 15 percent of net digital receipts and single title ebooks to 25 percent.

[79] The wording of such a clause is fairly simple: "Notwithstanding the foregoing [royalty rate], during the term of this Agreement, should the Electronic Book royalty in the Publisher's contract boilerplate [or, "in any other contract offered by Publisher to an author"] reflect a change to the Author's advantage, the contract shall be automatically amended to replace the current royalty with the new royalty."

a purchaser not ordinarily engaged in the business of bookselling" or "outside of normal trade channels" (i.e., "special sales"). If your publisher will not agree to this limitation, your best option is to try to increase the triggering discount percentage so that it exceeds the publisher's standard discount by as much as possible. Another reasonable compromise is to agree to reduce your royalty rate by one-half of 1 percent for each 1 percent that the publisher increases the discount over the triggering percentage. Many authors have negotiated this kind of "shared-loss" royalty provision. The Authors Guild Model Trade Book Contract and Guide has appropriate wording if your publisher or agent cannot provide it.

Publishers' contracts vary in the royalties for mail order, book club, export, "small printings," and other sales outside normal trade channels, but all these categories tend to be lower than retail sales rates. You might be able to achieve increases in the offered rates, and it is worth attempting if you think the book will sell significantly through any of these channels. If you have granted the publisher foreign rights in the English language, it is important to ask it to match, or at least approach, your US rates for export sales.

REMAINDERS

"Remainders" are overstock copies that are sold to remainder houses and resold to consumers for a fraction of the retail price. Most contracts offer the author at most 10 percent of the amount received for the sale of remainders—a very small amount. Your best alternatives are to increase the royalty for remainder sales, and/or to get the right to purchase remainders at the lowest price offered to remainder sellers and to arrange to sell them yourself. If you want the latter option, provide that the publisher must notify you before it remainders the work in any format or edition and allow you to purchase the remainder copies at cost or the remainder price. Many publishers will agree to this but will also specify that they will not be in breach if they mistakenly fail to notify you.

FREE COPIES AND AUTHOR'S DISCOUNT

Most publishers give the author twenty-five free copies (hardcover) and twenty-five free copies (paperback), and a 50 percent discount to you to buy additional copies. This clause might also provide that copies you purchase must be for "the author's own use, and not for resale." If you think you might want to sell your own copies, negotiate that right into the contract, but do not expect to earn royalties for copies you purchase, whether or not you may resell them.

AGENCY CLAUSE

Your agent will make sure that an agency clause is added to the publishing contract. Make sure it embodies your agreement with your agent (see chapter 15), and that you have negotiated your arrangement with your agent before she negotiates with the publisher on your behalf. The typical agency clause authorizes the publisher to discharge its payment obligations to you by paying your agent, and allows the agent to take her commission from said payments.[80] The publisher has little or no stake in your deal with your agent, so it is unlikely to argue over the terms of the clause your agent requests.

ACCOUNTING AND STATEMENTS

Most trade publishers send semi-annual statements accounting for sales and include a check for the royalties and license fees owed. Some traditional trade publishing might offer quarterly accounting, but this is rare. In no event should you accept statements and payments less frequently than twice a year. Accounting periods depend on your publisher's fiscal year. It is not uncommon for publishers to send statements and payments three or even four months after the end of the accounting period.

Some publishers' statements are clearer than others, but you ought to be able to understand the number of sales made and royalties due for each edition. Some publishers will agree in the contract to disclose the number of copies of the work that were printed, bound, and given away, as well as the number of copies on hand at the end of the accounting period.[81] Statements should also include all subsidiary rights income received in each category and the identity of the licensee. Review your royalty statements carefully and do not hesitate to ask (or have your agent ask) for any information needed to verify the statement's accuracy or if it contains anything you do not understand.

---

[80] This is obviously not as good for you as an agreement to pay you and your agent your separate shares of the amount due.

[81] When requesting this, you could argue that this information will have to be revealed if you exercise your right to audit the publishers' records.

RESERVES AGAINST RETURNS

Almost every publisher offers a full refund to retailers and distributors for books ordered and returned unsold. Royalties are not due to you for returned books. For that reason, virtually every contract allows the publisher to withhold a "reserve against returns," that is, to hold royalties otherwise due in order to avoid overpaying for returned books. Although reasonable in theory, some publishers withhold far more than a reasonable estimate of future returns for too long, thus depriving you of money that is rightfully yours. The Authors Guild recommends that reserves against returns for hardcover and trade paperback books not exceed 15 percent of reported sales in a given accounting period. The reserve should be withheld no longer than eighteen months after first publication. For mass market paperbacks, it recommends reserves of 35 percent or less. If the publisher will not agree to these limits, ask it to agree to withhold a "reasonable reserve." The Guild recommends limiting reserves to the first three accounting periods or eighteen months after initial publication. After that, it is unlikely the publisher will receive significant numbers of returns.

JOINT ACCOUNTING

Watch out for language saying that "all" amounts the author owes the publisher under contracts for other books may be deducted from royalties due under your current agreement. Such "cross-collateralization" or "joint accounting" clauses allow the publisher to deduct from this book's earnings all amounts owed by you for page-proof alterations, permissions payments, books purchased, or other obligations associated with different books. Some publishers might even claim the clause entitles them to deduct unearned advances for other books, although this is less likely if each contract describes the advance as "nonrefundable."

Try to strike joint accounting provisions from the contract. The concept can appear in various places in the payment terms and is manifested in words such as "this or any other agreement between the parties" or "any other amounts owed to the publisher." If your publisher will not delete the clause, it is important to add that "amounts due under any other agreement between the parties will not reduce the advance, including flow through amounts due for subsidiary rights licenses." It is equally important to make clear that an unearned advance under another contract is not a debt to be repaid out of earnings from the current contract.

SUBSIDIARY RIGHTS PAYMENTS AND ACCOUNTS

The complexities of subsidiary rights accounting have plagued publishers for years, leading to inadequate and undocumented payments to authors for their share of income from such sublicenses as book clubs, foreign publishing, and audio books. In response to this problem, a committee of the Book Industry Study Group created the Subsidiary Rights Payment Advice Form that appears as Appendix D at the end of this chapter. Try to provide that the publisher will require sublicensees of your work to include this form or its suggested explanations with their payments.

EXAMINATION OF THE PUBLISHER'S RECORDS

It is very important to make sure your contract contains the right to audit the publisher's records regarding your book's financial performance. The audit clause should allow you or your representative to conduct the examination and should not limit who your representative may be or how she may be paid. For example, it is unreasonable to require the examiner to be a CPA, that she sign a nondisclosure agreement covering your book's information, or that she not be compensated through a contingency fee based on the amount of underpayment she detects. The audit clause should provide that the publisher will pay your examiner's fee if the audit reveals that it erred to your detriment by more than 5 percent of the amount due on the statement(s) examined. It should not limit the period in which you have to examine the records. Many publishers want to limit your "look back" period to two years after you receive a royalty statement. This is unreasonable; if your examiner detects a discrepancy in payments that extend back to the beginning of the contract, you should be able to correct it at any time. At the least, provide the right to audit the records back for the length of the statute of limitations for breach of contract (currently six years in New York).

LEGAL RISK ALLOCATION

Publishing a book entails risk. One category of risk is legal. The publisher could be sued based on the content of your book for copyright infringement, defamation, invasion of privacy, or other personal injury. Unpublished writers have sued Michael Crichton, J. K. Rowling, and other successful writers and their publishers alleging infringement; although these suits were thrown out of court, the costs of defending even frivolous suits are significant.[82] This section will examine how the contract allocates the legal risks of publishing your book.

WARRANTIES AND INDEMNITIES

The author's representations, warranties, and indemnities appear in every publishing contract. The representations and warranties are your promise to the publisher that you are free to enter the contract, that you own the rights to the work you are granting, and that no third parties can allege the work infringes their rights or causes them harm. The indemnification obligation requires the author to defend and pay all costs and losses of the publisher, including payments to investigate and settle claims and attorneys' fees, arising out of any third party's claim against the publisher based on the book. If you fear such an accusation might be made about your book, you should discuss it with your publisher early and work together to decrease the risks.

Doing so will not eliminate your risks, unfortunately. The typical contract requires the author to indemnify the publisher (and its employees, agents, and sublicensees) not only against legal judgments resulting from an actual breach of warranties, but for all expenses incurred for an alleged breach, no matter how little merit the claim has. This term places all the risk squarely on you, which is unfair and unreasonable unless you knowingly infringed copyright or defamed a person. There are ways, however, to balance the risk allocation more fairly.

Try to limit your indemnity obligation only to cases of a final judgment resulting from an "actual," not an "alleged," breach of warranties.[83] Require the publisher to submit any proposed settlement with a third party to you for your approval. Exclude third party content and changes required by your publisher from the material you warrant. Scrutinize the warranties carefully. It is reasonable to warrant that your work does not infringe intel-

---

[82] Claimants almost always sue the publisher, the perceived "deep pocket," whether or not they name the author.

[83] Sometimes this takes only the substitution of "actual" for "alleged" in the contract language.

lectual property rights, defame, or otherwise legally injure a third party, but if your work contains recipes or formulas, you should not have to guarantee that no harm will come from a reader's misuse of the content. Most publishers are reluctant to change their warranty and indemnity clauses, sometimes claiming their insurers have approved the boilerplate and will not cover claims for contracts that have altered the language.

In practice, no matter what the contract says, publishers often treat expenses, settlements, and liabilities from legal claims, especially meritless suits, as a cost of doing business. In most cases, it will seek to recoup its costs from royalties due instead of requiring outright payments from their authors. Unless the publisher specifically agrees to this in the contract, however, it has no legal obligation to do so. Fortunately, most publishers also agree to name their authors as "additional insureds" under their liability insurance policies, which costs little or nothing. But deductibles are high and your indemnity obligation could still require you to cover the deductible and other expenses not covered by the insurance. If the publisher agrees to add you as an insured, make sure this appears in the contract, and try to limit your share of the deductible to an amount you can realistically cover or to a percentage of your advance, and to have amounts due from you withheld from royalties instead of directly payable. If the publisher does not have media insurance or requires you to pay the entire deductible, consider obtaining your own liability insurance. Your writers organization might be able to refer some insurers.

BANKRUPTCY

If your publisher files for bankruptcy, control over its business and its assets is placed in the hands of the bankruptcy court. All rights in books held by the publisher are considered assets, and no bankruptcy clause in a contract can override the court's control over those assets. For that reason, do not spend too much capital negotiating the bankruptcy clause. Other kinds of financial calamity for a publisher do not lead to court control, however, so it is a good idea to provide that your rights will revert automatically upon the publisher's insolvency or liquidation. Even better, try to agree that the publisher's failure to remit statements or royalties for a specified period will lead to automatic termination of the contract without limiting your other remedies.

TERMINATION

Unless you provide for the right to terminate your contract upon the publisher's breach, your remedies against it, even for breaching its most important obligations, are limited to money damages, which you must sue to receive. It behooves you, therefore, to provide for the right to terminate the contract and retrieve all rights granted if the publisher fails to provide royalty statements, make required payments, or publish by the agreed deadline.

ADJUDICATION OF DISPUTES

Consider asking for an arbitration clause to address disputes. Arbitration is cheaper, more direct, and faster than litigation in court; in simple cases you do not need a lawyer. Larger publishers usually refuse arbitration clauses, because they can afford the cost and delays of litigation better than their authors. Smaller publishers might agree more readily.

THE FUTURE

As noted, the contract likely provides that the grant of rights, and therefore all the other contract terms, extend for the entire term of copyright. Even if your book becomes a perennial seller and earns both parties a nice income for many years, you do not want the publisher to control your career. If the book stops bringing in income, you should have the right to end the contract and get the rights back. The following terms address the future of the book and of your writing career in either circumstance.

OUT-OF-PRINT/REVERSION OF RIGHTS

Virtually all book contracts include an "out-of-print," or "reversion of rights" clause. The out-of-print clause encourages the publisher to sell the work for as long as it is profitable for both parties. It provides that the rights granted to the publisher will revert to you and the contract will terminate when the work is no longer "in print," thus allowing you to remarket or repurpose the book freely. In negotiations, focus on the definition of "in print." When the publisher stops investing in printing, distributing, and marketing the book, it should also relinquish the right to profit from it (except for the right to profit from existing sublicenses). Logically, your book should therefore be deemed "in print" only if copies of an English-language hardcover or paperback edition are offered for sale in the United States through regular trade channels and the book is listed as such in the publisher's catalog. But the publisher will want to keep the rights for as long as it can, so it is not likely to agree to define "in print" so restrictively.

Some contracts do not define "in print" at all, and the publisher can use that obscurity to argue that the existence of a foreign edition or non-book version renders the work "in print." It is perfectly reasonable for you to insist on a definition that includes the book's availability through regular trade channels in the United States. The publisher will likely want formats such as ebooks and "print-on-demand" versions to constitute "in print," but will likely agree to revert the rights if the work is not available for sale in printed book editions in the United States and the author has not earned a certain minimum in royalties (e.g., $500) in two succeeding accounting periods. If you do not include this, the publisher can claim the work is "available for sale" even if no print editions exist and few digital copies are sold. Also, consider requesting reversion to you of specific rights, such as hardcover or paperback editions, if the publisher stops producing and selling them, even if it retains digital rights.

The typical out of print clause does not require the publisher to inform you that the work is out of print; unless you include this, you must determine that for yourself through your royalty statements. Many contracts require the author to request that the publisher put the work back into print and to give the publisher several months to comply before rights revert. If yours has this term, give the publisher no more than sixty days to respond to your request and no more than six months from the date of your request to re-issue a printing. Also, provide that the rights will revert automatically if the publisher does not put the work back into print instead of relying on the publisher to confirm that the rights have reverted.

REVISED EDITIONS

Contracts for textbooks, technical books, and some children's books often contain a clause that requires the author to revise the book for later editions upon the publisher's request, sometimes without further payment (except for the continued payment of royalties).[84] Typically, the revised

---

[84] Revised edition clauses should not appear in contracts for nonfiction trade books and novels. If the parties in these cases believe a new edition is warranted, they can mutually agree to amend the contract.

edition clause states if the author will not or cannot make the revisions, the publisher may hire another author to do so and charge that person's payment (on a flat fee or royalty basis) against the original writer's earnings. To protect yourself from losing control of your work and money owed to you, include the following terms: (1) that the publisher's requests for revisions must be reasonable and subject to your approval; (2) that the second author must be subject to your approval; (3) that in no event shall your compensation be reduced below a specified minimum; (4) that the authorship credit to you and to the subsequent author shall be subject to your approval; (5) and that you shall have the right to remove your name from later editions.

THE OPTION CLAUSE

Giving the publisher an option to publish your next book helps the publisher, not you. It gives the publisher the privilege of publishing your next book or books only if it chooses. If not properly limited, an option can bind you to the publisher for all your subsequent works, even if it performs badly, your editor leaves, or you can get better terms elsewhere. It prevents you from seeking other opportunities for a period of time that, if not curbed, could be fully controlled by the publisher. Ideally, therefore, you should strike the option clause from the contract.

From the publisher's perspective, investing in a book by an unproven writer is financially risky. Having the option to publish her future works on terms over which it has some control hedges the risk. Even so, some publishers are willing to delete the option clause altogether. If your publisher will not strike it entirely, it is important to negotiate revisions to the typical clause to neutralize its most harmful effects.

An option to publish your next work on the "same terms" as the current contract is unacceptable because it effectively gives away your ability to negotiate the terms of your next—and all future—publishing contracts. Change any such clause to state the next contract will be on terms "to be mutually agreed" at the time the second contract is negotiated.

Granting the publisher "last refusal rights" allows it to acquire your next work by matching another offer received. This effectively prevents you from getting other publishers to consider your next work; no publisher will invest in making an offer if it knows a competitor can take the work on the terms it worked out with you. At most, permit the publisher a "right of first refusal," or give it the right to "top" another offer by at least 10 percent.

Do not agree to an option that requires you to submit a complete manuscript for consideration. At most, agree to submit a summary and sample chapter or two or a proposal for the optioned work. Do not allow the publisher to consider your next work for any period of time that begins after publication of the current work, which by definition could be years from now. The consideration period should begin no later than on acceptance, not on publication, of the current manuscript, and should not exceed six weeks. The negotiation period should also be reasonable, not more than four to six weeks, before you can walk away and freely shop the work elsewhere.

Finally, limit the option to cover only books that are similar to or in the same market as the current work (e.g., "biography for children" or "technology industry study"), or if applicable, only to works written under your pseudonym or by you and a collaborator together, not separately.

NONCOMPETE CLAUSES

Standard contracts contain clauses restricting the author from publishing another book based on material in the current book, or from publishing material that competes with the sale of the current book. Some also state that the book to be delivered will be the "author's next work." A broadly worded noncompetition clause can harm your interests. For example, the publisher could try to prevent you from using your characters in sequels and prequels, or claim that the author of a textbook, cookbook, or other educational work may not write other works on the same subjects while the contract is in force. Although courts require noncompetition clauses to be reasonable in scope and not unduly restrictive, it is best to change the contract to limit the definition of what is "competitive."

First, if your work is fiction, your next novel cannot logically "compete" with it, so you should try to delete the clause entirely. If the work is nonfiction or if the publisher will not strike the clause, describe the type of work to which the clause applies as specifically as possible as to subject matter, market, and format. Do not give the publisher the discretion to decide whether a work will compete with the contracted book—limit the restriction to works that "actually" compete with the primary work.

By the same token, if you deliver your manuscript on time, the publisher should not care whether the work is the author's "next work." If the publisher will not agree to delete either the "next work" or "noncompetition" clauses altogether, you can protect yourself by adding the following sentence:

Notwithstanding the foregoing [noncompetition and/or next book clause], it is understood and agreed that the author may write and publish [TYPE OR GENRE] books in the field of [SUBJECT], and this paragraph is not intended and shall not be interpreted to prohibit or limit such writing and publishing activity by the author.

AUDIO LICENSES

Interest in audio rights has grown dramatically over the past fifteen years. In the past, audio rights were nearly always granted to the publisher as a subsidiary right, but with the recent popularity of downloadable audio books, established authors are now attempting to reserve the rights. Consider whether or not your publisher will be able to sell audio rights better than you or your agent or whether it can produce its own audio books. If so, you might want to grant an option or a right of first refusal to your print publisher.

There are a number of issues that arise in audio rights licensing, whether they are included in your book publishing contract or separately licensed. Limit the grant of rights with respect to duration, territory, language, and exclusivity. Unlike book rights, which are usually tied to the term of copyright (provided that the book remains in print), the duration of audio rights is often shorter. The reason for this is simple: as with digital book formats, audio books need never go out of print because it is relatively inexpensive to make single copies. Thus, it is not uncommon for agents to limit the grant of audio rights to a term of seven to ten years after initial publication. The publisher might require an option for sixty days or more in which to negotiate for an extension or renewal of the audio rights.

Publishers generally want the widest possible territory, i.e., worldwide rights, and all languages, but might settle for English-language rights. Again, make sure that your publisher has access to all the markets included in the grant. One way to do this is to ask the publisher for a breakdown of gross sales by country.

The question of whether to grant exclusive or nonexclusive audio rights turns on similar factors as the scope of territories and languages granted. Is the publisher better situated than you or your agent to sell audio rights? If you believe the book will have strong sales, consider retaining at least a nonexclusive right to audio versions because the value of the rights, and the potential players in any sale, will change dramatically if the book is successful. On the other hand, granting only nonexclusive rights will affect the publisher's incentive to market them because they are worth less and harder to sell. Either way, specify that the audio version of the book will be a nondramatic verbatim reading of the entire text of the work. This is important to ensure that there is no confusion as to rights in other possible forms of audio or audiovisual works, such as multimedia productions, the soundtrack to a movie, or even a film itself.

If you enter into a separate contract for audio rights, you should receive an advance against royalties. The standard royalty rates in audio book contracts are generally low, typically escalating from 5 to 10 percent (sometimes with 1 percent added per 10,000 units sold). They also are based on net receipts rather than retail price. Thus, you should generally negotiate for a substantial advance on the theory that there might not be much more income forthcoming for your audio rights. Most trade book contracts with traditional publishers now offer an audio download royalty of 25 percent of net receipts. However, as discussed earlier with respect to ebook royalties, the Authors Guild and other advocacy groups believe a 50–50 split of proceeds would represent a more equitable balance.

FINAL NOTE OF ADVICE

Asking for changes to your contract will not harm your publishing relationship. If anything, demonstrating your business and industry savvy will increase your publisher's respect for and confidence in you. Even if it rejects most of your requests, it is likely to accept some of them and this benefits you. In any case, protecting your interests, especially control of your writing career, is the right thing to do.

APPENDIX D
(To be sent by Publisher to licensees)

SUBSIDIARY RIGHTS PAYMENT ADVICE FORM

This form must be completed and delivered to us when you send payment pursuant to licenses granted by us to you. You may deliver this form to us by mail, including it with your check, or you may scan the form and attach it to an email sent to _____ or fax it to _____ .

Failure to do so may result in our inability to record your payments and prevent us from determining that you are in compliance with the terms of your license(s).

- ◆ Amount remitted: _____

- ◆ Check or wire transfer number: _____

- ◆ Check or wire transfer date: _____

- ◆ (for wire transfers) Bank and account number for which moneys were deposited: _____

- ◆ Publisher/agent payor's name _____

- ◆ Title of the work for which payment is being made: _____

- ◆ Author(s) of the work: _____

- ◆ Our Unique Identifying Number for the work as it appears in the Appendix to the relevant contract. If none, the original publisher's ISBN number of the work: _____

- ◆ The period covered by the payment: _____

The following information will be very helpful, so we ask that you also provide it:

- ◆ Reason for payment (guaranteed earned royalty, fee, etc.): _____
_____

◆ Payment's currency: _____

◆ Type of right (book club, reprint, translation, etc.): _____

_____

_____

◆ Summary justification of your payment:

Gross amount due: _____

Taxes: _____

Commissions: _____

Bank charges: _____

Net amount paid: _____

CHAPTER 12

NEWSPAPER, MAGAZINE, AND

SYNDICATION CONTRACTS

P rior to the mid–1990s, freelance contributions to newspapers and magazines were routinely sold without a written contract. Matters such as the scope of the rights granted and secondary use rights, payment terms, discretion to edit, acceptance for publication, and allocation of legal risks were addressed, if at all, by verbal agreement and industry practice. In those days, publishers did not routinely use contributions after first publication, and it was understood that writers had the rights to resell and reuse their stories freely. Established freelancers could make substantial extra income from reselling their pieces after first publication.

This arrangement changed after publishers discovered the lucrative electronic database market for their publications and began to license their publications, including the freelance contributions, to firms such as LexisNexis and Westlaw. In 1993, six freelance writers sued several publishers and databases over this practice, and, although they eventually prevailed in the Supreme Court, the victory proved to be a Pyrrhic one. Beginning in 1994, newspapers and magazines began to pressure freelancers to give up many—or all—of their rights through written contracts. The *New York Times*, one of the defendants in the writers' suit, introduced a nonnegotiable contract for all its freelancers that purports to cover both previously published and all future articles sold to the paper. Most newspaper chains quickly followed with written contracts that were structurally similar to the *Times'*, though not as extreme. Written contracts with newspapers and magazines are now the order of the day for most freelance articles. The terms of these contracts vary among publishers; prestigious magazines and smaller publishers appear more willing to agree to better terms than the bigger chains. The common terms in the contracts currently offered by major newspapers and magazines, and revisions you might want to request, are explained below.

You might receive the assignment via an email or telephone exchange with an editor, in which the topic, word count, and fee are agreed. Typically, the publisher will follow with a formal contract that is likely to say that its legal terms apply both to the current assignment and to any future work you sell to the publisher. This gambit has both advantages and disadvantages for you. On the one hand, you will only need to negotiate the terms once no matter how many articles you sell to the publisher; on the other, you might have more leverage to negotiate later, after proving your value as a contributor. Remember, though, that you are never really "locked into" your original agreement. You can always ask to revisit your contract in the context of a later assignment.

Ideally, the written contract will confirm the nature of the assignment, due date, fee, the extent to which expenses will be covered, how and when payment will be made, the effect of killing the piece, and how revisions will be handled. If the document lacks any of those terms, ask about them. The contract will also contain legal terms that you should not neglect: the grant of the rights in the work, warranties and an indemnification obligation, a noncompetition clause, and a right of the publisher to use your article, image and likeness to advertise the publication.

While it is in your interests to have the understanding in writing, keep in mind that the document you receive is an offer and that the terms are open to negotiation. If the editor does not send a contract, consider providing your own confirmation of the assignment. It need not be long or formal. (A sample is included at the end of the chapter.)

THE SCOPE OF RIGHTS GRANTED

Before accepting an assignment, ask yourself whether you might want to reuse the piece, either as published or as the basis for other work. If so, then you will need to secure the rights to do so in your contract.

The rights in your work that are granted to the publisher are defined according to exclusivity and duration, format, languages, and territory. Many publishers will agree to take only the rights that are necessary to meet their business needs; others will ask for a broad scope. If the contract requires you to grant "all rights of whatever nature" on an exclusive basis or similar, ask the publisher to parse the rights as suggested below.

Exclusivity and Duration. Most contracts require the writer to grant the publisher the exclusive first right to publish the piece for some period of time that starts on publication date; this is reasonable and fair. Because secondary uses of your stories are potentially lucrative, the *duration* of the exclusivity period is the key point. If the publisher's exclusive period is too long, or even permanent, you will effectively be prohibited from reusing your work for its useful life. The most draconian contracts (including the *New York Times*') deem the freelancer's contributions to be "works made for hire," meaning the publisher is legally considered the sole original author or require an exclusive assignment of the copyright; without an affirmative reversion of rights, the writer would never be able to reuse the work.[85]

The prestige and reliable pay offered by the *Times* have allowed it largely to succeed in taking all rights permanently to its contributors' work. But "work for hire" contracts and assignments of copyright are rightly considered by most in the industry to be retrogressive, unfair, and unnecessary and many authors (and their agents) refuse to sign them.[86] In fact, most newspapers and magazine publishers offer fairer contract terms. Most of them limit their exclusivity period to thirty up to ninety days, after which, the writer receives back the rights (usually nonexclusively) to reuse the piece in any way she wishes. Some publishers even agree to revert exclusive rights to the author to make some uses of the story, although this is becoming rare. Receiving back nonexclusive rights is not ideal because they are generally harder to sell than exclusive rights and you might find yourself in effect competing with your publisher in secondary use markets. For that

---

[85] Chapter 4 explains the meaning and implication of works made "for hire" under copyright.

[86] In fact, the employees of newspapers (who are members of the Newspaper Guild) work under a collective bargaining agreement that provides them a share of the publishers' revenues for reuses of their columns. Freelancers have neither the benefits of employment nor the opportunity to earn anything for reuses of their work under "work for hire" agreements.

reason, it is worth trying to negotiate for a reversion of exclusive rights to make certain uses (such as reprints, inclusion in anthologies, and syndication) that offer the opportunity for real income, and nonexclusive rights to reuse and relicense the piece in all other ways permitted under copyright. If you cannot persuade the publisher to give you back some rights exclusively, getting nonexclusive rights is much better than nothing.

Formats. Typically, the contract will allow the publisher to exploit your story "in all media now known or hereafter invented" or "by any and all means, methods, and processes, whether now known or hereafter invented." Although retrieving rights back after a reasonable exclusivity period is more important than limiting the formats the publisher may exploit, if you have enough clout, you might be able to change the "all media" language. For example, the grant of rights section might list the publisher's allowed uses as follows: print and online publication of the periodical, the right to exploit the verbatim text in electronic and digital media, to authorize photocopies, and to license reprints (for a share of the fees).[87]

Whether you limit the permitted formats or not, it is important to add a statement that the grant of rights does not include the right to make derivative works from your story except as needed to edit and exploit it in the authorized formats, and that all rights not granted to the publisher are reserved to you.

Language and Territory. Depending on your plans, you might try to limit the language and territory in which your publisher can exploit your work. For example, you could specify that the publisher may exploit the piece in English (and/or other languages). You might allow distribution only in North America or other specified territories. If you do this, you should also place limits on the publisher's right to license the story to its foreign language or other affiliates.

Syndication Rights. In a sense, a syndicate is another publisher, one that gathers written materials by a number of writers and distributes them to a geographically broader periodical market. Once an article is picked up for syndication, it might appear in many newspapers and periodicals. If you reserve these rights, syndication gives you an opportunity to make extra income and to be read by more readers. If you do not reserve these rights, ask your publisher about sharing the income from syndication with

---

[87] You are more likely to get concessions like this from a magazine than from a newspaper.

you. The ideal share of syndication income is 85 percent to you, 15 percent to the publisher, but you are more likely to get a 50-50 split. More information about negotiating directly with a syndicate is at the end of this chapter.

Transfer on Payment. Given the prevalence of slow payment by some periodical publishers, you should add a line that says the grant of rights is not effective unless and until payment is made in full.

THE ASSIGNMENT AND DUE DATE

The contract should describe the assignment in enough detail, including content and word count, to limit the possibility of a misunderstanding. Avoid language that has you agreeing to submit a "satisfactory manuscript" or that allows the publisher to reject the work "in its discretion." Whether the work is acceptable should be based on objective, not subjective, criteria—length, topic, professional competence, and fitness for publication. If the publisher's plans change and it decides not to run your piece, you should still get paid something for it unless you failed to deliver adequate work.

Where the assignment involves some affirmative act by the publisher, such as supplying reference materials, arranging interviews or the like, your deadline should be expressed as a certain number of days from your receipt of such input. Strike any reference that makes the deadline for delivery "of the essence." Give yourself some flexibility in meeting the deadline, understanding that in periodical publishing, your grace period will necessarily be significantly shorter than in book publishing. The contract should provide for an extension for delays beyond your reasonable control, such as illness or travel delays, although the publisher will understandably resist allowing this period (called *force majeure*) to exceed a specified period of time.

EDITING AND PUBLICATION

Magazines and newspapers often edit articles extensively for length and style, but it is reasonable to request the right to review and discuss modifications made to your work. Due to time constraints, the publisher might be reluctant to give you a right of approval—or even review—over changes, so make the amount of time you request for review reasonable in the circumstances. If you wish, ask for the right to make substantial changes yourself if they are required and ask for a chance to revise the piece if it is deemed unacceptable for publication. You should also be able to have your name removed from the byline if you really disapprove of the publisher's revisions.

To avoid waiting indefinitely for payment and publication, consider asking for a clause stating that the publisher will inform you whether or not the work is acceptable for publication within a specified period of time after delivery and will publish by a certain date or period of time after acceptance. Because the publisher's exclusive ownership period usually begins on publication, it is important to ensure the clock will start within a reasonable time. One way to ensure this is to provide that if the publisher does not publish the work within a certain period of time after acceptance or delivery, the rights will automatically revert to you.

EXPENSES AND KILL FEES

Expenses. There are two ways to deal with the expenses you might incur in researching and writing your piece. One way is to include them in the fee. The second way is to have the publisher agree to reimburse you for expenses incurred. When negotiating your fee, ask whether and to what extent the publisher will cover your expenses. If it will not, build your expected expenses into the fee. If the contract is silent about your expenses, your publisher will consider them your responsibility.

By their nature, some articles will require extensive research, permission fees for third party materials, fees for privacy releases, and the like; the publisher should agree to cover these. For such pieces, before agreeing on the fee, discuss an expense budget. If the publisher requests that you provide a budget, allow for a variance such as 10 percent in the event of unforeseen costs. For extensive or long-term projects, a progress payment schedule for expenses incurred and a part of the fee, made every thirty days or so, is not uncommon. Or consider asking for a nonreturnable advance for the expenses to be covered. Depending on the nature of the assignment, you might also want to request a term that makes unforeseen or extraordinary necessary expenses the publisher's responsibility, subject to its reasonable approval.

Kill Fees. There are many reasons why a publisher might decide not to run a story it has commissioned; the inadequacy of the work product is only one possibility. The practice of "killing" a piece is common enough to have given rise long ago to the industry standard practice of the "kill fee." There are several ways to protect yourself from getting an unfairly low, or worse, no payment in the event your story is killed. First, as previously noted, you should provide in the contract that your fee is due upon delivery of a "professionally competent" article that meets the assignment terms and is fit for publication. The contract should ideally provide that payment will be issued within thirty days of delivery or acceptance, not on publication, of the article. If the publisher cancels the assignment before completion, it might seek to tie the amount of the kill fee to the stage of the work at the point of cancellation. If the project is half complete or more and the publisher's reason for terminating the contract has nothing to do with quality, you deserve to be paid the full fee plus all expenses agreed. If the contract provides payment is due on acceptance, add that the payment is "nonrefundable," meaning it need not be returned if the publisher does not use the article. Less desirable but more common is a promise to pay a kill fee of 50 percent (or higher) of the agreed fee. In either case, the contract should provide that if the publisher kills the piece, your expenses will be reimbursed in full and all rights granted will revert to you automatically. A kill fee of less than 50 percent is unacceptable unless the publisher cancels the contract before you have put any time into the assignment.

CREDIT AND PUBLICITY

The contract should specify how your story will be credited. Most periodicals credit the author by name, but make sure the obligation to do so appears in the contract if you want to ensure it. Many contracts allow the publisher to use the writer's name and likeness and to use excerpts from the article to promote the publication. Try to ensure that the publisher will consult with you before making use of your persona and that you will have the right to approve of the photo and bio. Sometimes this clause as written is overbroad; if you do not want the publisher to use your persona to sell its other publications or later issues, refine the contract language accordingly.

WARRANTIES AND INDEMNITIES

Most contracts require the writer to represent and warrant that the article does not infringe on any third party's rights, such as copyright, or cause them harm, such as through libel or invasion of privacy. Further, they oblige the writer to defend and pay all costs and losses of the publisher arising out of any legal claim based on the story. If the nature of your article raises concerns about libel or other legal risks, discuss it with your editor early and work together to decrease the risks. [88]

It is worth making clear in the agreement that you are liable only if and when there is a final judgment based on an actual, not an "alleged" breach of a warranty. Nor should you be responsible for anything the publisher changes or adds to the piece. In practice, publishers often treat expenses from legal claims as a cost of doing business, and most of them carry media liability insurance. But deductibles are high and your indemnity obligation might still require you to cover the deductible and other expenses not covered by insurance. Try to limit your indemnity to an amount you can realistically cover or a percentage of your total fee. If the publisher will not agree to limit your liability, consider obtaining your own insurance. Various writers' organizations can refer you to appropriate insurers.

NONCOMPETITION

Some contracts restrict the writer from publishing a story with another publisher in the same market on a similar topic or one that is "reasonably likely to compete with the article" for some period of time after first publication. One way to control this restriction is to limit the publisher's discretion to decide whether a new article competes with the first one. Specify that the restriction applies only to works that "actually" compete with the first. Some contracts list those competing publications with which the author may not enter a contract for the restricted period. This might be preferable if you can live with it because it creates knowable parameters; you can interpret it as letting you publish in any publication that is not listed or described. In either case, the restricted time period should be reasonable for you and your plans; if it is not, ask to shorten it.

INDEPENDENT CONTRACTOR STATUS

The contract might state that you are an independent contractor. Unless you are on the publisher's staff, there is no harm in agreeing to this. It protects the publisher from any argument that you deserve benefits, that your acts should be attributed to it, or that it should withhold payroll taxes from your payment. It protects you by helping avoid disputes over whether

---

[88] Chapter 8 reviews defamation and privacy laws.

your story is a work made for hire (unless you expressly agree in writing that it is).

SYNDICATION

The terms of syndication agreements cover similar ground as periodical contributor agreements. If you reserved syndication rights and are negotiating directly with a syndicate, keep the following in mind. Limit the grant of rights only to those that the syndicate needs—the right to relicense print and digital versions of the articles you make available. You need not and should not transfer the copyright to your works. As well, grant only subsidiary rights that the syndicate demonstrates to you it is able to exploit directly. Limit the duration of the syndication deal to one or two years. This will give you the ability to renegotiate if you are very successful or to walk away from an unsuccessful venture. Any kind of automatic renewal would defeat the purpose of a short term, so agree to this only if each renewal term comes with increased compensation.

Consider how much control you want to retain over the selection of the organizations that will run your work, the markets in which the work will appear, and how much the re-publishers may change or abridge your work as it was originally published. If having an approval right to any of these is important to you, include it in the contract.

Another key term to include is a guaranteed minimum payment for each of the works you have licensed. The guaranteed minimum should not be contingent on the success (or lack thereof) of the syndication. The amount of the guaranteed minimum will depend on the nature and success of the syndication relationship. For example, are you selling one feature or column, or a continuing series? Which newspapers or periodicals are picking up the work? How much above the guaranteed minimum will you earn?

As for royalties, the syndicate can be expected to keep 40 to 60 percent of the gross receipts, and to pay the remainder to you. Consider limiting the syndicate's ability to include your work in packages to be sold at a special price, which would obscure the value of your individual work and lower your share of the fee. Finally, as in book publishing contracts, noncompete and option clauses can seriously hamper your ability to place your work elsewhere and should be carefully limited to those markets in which the syndicate is active.

SAMPLE ASSIGNMENT CONFIRMATION TO A PERIODICAL PUBLISHER

Dear Ms. Editor:

I am delighted by Happy Periodical Publisher's offer to publish my article, The Great American Article. I would like us to come to a more specific agreement over a few important issues:

1. Happy Periodical Publisher's exclusive right to publish the article in print and digital formats will be limited to first serial rights in the English language to be sold in the United States, its territories and Canada, and placed verbatim on Happy Periodical Publisher's website, for a term of 90 days beyond the US sale date of the issue in which my article is first published. The right to publish the article in other countries, languages and formats shall be nonexclusive.

2. I agree not to publish the work elsewhere, in whole or in part, until Happy Periodical Publisher has published the work in [Periodical] and for [X] days thereafter.

3. Happy Periodical Publisher shall remit my fee in the amount of [Y] within 30 days of acceptance of the article for publication, and, after acceptance, if it decides not to publish the article, I shall be entitled to keep the entire payment agreed upon.

4. Happy Periodical Publisher agrees to reimburse me for the following reasonable expenses: _____, for which I agree to submit receipts, within thirty (30) days of the delivery of my article.

5. I agree to allow Happy Periodical Publisher to use my name, biography, and likeness for promotional purposes, subject to my right of approval, not to be unreasonably withheld.

I appreciate your attention to these concerns, and look forward to working together on my article. Please contact me if you wish to discuss any of these issues. If these terms are acceptable, please sign this letter where indicated below and return it to me.

Sincerely,

Accepted by: _____

CHAPTER 13

SELF-PUBLISHING OPTIONS:

EBOOKS AND PRINT

ON DEMAND

E ven writers who have enjoyed commercial success in the past face daunting odds against landing a commercial publisher today. In the United States, trade publishers buy some 10 percent or less of the books that are offered to them. Literary merit has less to do with what editors decide to publish than whether a book is likely to generate a profit, and traditional houses are very reluctant to take risks on commercially unproven writers.

One of the bright spots in the otherwise grim publishing landscape is the recent rise of viable and inexpensive self-publishing options. In the past few years, thousands have resorted to self-publishing and placed their books on virtual shelves alongside commercially published titles. Some have even earned a profit (although profits are usually small). If approached with realistic expectations and proper precautions, self-publishing can be a good alternative to a deal with a commercial publisher. Self-publishing lets you control more elements of publication than traditional publishing allows, such as the book's appearance and format, retail price, and how long it will stay in print. Some recent self-published titles—largely in the non-fiction niche and religious markets and the romance/erotica genres—have achieved remarkable success. The blockbuster *Fifty Shades of Grey* trilogy started life as a self-published ebook. A popular self-published book can often bring an offer from a major publisher, as *Fifty Shades* and others have, because a book that succeeds with the public is the holy grail of publishing. When the commercial houses see such a title resonating in the marketplace, they invariably will approach the writer with a generous offer.

The information in this chapter will help you navigate the self-publishing options available for both the print-on-demand (POD) and ebook formats. Be aware that, more than any other part of the industry, the market, players, technology, and services offered in this area are in a constant state of rapid change. Currently, competition among the players is fierce, Amazon wields mighty market advantages, and the costs of formatting and distribution continue to decrease as technology advances. As a consequence, there are opportunities—but also pitfalls—for writers. If you are considering self-publishing, your due diligence should include researching and comparing the various services offered and examining the titles published by several different providers[89] before choosing how to proceed.

A simple online search for self-publishing companies will yield dozens of options. To cut through their marketing hype and create the optimal scenario for your book, you should have some background knowledge about what publishing a book entails.[90]

PUBLISHING BUSINESS MODELS

Trade book publishers pay authors for the right to publish their work and incur the entire cost of producing, marketing, and distributing the books. Their profits come solely from sales of the books and some subsidiary rights, so their financial incentive, which their writers share, is to sell as many copies as they can. By contrast, self-publishing firms make money by charging authors to make their books available to the public. Among the firms, the fee structures and services offered vary, but for most of them, their main source of profit is in the services sold to authors. No matter

---

[89] For simplicity, the entities offering self-publishing services will be called "publishers" here.

[90] Part of what is exciting in this arena is the changing definition of a "book." The available services work well for long-form articles, fan fiction, and fictional "shorts," none of which are typically taken on by traditional publishers.

what their sales associates tell you, most of these firms have little financial incentive to sell many copies of your book.[91]

A writer who wants to self-publish can easily do so by signing a contract with an ebook or POD publisher (several of the firms offer to publish in both formats as part of a bundle) and handing over a digital file of the manuscript and—depending on the services purchased—a pile of money. A number of the firms offer tiers of package deals that include a menu of various services: editing, copyediting, formatting the manuscript, creating a cover, assigning an ISBN (unique identifier), listing it for sale with various wholesalers and retail sites, distribution, promotion, and collecting and paying royalties. Other firms allow you simply to convert your manuscript into an ebook format —there are several formats, including PDF—and offer it for sale in various forums. They collect and account for your royalties, and do little else. Some of these charge a modest flat fee and let you keep most or all the royalties. Others do not charge up front, but take a larger cut of the royalties. The bare bones services do not provide editing, copyediting, cover and interior design or formatting.

Whichever you choose, it falls to you to evaluate each service and fee structure offered by the publishers you are considering, and to ensure that every element of your book is acceptable to you. Moreover, even if you pay for promotional help, prepare to market the book on your own. Because it is so easy to self-publish, your book will be competing for readers with many others and your publisher will do very little, if anything, to help you break out of the crowd.

PRINT ON DEMAND

On a per-unit basis, printed books are much more expensive to produce than ebooks, so they cost significantly more at retail and face longer odds in the marketplace. For that reason, many writers prefer to publish first in ebook form and then add a print component if circumstances warrant. Other writers literally want to see and sell their work in print. For them, there are several credible companies that produce and sell books on demand (most also offer the ebook format option). Readers can find these titles

---

[91] True, if the publisher takes on a high enough volume of titles, as Amazon and others seek to do, they can earn a profit from royalties on sales of each title. But their incentive is to sign you and many others up, not to make your book a bestseller.

at most online bookselling sites, order them, and receive them in quality paperback or hardcover form just as they do trade publishers' books. The difference is that POD books are printed, bound, and shipped individually only after the reader has ordered them. There is no print run, the books are not waiting in warehouses to be shipped, and retail stores do not order them for their inventories.[92]

Many credible firms offer POD services.[93] These firms charge an upfront fee, ranging from around $1,000 to $15,000 depending on the services chosen, and also take a percentage of the net royalty on copies sold. They set minimum prices for the titles. Theoretically, the high unit costs to these firms of producing and shipping single copies justify these terms, but whether any individual firm's terms are competitive is another question. Fortunately, it is not hard to compare publishers' terms—most are posted on their websites. To compare quality, look at the books they publish and look for reviews on bookstore websites and elsewhere.

EBOOKS

Ebooks are digitally formatted books available for download to a computer or dedicated reader such as the iPad, Kindle, Nook, or Microsoft Reader. Because they cost so little to produce on a per unit basis, ebooks can be priced quite cheaply—thousands of self-published titles are offered for less than a dollar, and many are free. A writer seeking to self-publish in ebook form can readily do so by creating an account with an ebook publisher, formatting the manuscript from a digital file into the required format, creating a cover from a jpeg file, deciding on the retail price, and sending it. Most ebook publishers take a royalty on sales, charge a modest flat fee to format and post the book, or use a combination of fee plus royalty share.

---

[92] Some bricks and mortar retailers have begun to offer POD in their stores.

[93] If your work was ever published with an established US publisher and is now out of print, the Authors Guild offers Backinprint.com, an online bookstore and POD service for out-of-print books (www.backinprint.com). Through Backinprint, POD publisher iUniverse prepares a digital file from a physical copy of the original edition, allowing for production of quality paperbacks with original cover designs and perfect bindings. The books, which sell for about $10 to $20, are listed for sale at Backinprint.com, iUniverse.com, Amazon. com, BarnesandNoble.com, and every other online bookstore. Writers receive a royalty of 20 percent of net receipts. The up-front cost to participants (who must be Guild members) is free in most cases.

Of course, it is not quite as simple as it sounds if you want your book to be your best possible offering to the marketplace. Whether you choose to publish in ebook, POD, or both formats, if you are going to self-publish, you should understand how to make a book. A shoddy-looking product is almost worse than nothing; it is unlikely to sell many copies and will not gain favorable attention from reviewers or commercial publishers. The first decision you will need to make, then, is whether to let the publisher provide the essential elements of the book or to do it yourself. When deciding on the candidates for your business, examine books they have designed, edited, and published and decide whether you want yours to resemble theirs. You might decide that the financial terms and distribution services offered by a firm work for you but that you would rather provide editing and design yourself. Of course, hiring your own editors and designers costs money and time, too, but having control over the end product might be worth it to you.

EDITING AND COPYEDITING

Substantive and meaningful editorial input by a professional is one of the great advantages offered by commercial publishers. Realistically, every writer, even the great ones, needs a good editor to make her work the best it can be. Some publishers offer editorial services in their packages, but you should assess the proposed editor's skill and your rapport before you commit to working with her. When speaking to the publisher's sales associate, ask about the editor's experience and past success, and the exact services included for the price. Will you be in direct contact with the editor, or will you receive written comments only? Make sure the editor's area of expertise is right for your project. Try to get a sample of her editorial feedback on past projects. You should also nail down an acceptable deadline for receiving editorial feedback. Remember, the publisher is trying to make money from your purchase of services; it is not as motivated to get your book into print as you are. Consequently, the editors on staff could have large backlogs of projects, meaning you might wait longer than you expect for a job that ends up being rushed.

Finding your own editor is not hard to do; many professional editors freelance. Your writers' organization might have a list of recommendations for book doctors or freelance editors. The Independent Editors Group (www.bookdocs.com), a group of distinguished former editors at commercial publishers, is another good resource. The members are available for hire for freelance editing and evaluation and to give guidance throughout the self-publishing process; they can also recommend copyeditors and indexers. If you work with a freelance editor, you should have a contract with her that sets forth the fee structure (i.e., per project or by the hour or page count) and the services to be provided in detail. The contract should also make clear that all rights in the ultimate manuscript are and remain yours and that the editor and her associates will keep your project strictly confidential.

COVER AND DESIGN

Another hallmark of commercial publishers is the highly professional look—covers and interior designs and layouts—of their books. Badly designed or rendered covers and sloppy layouts are dead giveaways that a book is self-published. If you agree to have the publisher you have chosen design your book's layout and cover, it should give you the option to supply your own cover image if you wish and to approve of or choose the cover and possibly the interior design, at least from a menu of design options.

If you choose to provide your own cover and interior design, consider hiring a professional book designer to lay out and typeset the book. There are many freelance professionals who produce excellent work. Before deciding whether to retain a designer or to pay your publisher to design the book, ask to see samples of each of their work and to talk with previous clients. If you hire a designer, you should have a contract that describes the book, the specifications, including its dimensions and the number of pages, and whether the engagement will include cover design (for POD, this includes the front, spine, back, and flaps), the interior, or both. The contract should also:

Specify the format in which the designer will deliver the finished product (e.g., mechanicals ready for printing or specifications to be followed by the publisher).

Grant you all rights in the design (and any art included) to make any and all uses you wish to make, including promotional and advertising uses.

Include the right to terminate the contract at any time without being liable for expenses not yet incurred.

Provide that changes required because of the designer's error are the responsibility of the designer to correct.

ISBN NUMBER

"ISBN" stands for "International Standard Book Number" and it is exactly that—a unique identifier for every edition of a book that is used throughout the book industry. You cannot sell a book in any format in the marketplace without an ISBN. Most publishers will provide your book with an ISBN number as part of any package you buy, which has the advantage of saving you money. Because it is so much cheaper to buy ISBNs in bulk (as of this writing, they cost $125 for one, $250 for ten, $1,000 for one thousand), the publisher should charge you very little, if anything, to assign one to your book. The downside of having a self-publishing firm supply the ISBN is that the firm is named as the publisher of your book on the cover and all retail listings. The only way to avoid that is to purchase your own ISBN number and create your own publisher name. Be aware that if you publish in more than one format (i.e., POD and ebook), you will need a separate ISBN for each. Only one organization sells ISBNs directly: Bowker. You can buy ISBNs online at www.bowker.com.

DISTRIBUTION OUTLETS

There are many online retail outlets that sell POD books and even more that sell ebooks. No matter which publisher or format (POD and/or ebook) you choose, it is important to ensure that your book will be available for sale on all of them. When choosing a publisher, a key question to ask is on which retail sites the potential publisher will list your book.[94] Some ebook publishers are aggregators for Apple's iBooks platform, and they take a percentage of the royalties earned through iBooks in exchange for listing the book there (but they still should also list the book on the other sites). Other publishers will list your book on all available outlets as part of your package. Some, such as CreateSpace (Amazon), charge an additional fee to distribute through channels other than its own US and international sites.

Amazon offers higher royalties and a chance to gain exposure for ebooks through its Kindle Lending Library program if a writer agrees to list

---

[94] Very few, if any, bricks and mortar stores stock self-published titles, although this might change as the market changes. If you live near an independent retailer, it is worth approaching it about stocking your title, especially if you demonstrate that you can bring customers into the store.

exclusively with Amazon for at least ninety days. As of this writing, Amazon has 60 percent of the ebook market (including self- and commercially published titles), and this market share will probably rise. The pros and cons of casting your lot with Amazon on an exclusive basis, to the exclusion of every other outlet, will depend on your outlook and specific circumstances.

MARKETING AND PROMOTION

Although some publishers include promotional help in their packages, it is virtually impossible to generate significant sales unless you aggressively seek on your own to promote your book and/or employ expert help. It might make sense to include a publisher's promotional service in a package deal if it is not too expensive, but in order to gain attention in the market, you book will need more attention and active promotion than any self-publisher provides.

Many books and articles on this subject exist. One of the best is literary agent Noah Lukeman's *How to Land (and Keep) a Literary Agent*. He argues that an author must establish effective promotional platforms in order to interest an agent and describes many ways to do so. His advice applies equally to marketing books. Other ways to generate attention and sales are:

If you do not already have one, establishing your own website (with your name and book titles as the domain names) is a must. The Authors Guild provides site-building software and domain name registration services at very low cost to members. It is relatively simple to do, and the promotion and marketing possibilities this essential platform provides are many.

Independent services for hire focus on social media, blogs, and other platforms, both online and offline, to promote titles. If you do not have the time and knowledge to do so yourself, consider retaining a reputable book marketing consultant.

Google Adwords/Keywords, social media-based promotion and paid ads, and other self-serve ad networks are considered necessities in the self-publishing arena.

Publications such as *Publishers Weekly* and *Kirkus* now review self-published books for a fee. Neither of them guarantees a favorable review, however, so you risk spending money for a result that might be worse than being ignored would have been.

Amazon's stature in the industry also offers benefits. Its Amazon Author Central page, for example, explains how writers can position their titles so that they surface in response to particular searches by users.

Explore the possibilities of social media. Twitter, Facebook, Pinterest, YouTube, and the like are potentially excellent platforms.

YOUR SELF-PUBLISHING CONTRACT

Your chosen publisher will offer you a contract, likely through its web-site, and expect you to "click" your acceptance of the terms. This makes it unlikely (though not impossible) that you will be able to negotiate changes to the boilerplate in these agreements.[95] Even so, you should read what you are agreeing to before you proceed so that you ensure the publisher observes basic industry standards and that you understand the transaction.

THE CONTRACT

You should seriously rethink signing with any publisher if its boilerplate contract deviates from the following fundamentals:

It should not include a broad grant of rights. No publisher should obtain rights that it does not have the means or intent to exploit to your advantage. The publisher needs the rights to create and sell ebooks and/ or POD books, but the grant of rights should not define digital rights so broadly that it includes multimedia or audio book rights. If you are publish-ing in ebook format only, the grant of rights should not include "print" or "book publishing" rights.

No rights should be given on an exclusive basis. The grant of rights should explicitly say that they are nonexclusive. You are paying for a service, not to limit your options for the work.

The publisher should undertake to collect and remit all amounts due to you from sales and issue a report of sales and earnings at least once per quarter, if not more often. You should be able to access your account on the publisher's website and sales data should be available there in real time.

---

[95] These firms also commonly allow themselves the right to change the boilerplate at will; by continuing to use the service, customers are automatically agreeing to these changes.

If royalties are based on "net proceeds," "net" should be explicitly defined. Most contracts define net as the retail price of the work sold, less third-party discounts and fees and the cost of conversion and encryption, but these should be reasonable.

Perhaps most important, make sure you have the right to terminate the contract on reasonable notice—no more than thirty days. You need the freedom to take your work elsewhere at any time you wish. If a commercial publisher takes notice and offers to publish your book, it will likely require you to grant ebook rights, and you should be free to accept the offer. It is fair for the contract to stipulate that upon termination, your publisher will have the right to continue selling copies for a reasonable period (no more than thirty days). This should not harm your dealings with a new publisher.

THE NEGOTIATION

Aside from the boilerplate terms, you should be able to negotiate the various components of the package deals offered by the full service companies, if you decide to go with one. Because they want your business, and presumably to sell you as many services as they can, they will have a sales associate contact you. Ask whether the firm will discount some of its offerings, or even throw in some services gratis. Other questions to ask:

How and to what extent will the publisher consult with you regarding, or allow you to choose, the appearance, format, production, copyediting, style, and promotion of the book? If you are paying the publisher for these services, do not be afraid to ask for samples and to speak with other clients before signing on.

Does the company's business model rely on the fees charged to writers to participate, on royalty revenue from sales of the books, or from a combination? Does it offer flexibility in the fee structure? For example, can any of the up-front fees be recouped from royalties earned? If you are counting on selling as many copies as you can, the royalty share model is generally preferable because it gives the publisher an incentive to sell the book. On the other hand, if your book becomes a runaway bestseller, you would be better off earning the lion's share of royalties.

Are the costs reasonable for the services provided? For example, what is the charge to convert a previously published work to ebook form and make it available for distribution through online retailers? If it is not available in digital form, the publisher will incur costs to convert and proofread it. If you are sending your work in digital form and the publisher is not editing the book, conversion should be a minimal expense.

Retail price: for ebooks, the publisher should not dictate a minimum or maximum price. You should be able to give copies away if you choose, or to charge well over the market average if you choose.

Retail pricing for POD is different, because it costs the publisher to print, bind, and ship a hard copy, and it should be able to recoup its outlay. It is fair for POD publishers to dictate a minimum, but not a maximum, price.

For both formats, it is fair for the publisher to set your royalty rates based on the retail price you dictate, although not all of them do.

Does the company offer adequate piracy protection? Even though most companies use encryption protocols that are standard in the industry, unauthorized ebook sites are fairly rampant. Ask about the publisher's encryption protocols and whether and to what extent its titles have been pirated.

Keep in mind that the self-publishing industry is constantly changing. Currently, a lot of competition for your business exists. The best way to serve your interests is to apprise yourself on a regular basis of the current state of the industry. Compare books you admire and the ease with which you can find and access them. Amazon has a great competitive advantage in this arena right now, but there are other nimble and smart players out there that might be better for your needs.

CHAPTER 14

ELECTRONIC RIGHTS AND WRONGS: BATTLES OVER DIGITAL RIGHTS

"The parties . . . may enter into an agreement allowing continued electronic reproduction of the Authors' works; they . . . may draw on numerous models for distributing copyrighted works and remunerating authors for their distribution."

The US Supreme Court made this optimistic pronouncement in 2001, when ruling in favor of a group of freelance writers who claimed that their publishers had infringed their copyrights electronically. Since then, however, the information industry—writers, publishers and the enterprises that aggregate and distribute content digitally—have largely failed to come up with a model that allows each participant to capitalize equitably on the potential of digital technology.

The changes in the industry wrought by the rise of the Internet have raised complicated issues about ownership, control, and monetizing of literary content, some of which remain unresolved. The publishing industry was slow to realize the potential of digital rights, but as it did, litigation ensued among publishers, writers, aggregators and retailers, and the US Justice Department. This chapter will examine the various legal skirmishes among industry actors over digital rights and fair remuneration and explain how the outcomes are affecting the players, especially writers.[96]

Today, literature can be disseminated in formats and to an extent unimaginable twenty years ago. The proliferation of free and pirated content on the web has made print, and payment, obsolete for many forms of information. In 2007, advances in technology finally made ebooks palatable and convenient to readers, and they have become very popular. The range of books, long-form journalism, and articles published and accessed through ereaders, on mobile devices, and on websites is projected to increase dramatically, if not exponentially, in the coming years. By 2011, among major publishers' products, ebook sales revenue had surpassed hardcover sales revenue and was hard on the heels of paperback revenue.

The lower cost of entry into digital publishing has increased competition for traditional publishers from start-ups and self-published writers, who now have cheap and low risk self-publishing alternatives to reach readers. At the same time, the reading public, inundated with free content through the Internet and encouraged by Amazon's aggressively low pricing of popular ebook titles, already expects to pay little or nothing for books and articles. This downward price pressure not only harms established publishers' revenues, but it has sliced into the market for printed books. On the periodical side of the business, newspaper and magazine publishers have for years been losing advertising revenue to Google and Craigslist and from the cannibalization of their subscriber base by their own presence online.

Since the mid-1990s, traditional publishers have reacted to the threat and promise of technology by trying in the first instance to obtain as many rights to their writers' content as they can get for as little money as possible. They used various soft and hardball tactics, including litigation, to accomplish what would amount to realignment in the traditional division of rights between writer and publisher. In the major lawsuits over these issues, courts have recognized in theory that creators should control and be compensated for new uses of their works, but the practical results of the cases have not led to meaningful economic rewards for writers.

Over the past two decades, three seminal lawsuits over digital rights in literary works have made their way through the courts: *The New York*

---

[96] Chapter 13 describes the current market for ebooks and "print on demand" books and explains how writers can sell their works in these formats.

Times, et al. v. Tasini, et al. and its progeny (regarding freelance contributions to periodicals, begun in 1993), *Random House v. Rosetta Books* (regarding ebooks, 2001), and the *Google Books* litigation (regarding digitization of books for a searchable database, begun in 2005 and ongoing). More recently, the Justice Department shocked the industry in 2012 when it sued five of the Big Six book publishers[97] and Apple over an alleged scheme to fix the retail price of ebooks. The outcome of this case is likely to reverberate through the industry for years to come. If the Justice Department prevails, the likely winner is Amazon, and the likely losers are bricks and mortar bookstores and the publishers and writers who need them.

FREELANCE CONTRIBUTIONS TO PERIODICALS

In 2001, the Supreme Court ruled in *The New York Times, et al. v. Tasini, et al.* that newspaper and magazine publishers do not presumptively have the right to include freelance articles in electronic databases, such as LexisNexis. The Court held that the publishers must obtain permission from their freelance contributors to reproduce and distribute their articles in this new form of media. The defendants, three publishers and two databases, had argued that the Copyright Act gave them a "default license" to deal directly with the lucrative databases without sharing with the authors of the contributions. The section of the Act the publishers relied on says:

> In the absence of an express transfer of the copyright or of any rights under it, the owner of copyright in the collective work [here, the publisher] is presumed to have acquired only the privilege of reproducing and distributing the [freelance] contribution *as part of that particular collective work, any revision of that collective work, and any later collective work in the same series.* (emphasis added).
> Copyright Act, Section 201(c).

The defendants argued that the "privilege of reproducing and distributing the contributions as part of [a] revision of that collective work"

---

[97] The major US trade publishers, each of which is a conglomerate of "imprints," are Random House, Penguin Group, Simon & Schuster, Hachette Book Group, HarperCollins and Macmillan; Random House and Penguin Group are in the process of merging their trade book units.

included selling freelance contributions to the databases. They reasoned that a database was a "revision" of each of its constituent publications, or that when a freelance article was located, purchased, and read by a subscriber to the database it was at that point still a "part of" the original periodical. They also urged that the databases, to which most academic institutions and many businesses subscribe, had become so necessary to modern research that requiring the publishers to obtain permission from their contributors would devastate scholarship by leaving holes in the historical archive.

The Court rejected these arguments. First, the freelance articles "as presented to and perceptible by" the users of the databases were not presented in their original context, but instead were disconnected from the original publication. They could not, therefore, be reproduced "as part of" the original publication or a revision of it, and the publishers' relicensing them went beyond the permitted uses and infringed the freelancers' copyrights. To the argument that a ruling for the writers would decimate the nation's historical archives by requiring the removal of freelance materials, the Court observed that the parties could "draw on numerous" existing models to ensure both fair compensation and continued dissemination of the works.

Important as the Supreme Court's ruling was for establishing the preeminence of freelancers' digital rights in their work, to this day, the affected writers have never received an effective financial remedy. Soon after Tasini and his fellow plaintiffs filed suit in 1993, the *New York Times* and other major newspaper and magazine publishers changed their long-standing practice and began to require freelancers to sign away their copyrights in their past and future contributions to their publishers. In response to these hardball tactics, a group of freelancers and three writers groups brought a class action suit in 2000 on behalf of all freelancers against all the entities that had placed their articles in electronic databases without permission. The plaintiffs and defendants negotiated for almost two years to find a means to achieve a blanket release from the writers' claims and fair compensation through a negotiated settlement. The parties ultimately agreed to a settlement of up to $18 million that would have restored most works to the databases, but the Second Circuit Court of Appeals surprised the industry and rejected the settlement on the grounds that it was not fair to all of the class members.[98]

---

[98] A few class members had objected to the settlement on the grounds that the payment was not sufficient, but the Second Circuit rejected it because most of the class members

Two later lawsuits challenging *National Geographic's* release of an interactive CD-ROM containing exact digital replications of the magazine led to a significant diminution of freelancers' rights. The Second and Fifth Circuit Courts of Appeal distinguished the electronic databases disallowed in *Tasini*, which present articles disaggregated from their original context, from the more advanced technologies that present contributions as images in their original context. These courts held that collective works publishers are permitted to make such uses under the Copyright Act without the contributors' permission. The Supreme Court did not review these rulings, tacitly approving them. Settlement of this class-action lawsuit is still pending.[99]

EBOOKS AND BOOK CONTRACTS

Ebooks are digital versions of printed books that are purchased and downloaded to computers or dedicated reading devices such as the Kindle, the Nook, and the iPad. Although the text of an ebook might be the same as the text of the print version, ebooks have different features and more functions than a printed book. For example, an ebook can be searched for specific words and phrases. Readers can highlight and bookmark certain text to be indexed and reaccessed, jump to specific chapters through links in the table of contents, type electronic notes that are automatically indexed, sorted, and filed with related text, change the font size and style, and link to a definition of words in the text. Most ebooks contain encryption code to prevent unauthorized printing, copying, and file-sharing. These distinctions between print and ebooks became legally significant in 2000 when a court was asked to interpret older book publishing contracts that do not mention "electronic rights" or "electronic books."

---

had not registered their copyrights and so should not have been included in the class. The Supreme Court reversed that holding and told the Second Circuit to reconsider. On reconsideration, that court again rejected the settlement because the subclass of unregistered freelancers were slated to receive far less than writers who had registered their works, and therefore the settlement treated them unfairly. The parties continue to work towards a settlement.

[99] Chapter 12 covers newspaper and magazine contracts and how to negotiate them.

Most book publishing contracts signed prior to 1995 do not include a specific grant of ebook rights to the publisher. Does the lack of a specific grant mean the writer may freely grant ebook rights to a third party without the publisher's consent? The leading court decision answered this question in the affirmative in 2001. In *Random House v. Rosetta Books*, a federal court rejected Random House's lawsuit seeking to bar its writers from licensing ebook rights to Rosetta Books, a start-up ebook publisher. Rosetta had made deals with William Styron, Kurt Vonnegut, Jr., and Robert Parker to publish ebook versions of their novels, all of which were under standard book contracts from the 1960s through the 1980s. (Because the works were still in print, the original contracts remained in force.) Although the book contracts contained the traditional grant of "the right to print, publish and sell the Work[s] in book form," they did not mention electronic or digital rights or ebooks, and the authors had reserved all rights not specifically granted. Random House argued that its right to publish in "book form" necessarily included ebooks. Given that the publisher had approximately twenty thousand current contracts in force that did not specifically mention ebook or electronic rights, the significance of the ruling would be felt across the industry. Numerous publishers with similar terms in their contracts appeared as "friends of the court" to support Random House's position.

The district court had to discern the parties' intent at the time they were negotiating by relying on the language of the contracts and basic principles of contract interpretation. It concluded that the traditional grant of the "exclusive right to print, publish and sell the Work in book form" could not be interpreted to include electronic books. In part, the enhancements that ebooks offer over printed books convinced the court that the parties could not have intended "book form" to include ebooks. The Second Circuit Court of Appeals affirmed the conclusion without analyzing it.

This decision was a big victory for writers. At stake in the case was the fundamental interpretation of book contracts, which carefully and explicitly define the rights and formats that are granted to the publisher and spell out the royalties to be paid for the exploitation of these rights. By reading the contract as it did, the court preserved writers' ability to control whether and how to exploit their works in a new format. Publishing insiders are carefully watching the progress of a lawsuit that may revisit the issues raised in *Rosetta*. HarperCollins has brought a suit against Open Road Integrated

Media, a standalone ebook publisher, involving the 1972 children's classic *Julie of the Wolves*, written by Jean Craighead George and published in printed form by HarperCollins. Ms. George, who has since passed away, contracted with Open Road to publish an ebook edition of the work, and HarperCollins subsequently filed suit against the e-publisher in December 2012. As the legacy publisher, HarperCollins argues that it holds exclusive right to publish the ebook, but given the advanced age of the contract (drawn up long before the existence of ebooks as we know them today), the defendant, Open Road, believes Ms. George was free to exploit the electronic rights for her work without interference from HarperCollins. A hearing in the United States District Court for the Southern District of New York is scheduled for later in 2013.

The practical result of *Rosetta* today is less important than it was in 2001 because since the late 1990s, virtually every book contract contains a grant of ebook rights. But writers with older contracts that are still in force might be able to sell their ebook rights separately or to self-publish in that format. This right gives leverage to ask for an advance against ebook royalties, higher royalties than the low-ball standard of 25 percent of net (discussed in chapter 11), and a veto over changes or abridgements in the text. Still, if this applies to you, exercise caution and consult with your agent or a publishing lawyer before proceeding to contract with another publisher for ebook rights. Your current publisher might offer you at least as good a deal as a third party would. You also need to consider whether your current contract has a "noncompetition" clause that might interfere with your plans. Although the court in *Rosetta Books* held that noncompetition clauses did not preclude granting ebook rights to a new publisher, the market for ebooks was still nascent in 2001, the year of the holding. The conclusion might be different today in light of the past several years of growth in the market.

SCANNING BOOKS, ORPHAN WORKS, AND THE "DIGITAL LIBRARY": THE GOOGLE BOOKS LAWSUITS

In the past decade, the traditional news media has lost much of its advertising revenue to search engines such as Google, which has profited enormously by aggregating information that others create and make available on the Internet. By 2004, however, Google wanted to grow its search database by adding books. It made deals with five large libraries to scan and digitize their holdings and put them to the Google database. With some 20 million books scanned to date and counting, the "Google Books" project has vastly increased the information in the search giant's database. Google makes only "snippets"—a few words—of the scanned books available in search results to end users, and argues that this limited use helps market the titles and makes its digital copying fair use under copyright. In exchange for letting Google digitize their collections, the libraries received one digital copy of each of its books and agreed not to sell or give digital copies to any commercial enterprise.

Not surprisingly, the authors and publishers that own the copyrights and were excluded from the deal were alarmed by the wholesale copying of their books into digital files for a database that could be hacked. They had seen the music industry's decline at the hands of mass file-sharing and cried foul at Google's scheme.[100] In 2005, varioius parties filed lawsuits against Google for copyright infringement. The Authors Guild and several named authors filed a class-action suit on behalf of rightsholders, and the Association of American Publishers filed another suit. The parties quickly began settlement negotiations, and after two years, they announced a major deal, one that would have made the entirety of most of the digitized books potentially available to the world, while allowing the copyright owners to get compensated for every use made. The court examining the settlement for legal adequacy listed the "many" benefits of the settlement:

> Books will become more accessible. Libraries, schools, researchers, and disadvantaged populations will gain access to far more books. Digitization will facilitate the conversion of books to Braille and audio formats, increasing access for individuals with disabilities. Authors and publishers will benefit as well, as new audiences will be generated and new sources of income created. Older books—particularly out-of-print books, many of which are falling apart buried in library stacks—will be preserved and given new life.

---

[100] The Google Books project is not to be confused with the "Search Inside the Book" marketing plan by which Google, Amazon, and Barnes & Noble are allowed by publishers to make up to 20 percent of books digitally available to users. The publishers include only books to which they have electronic rights and will not include a book if the author objects.

The complicated settlement arrangement went beyond compensating the owners for scanning the books and making a few words available. Had it succeeded, it would have given Google the right to continue digitizing books, to make the entirety—not just "snippets"—of the vast majority of the works available by subscription to institutions and by individual sales of online access to the public, to sell ads on pages from the books, and to make other uses of the database. The copyright owners could choose to have their books included in any or all of the possible uses and would receive the lion's share of the proceeds. Google would create the infrastructure for the project, which the parties had carefully designed.

Notwithstanding these features, the proposed settlement caused a vehement backlash from foreign writers, Google competitors, the Justice Department, and numerous US writers. Even though any owner of the rights to a book could remove it from the Google database, many writers were offended that their right to control the fate of their books had been negotiated away unless they took affirmative steps. More than 6,800 writers opted out of the proposed settlement.

The Justice Department, the Copyright Office, some Google competitors, academic and other writers' groups, and advocates for liberalizing copyright argued that the settlement would give Google a monopoly over the digital use of millions of books, including millions of so-called "orphan works," i.e., books and other writings covered by copyright for which no owner can be located. Under the settlement, Google would have been allowed to exploit orphan works and fully released from infringement claims for including them—an advantage that no other party could possibly gain, unless it chose to digitize books without permission and to settle a lawsuit on the same terms as Google.

The court concluded that it was not appropriate to use the mechanism of a class action settlement to create a forward-looking business arrangement that benefited Google at the expense of potential competitors. It opined that Congress is more suited than private litigants to address how to make "orphan books" available to the public (even though Congress has made no progress on that score). It concluded that most of the legal concerns would be ameliorated if the settlement included only books licensed on an "opt in" rather than an "opt out" basis, but Google had no interest in such an arrangement. For these reasons, the court rejected the proposed settlement.

The authors' and publishers' infringement lawsuit against Google continues. The authors won the most recent legal skirmish as of this writing when the court certified the case as a class action and allowed the Authors Guild to remain a party in the case. Google has appealed the class certification decision and has moved for summary judgment dismissing the lawsuit based on its argument that scanning and using the books is fair use that causes no financial harm to copyright owner. The court has not yet ruled on the fair use argument, but no matter how it decides, the vision the Supreme Court articulated in *Tasini* of a digital repository of commercially available literature that generates royalties for its owners appears to be dead.

THE LIBRARIES AND HATHITRUST

The Google Books project recently led to another lawsuit over digital exploitation of books. The four university libraries that allowed Google to scan their collections received digital copies of an estimated 7 million copyright-protected books. Although prohibited by their contracts with Google from using them commercially, these universities announced a year ago that they had pooled their files in a repository organized by the University of Michigan called HathiTrust. In June 2011, the University of Michigan announced plans to permit its students and faculty to make unlimited, complete downloads of what it decides are "orphan works" in the Trust. Other universities announced they would use the Trust for the same purposes.

A number of foreign and US writers objected to the universities asserting the authority to decide which writers had forfeited their copyrights. The writers expressed great concern at the potential for all other domestic and international colleges and universities to follow suit. A number of writers' organizations and individuals from several countries sued the participating universities and HathiTrust for copyright infringement. Among their claims, the plaintiffs questioned the security of Michigan's database, which includes thousands of editions, in various translations, of works by writers from nearly every nation. Within days of the Trust publishing the list of "orphans" it planned to make fully accessible, the writers announced that they had located dozens of the owners of the "orphans." Although this led the Trust to shelve its orphan book plans for the time being, it has not scrapped it entirely.

In October 2012, a New York federal court ruled that the unauthorized scanning for the purposes of allowing readers to locate text is fair use under the Copyright Act. Its holding on this question was the first time a court has decided whether scanning works into a database without permission is legal, and its decision could well affect Google's fair use argument as well.

THE EBOOK PRICING WAR: JUSTICE PICKS A WINNER

Ebooks are upending the traditional economics of book publishing. On the one hand, they virtually eliminate the costs of printing, storage, shipping, and returns. On the other, they reinforce consumers' expectations that literary works should be available for free or at very low cost. In this environment, by 2010, Amazon had achieved 90 percent of the market for ebook sales for its Kindle. How did Amazon achieve this formidable position? Few industry watchers dispute that Amazon's decision to price ebook frontlist (i.e., current and prominent) titles at less than the wholesale price gained it market share. Its competitors simply could not afford to do the same. The publishers, which have the highest stake in the ebook market and in how it affects print sales, had no say in Amazon's gambit because they had sold ebooks to Amazon the same way they sell print copies—through the so-called "reseller model." In the reseller model, publishers sell ebooks to retailers at a wholesale discount of around 50 percent of the suggested retail price and assert no control over the ultimate retail price. When Amazon began selling the most popular titles in ebook form at $9.99 or less, publishers quickly saw ebooks begin to cut into print sales of the same title. More alarming still to publishers, low priced ebooks encourage buyers to expect ebooks to remain that cheap.

Amazon strategically priced only certain books—the frontlist titles that attract buyers to bricks and mortar bookstores—at a loss, and this has begun to discourage new entrants into the ebook market and to eliminate Amazon's retail competition. (The Borders chain liquidated in 2010, cutting by almost half the number of retail bookstores in the United States.) As they see it, traditional publishers have few defenses that might protect their businesses from getting consumed by Amazon.[101] One solution was

---

[101] As the Authors Guild described in a filing in the Justice Department case, Amazon currently controls about 75 percent of the print market for trade books, and through a series

to replace the reseller model with so-called "agency pricing" for ebook sales to retailers. The agency model was proposed in 2010 by Apple, which wanted to acquire ebooks to sell for its new iPad tablet reader. Under the agency model, the publisher decides the retail price for the ebook, and the retailer, acting as its agent, sells at the publisher's price and takes 30 percent. Apple's offer to use the agency model had one catch: the publishers could not allow other retailers to sell the books at a lower price.

Apple entered into contracts with five of the Big Six publishers in 2010 to sell ebooks based on the agency model, and the publishers in turn demanded that Amazon and other retailers adopt it. Amazon retaliated against Macmillan by removing the "buy" buttons from all of its titles, both ebook and print, for several weeks before it reluctantly acquiesced to using the agency model. Shortly thereafter, the Justice Department's Antitrust Division began investigating whether the five publishers, in agreeing to the Apple deal, had colluded to fix prices for ebooks. In April 2012, it sued all five and Apple, and quickly announced a proposed settlement with three of the publishers. [102]

The settlement requires that the publishers allow ebook retailers to continue selling ebooks at a loss, so long as they do not lose money over each publisher's entire list of ebooks over the course of one year. To many observers, this seems anathema to the goal of keeping ebook prices low in the long term, because it will allow Amazon to continue entrenching its market dominance over this format. Consumers of books are not likely to continue enjoying Amazon's below-cost pricing if the online juggernaut gains total market dominance.

Nonetheless, in September 2012, a federal court in New York ruled that the proposed antitrust settlement is in the best interests of consumers. The Authors Guild and more than 2000 others had filed comments objecting to those settlement terms that require the resumption of the reseller

---

of acquisitions, now controls the downloadable audio book market, the online market for used books, the market for self-published on-demand and ebooks, and is getting exclusive rights to thousands of titles by acquiring publishers themselves. The Guild describes this activity as "an unprecedented and dangerous balkanization of the literary marketplace."

[102] Random House did not originally sign on with Apple, but did so later, and is not named in the suit. Macmillan, Penguin, Simon & Schuster, Hachette Book Group, and Harper-Collins have all agreed to settle, and at least one of those publishers cites the high cost of litigation as its reason. All have denied that they fixed prices with their competitors.

model and allow retailers to continue to sell ebooks at a loss. Others opined that Amazon offers the best options for writers who want to self-publish ebooks[103] and that consumers should be offered the lowest prices for ebooks that the market will bear in order to build the market. This situation is fluid and will no doubt have evolved as of the publication of this book. One thing is certain, however: for better or worse, professional book writers have at least as much at stake in the outcome of this battle as any other part of the industry.

---

[103] Chapter 13 examines the on-demand and ebook self-publishing options offered by Amazon and others.

CHAPTER 15

LITERARY AGENTS AND

AGENCY AGREEMENTS

If you intend to sell even one book to a commercial publisher, you need a literary agent. You might be the next Stephen King, but you are unlikely to be read by the right editor for you, or by any editor, unless an agent submits your work.[104] Even if you get extraordinarily lucky and interest a commercial publisher without an agent, you probably lack the experience, industry acumen, contacts, and ability to negotiate effectively for yourself. Established literary agents are in the business of placing clients' works with the right publisher, negotiating the best possible contracts, and collecting and policing the fees, advances, and royalties due.

A good agent will know whether a manuscript or proposal can sell in its present form or needs work. Agents huddle with editors every day to keep abreast of the market and to talk up their clients' work, and they know who to target within a given publisher or imprint when shopping particular books. In turn, editors rely on agents to screen writers and manuscripts.

---

[104] The exceptions to this rule are authors of textbooks, professional or reference works, poetry, genre fiction, and children's picture books. But while they can sell their works without a literary agent, they would certainly benefit from having one. Some freelance journalists do well without an agent, but that is not the case when they are marketing a book.

Virtually no editor in a trade house will read an unsolicited manuscript unless it came from an agent; the major houses license the overwhelming number of the titles they publish through agents. Publishers typically return unsolicited queries with a form letter explaining that they do not consider unsolicited submissions unless they come through agents. Smaller and genre publishers might assign a harried intern or assistant to read through the slush pile, but, like all editorial assistants, they will be looking for reasons to reject what is in front of them as quickly as they can. Often, even a powerful agent has to make twenty or thirty submissions before a project finds an appropriate publisher. How many writers acting for themselves would have persisted through the twenty-ninth rejection? In short, the odds against your getting published without an agent are overwhelming.

Moreover, placing your work is only one of the important functions of an agent. Once a publisher expresses interest, agents are far better situated than writers to negotiate good deals without jeopardizing the parties' relationship. They can carry off auctions for rights that an author could not possibly set up alone. With their experience and clout, they are better able to negotiate the narrowest grant of rights, the most generous advance and royalties, and the most favorable delivery and "satisfactory manuscript" terms possible. Negotiating for herself, a writer would inevitably grant broader rights, accept lower pay, and keep less control over her work.

Most good agents would say that placing the works and negotiating the best deals are only two of the important services they give their clients. A third essential function is nurturing their clients' careers, their development as a writer in the industry. Agents know the business, and the good ones also understand the art and craft of writing. They want—and need—their clients to succeed and most of them believe that artistic success leads to commercial success. Your agent will read your work, tell you what she thinks of it and what it needs in order to sell, weigh in on your plans for future projects, help you devise your next move based on the performance of your last book, advocate for you with your publisher when things go wrong, and help you develop as a professional over the short and long term.

Finally, your agent is your representative to your publisher; she has a direct line to editors and others in the house and is your conduit to them. When you want to know what is happening with your manuscript or when you can expect editorial comments or payments, or to offer your opinion on the cover design, marketing plan, and so forth, your agent is the person to contact. The industry is small, and writers who contact their editors frequently to ask questions or to vent can quickly become known as "difficult" or worse. As your representative, your agent can shield you from such a possibility.[105]

The most important part of the process of professional writing is creating work that people want to read. A close second is finding a good agent to represent you.

FINDING AN AGENT

Your engagement with your agent is probably the most important business relationship of your career. So how do you find this important person? For most writers, unfortunately, it is not easy. Established agents are inundated with queries from your fellow writers, so many, in fact, that many successful agents do not accept new clients. You need to prepare for a lot of rejection and for a long journey to finding an agent, and at the same time, to protect yourself from being misled by unprofessional actors calling themselves agents.

Before reaching out to any agent, you must be ready to show your work, as good as you can make it. If your work is not ready to be shown to a publisher, then you are not ready to query the agent. Agents will most likely reject aspiring writers with great ideas or half-baked proposals but nothing tangible to market to editors. Unless you are a valued client of long standing (or a celebrity), you cannot expect an agent to edit your work or find you a ghostwriter. Keep in mind that agents who are accepting new clients get dozens of queries a day and are constantly committed to reading large stacks of manuscripts and proposals. If your query interests the agent, she is going to ask to read some or all of your manuscript or proposal. If it is not ready to show her, you will have wasted her time. Wasting an agent's time is a bad way to begin; you will probably not have a second chance with her.

CREATE A TARGET LIST

In his indispensable book *How to Land (and Keep) a Literary Agent*,[106] top literary agent Noah Lukeman describes hearing from many writers that

---

[105] Of course, you should also limit your calls to your agent, once you have one, to the minimum necessary.

[106] Lukeman is one of those agents who are not accepting new clients. But you can rely with confidence on his expert advice, *How to Land (and Keep) a Literary Agent* (Lukeman

they simply gave up after being rejected by the six or eight agents they queried. Given the buyer's market you are entering, it is fantasy to expect to land an agent in your first round of queries. You must create a significant list of appropriate candidates to target—and "significant" means long, at least fifty, according to many industry experts. That does not mean going through a directory of agents such as the *Literary Market Place* and querying them all in alphabetical order. It means researching to determine which agents are appropriate for your book and career ambitions, and prioritizing them in order based on who you think would be ideal. Agents specialize in specific kinds of books—fiction versus nonfiction, commercial versus literary, adult, young adult or children's, within genres, and within markets (such as business, technology, art, and science). Some agents are relatively new and hungry, while others are well established and so highly selective that they will read only queries from writers referred by an existing client. Obviously, you need to target agents who are willing to represent works that fall into your book's categories. As well, you should review the most recent deals these agents have made to help you prioritize who to query.

One of your first considerations is whether you want to work with a large agency (such as ICM or William Morris) or one of numerous smaller agencies. At a small agency, you might receive more personal attention, have calls returned faster, and have easier access to agency staff. On the other hand, a large agency has clout when dealing with a publisher or other licensee while shopping the work and negotiating deals. The downside is that you would be one of many clients, so your concerns would not always be foremost on your agent's mind, and she and her colleagues might well be trying to place more than just your work in the same market. There is no reason not to add candidates from both large and small agencies to your list, but these considerations might determine how you order your priorities.

Discovering which agents currently and successfully represent books in your category requires research and organization.[107] There are several ways

---

Literary 2009).

[107] Noah Lukeman recommends creating a spreadsheet to keep track of your candidates and their relevant information, their submission requirements, the status of your queries and submissions, etc.

to find good candidates for your target list, almost all of which are free or inexpensive. A few of the richest sources are described here, but you should dive into the web to find more.[108]

One tried and true method is to call on your network of fellow writers, through your writers organization, classes or critique group, and ask people whose work is similar to yours for referrals. An agent will notice when a writer she represents or respects has referred a querier.

Another excellent resource is the Association of Authors' Representatives ("AAR") (www.aar-online.org). Membership in the AAR is restricted to agents whose primary professional activity, as shown by a substantial number of concluded deals over the past two years, is as a writer's (or playwright's) representative. Anyone can call themselves a literary agent (no license is required), but being in the AAR is akin to having a professional seal of approval. Members must pledge to abide by the organization's Canon of Ethics (available on its website) and to conduct their business strictly in the best interests of their clients.[109] The AAR website lists its members and their contact information and links to their websites.

Publishers Lunch (www.publisherslunch.com) is a free daily and weekly email newsletter and, crucially for writers seeking agents, offers an inexpensive database containing reported book deals. The newsletter is compiled and written by Michael Cader, a former publisher and bookseller, on the *Publishers Marketplace* platform. More than 40,000 editors, agents, booksellers, and writers subscribe. Each "Daily Lunch" provides the key stories of the day for the professional trade book business. The "Deluxe" version of *Lunch* at *Publishers Marketplace* (www.publishersmarketplace.com) costs $25 per month. For that, you receive invaluable resources to help build your target agent list and learn what publishers are buying. Most agents and publishers subscribe, and they routinely report their deals, proposals, and acquisitions. As a subscriber, you can search the database of members' pages, discover which agents represents particular writers, and review thousands of reported acquisitions and deals, including the amount of the advance or license fee—key factors when ordering your target list. No other resource

---

[108] Refer to Chapter 1 for longer descriptions of various writers groups and many of the resources described here.

[109] This does not mean you should query only members of the AAR. Although they have proven experience and are manifestly ethical, it does not follow that other agents are not equally worthy. Many good agents simply choose not to join the AAR.

out there provides this information in one place in such an easily searchable format. Subscribers can also create their own webpages on the database with contact information, career highlights, proposals, and a checkbox to show they are looking for an agent. It also links you to various agents' blogs. While you are seeking an agent, the $25 monthly fee for *Publishers Lunch Deluxe* is a very worthwhile investment.

Publishers Weekly, the weekly industry magazine, sends several free weekly emails with news of the industry. If you subscribe to PW online (www.publishersweekly.com) for about $200 a year, you can access its searchable database of major reported deals, which names the agents who made the deals. This database only lists major deals, so is not as comprehensive as *Publishers Marketplace*.

The annual *Writers Digest Guide to Literary Agents* includes a blog (www.guidetoliteraryagents.com/blog) that is an excellent running source of agent information; it helps to cross-reference this resource against other sources.

The Literary Marketplace (LMP), an annual directory available in most libraries, lists agents that provide at least three references and every publisher currently in business, along with their contact information, areas of specialty, and submission guidelines. Be cautious when using the *LMP*. Although its publisher asserts that agents must submit client references prior to being listed as such, the *LMP* also contains advertising. Some of the entities that advertise as agents are not listed in the official directory.

Jeff Herman's annually updated *Guide to Book Publishers, Editors, and Literary Agents* is subtitled: "Who They Are! What They Want! How to Win Them Over!" As the name implies, the book offers in-depth information about what specific agents and publishers are seeking.

Another enterprising way to find candidates is to study the acknowledgments pages in your favorite books. If someone writing in the same field as yourself is so fond of her agent that she wants the world to know, that is a good sign that the agent is worth a look. You can then cross-reference the agent's name in the databases of the AAR, *Publishers Marketplace*, and/or *Publishers Weekly*.

Finally, attend writers' conferences and conventions. These forums provide opportunities to meet agents looking for clients and other writers and editors who might offer referrals. Many writers organizations arrange short meetings between members and appropriate agents. Although there are usually fees to attend the conferences and additional fees to have a one-on-one meeting, if you are ready to market your work and your research shows that this agent could work for you, it might be worth every penny.

QUERIES: SUBSTANCE, TIMING, AND MANAGING THE PROCESS

Your next step is to send query letters to the agents on your list, which in essence is an invitation to review your manuscript or proposal, in whole or in part. Industry experts advise that you query not more than five to ten agents at a time from your list, and logically, you want to query them in order of preference. Wait to hear from those you have queried (or six to eight weeks for agents who do not respond) before moving on to your next batch of five to ten. There are entire books and several blogs that focus on how to perfect a query letter. What follows here are only the basic necessities of your correspondence with potential agents.[110]

First, follow every agent's submission guidelines to the letter. If you do not, chances are the agent will reject you out of hand. Enclose a self-addressed, stamped envelope (SASE) with all queries (and later, with manuscript submissions). The query letter should be both engaging and professional in tone, no longer than one 8.5" x 11" page, and should describe your publishing track record, if any, and your areas of expertise. Describe the completed manuscript (for novels) or proposal (for nonfiction) that is ready to be shopped to publishers. Never send an entire manuscript or proposal until the agent explicitly asks for it. If your query interests her, she will ask for a full or partial manuscript or proposal. Do exactly as you are asked (and remember to include an SASE with all submissions).

When an agent requests a full or partial manuscript, she might ask if you are showing it to anyone else or even to give her an exclusive period to review it, meaning you pledge not to show it to any other agent during that period. Understandably, agents do not like to read submissions when they know others are also considering them. Depending on how many rejections you have already received, you might be willing to agree, but give it some thought. Your opportunity to have other agents consider your work will be in limbo for

---

[110] Do not deviate from these basics. Doing so will reveal a lack of professionalism and industry savvy that will turn off most agents.

as long as you agree to give one agent an exclusive.[111] Inquire up front how long an interested agent will take to read and respond to your submission. Depending on the kind and length of the submission, three to four weeks is reasonable; longer than that might be too long. If you do not hear from her within that period, you can then withdraw the submission or consider it no longer to be exclusive. If you send a manuscript for review without discussing exclusivity, and then receive a request from another agent, be clear with each before sending the work to the second agent. Above all, be forthright with everyone. The industry is very small and the agents could learn about your multiple submissions even if you do not mention it. Neither is likely to take on as a client anyone they think has not been honest with them.

READING FEES AND SCAMS

The Writer Beware website and blog published by the Science Fiction and Fantasy Writers of America (www.sfwa.org/for-authors/writer-beware/) will keep you up to date on the many scams aimed at hungry writers. Remember, there is no license required to practice as a literary agent, and predators know that aspiring writers are vulnerable to schemes aimed at separating them from their money. Beware of self-styled "agents" who ask you for money to read your manuscript ("reading fees") or who give your manuscript to a third party (who then asks you for money for "editorial services") or who suggest a publishing deal is imminent, if only you will pay for some "insider's" way to break into the business or to "fix" your manuscript. Gullible writers have been victimized many times by enterprises set up to exploit their aspirations by people who are not legitimate agents, editors, or publishers.[112]

In 1996, the AAR rejected the practice of charging reading fees by its member agents. That was done because while some respected agencies do charge reading fees—which can cost upwards of several hundred dollars—

---

[111] This is another reason why you should prioritize your list of candidates and query them in rounds of five or ten at a time. If you choose to grant exclusive reading periods, you want your top candidates to have them.

[112] This is not to say that an agent who recommends you have a professional freelance editor act as a book doctor to your manuscript before it is ready to be shopped is trying to con you; this happens often and is completely legitimate. What is not legitimate is when an agent gives or recommends the work to a "book doctor" without letting you choose, in exchange for a kickback. You should choose your own book doctor from among many good freelancers out there and pay a fair fee for their services.

many so-called agencies charge reading fees but do little more than cash the writers' checks. Even among legitimate agents that charge reading fees, an agent's income should be overwhelmingly comprised of commissions on the licenses they negotiate for their clients' work. Ask for a list of recent titles placed by any agent who asks for a reading fee (and confirm what they tell you through the resources described above). There are many ways to determine whether a proposed practice or assertion is true and complies with industry standards. If you cannot find out through Writer Beware or other industry research, ask an experienced author, another agent, trusted editor, or a writers' group or forum.

QUESTIONS TO ASK A POTENTIAL AGENT

If an agent expresses interest in representing you, arrange a personal meeting if possible, or a telephone conference at least. Do not be shy about asking to speak with current clients or other agents in the same agency. Prior to signing on with an agent, you need answers to some basic questions, either directly from the agent, from clients or colleagues, or from your own independent research:

How long has the agent been in the business? What is her recent track record in placing works similar to yours?

Specifically what services will the agent perform for you?

How many other clients does this agent represent in addition to you?

What size is the agency? Are there specialists in the agency who handle specific subsidiary rights, such as foreign or film deals?

How, and how often, are clients informed of the agent's activities in their behalf?

Are all offers brought to the client? If not, what are the criteria for rejecting offers without client consultation?

What is the agency commission for placing primary and subsidiary rights?

How and when are client funds distributed?

What expenses are charged to clients?

Does the agent have a standard author-agent agreement, or does she rely on a handshake to cement your business relationship?

How may the agency agreement be terminated, and on what terms?

The preferable answers to some of these questions are discussed in the following section.

AGENCY AGREEMENTS

As your representative, the agent has fiduciary duties to you, meaning that she is legally bound to protect and promote your financial and professional interests, to keep certain information confidential, and to refrain from acting in conflict with your interests. She also has legal control over your literary rights, meaning that she can legally bind you to most contracts dealing with your work even if you are not aware of them, and she might be entitled by virtue of those contracts to collect all funds due to you on your behalf. These are profound responsibilities, which is why you must trust the person you choose to represent you, and why you must also protect and police your own interests. Once you have done adequate due diligence and found a good match, it is worth asking for the author-agent agreement to be made in writing.

Traditionally, many agents and writers agreed to representation based on a handshake but documented the relationship in the publishing contracts for the client's work. Thus, virtually all agented book contracts include a clause that makes the agent a "third-party beneficiary" of the contract. The "agency clause" typically confirms that the agent represents the book, that all amounts due to the author are to be paid through the agent, and that the agent's commission is guaranteed. But these clauses leave out a lot of terms that are or could be critical to the relationship, and some agents now opt to ask their clients to sign a separate agreement delineating the relationship.[113] The explanation of agency agreement issues that follows applies both to agency clause/handshake arrangements and to more fully fleshed out author-agent agreements. For simplicity, it will refer to both as "agency contracts" unless the context indicates otherwise.

The material terms in a typical agency contract include the scope of the agent's right to represent you and your work(s); the right of either party to terminate the relationship and the implications of termination; commissions and expenses; and the agent's duties to you. Some, but not all, of these terms are specifically addressed in the typical agency clause. If you do not have a written author-agent agreement, discuss the issues that are

---

[113] The Authors Guild reviews proposed author-agent contracts for its members to explain their terms and help ensure that they are fair.

not addressed in the agency clause with your agent and at least get a verbal understanding on them.[114]

Exclusivity/Scope of Right to Represent. Most contracts give the agent "exclusive right of representation." This means that during the period of representation, even if someone other than the agent places the book with a publisher or other licensee, the agent is entitled to her standard commission on the work and remains entitled to represent it for subsidiary deals. This is fair because agents are obligated to use their best efforts to promote the work and dissatisfied clients typically have (and definitely should have) the right to terminate the relationship at will. But beware: neither an author–agent contract nor an agency clause should contain the phrase "agency coupled with an interest." This amounts to giving the agent an ownership interest in the work, and nobody but the author and her exclusive licensees should be entitled to an ownership interest (unless they actually helped create the work). If such a term appears in an agency contract, you should strike it. Similarly, avoid the "interminable agency" language that gives the agent the right to represent and collect commissions "on all proceeds from the work," as opposed to proceeds from the contracts negotiated by her. The agent is entitled to fair compensation for making specific deals for the work. If the agency is terminated, the writer should be free to market unlicensed rights using another agent.

By the same token, it is prudent to begin an agency relationship by allowing the agent to shop one or more specific works as opposed to all of your literary works. If the relationship is terminated, there will be fewer ties to sever. The one-work arrangement allows the client to retain a different agent to market a different work. Your agent might object to this arrangement, unless you have an objectively good reason for doing so (for example, if the works represented by each agent are of different types or genres). Ask her if she (or possibly another agent in her agency) can effectively market other works by you.

Also, before blindly giving your agent the right to represent your work in all formats, including nonprint rights (such as film, electronic, merchandising) and foreign sales, find out whether the agency has a practice of

---

[114] Because a verbal agreement is not ideal, you might consider following up your conversation with a letter confirming your mutual understanding of these issues if the agent does not want to enter an author-agency contract.

marketing such rights. Of course, many agents regularly and successfully use co-agents to place these rights, and industry standard commissions for the agent and coagent together are a maximum of 20 to 25 percent of the income from coagented subrights. That said, it makes sense to limit the scope of representation to those rights you know the agent can represent adequately, either independently or with coagents, based on her track record.

Services provided. Every contract should impose upon the agent the duties to use her best efforts to market your work, to submit all offers to the client (unless you specify otherwise), to obtain your permission before agreeing to or signing any contracts on your behalf, to take reasonable care of your materials, and to promptly forward royalty payments and correspondence. Agencies should segregate client funds from their own, which is a crucial protection in case the agency's bank or financial accounts are levied or it declares bankruptcy or shuts down. Insist on the agent's assurance that client funds are deposited in a separate account.

Commissions and Expenses. The vast majority of literary agents charge a commission of 15 percent on all earnings from the works they represent; this is the industry standard and is reasonable. (If they use a coagent for foreign or film/TV deals, they will take 20 or at most 25 percent, to be shared with the coagent.) A very few still ask for 10 percent. Most agents require their clients to cover the expenses associated with the representation. Your reimbursement obligation should be limited to specifically agreed expenses, and the agent should get your prior approval before incurring any single expense of more than $50 or $100. Agents who charge a commission of 15 percent (as opposed to the small percentage who take 10 percent) sometimes handle ordinary office expenses such as postage (but not FedEx or messengers), telephone, photocopying, and online research. If you agree to be responsible for such expenses, ask if you can undertake tasks that might save you money, such as providing photocopies of your manuscripts and proposals. The agent usually deducts expenses from the payments made to writers by licensees, and they should be accounted for on all client statements.

Most contracts say that the agent will collect all the proceeds for your work from the publisher and oversee the publisher's compliance with the contract (i.e., paying on time and correctly). This allows you to avoid administrative chores for which you probably have less expertise. The agent's standard practice should be to deduct commissions and expenses, if any, and promptly pay the balance to you. The agent should examine your royalty statements and, if necessary, obtain corrected versions and payments due from publishers. Royalties can arrive from other sources as well, and you should be able to rely upon your agent to check the accuracy of these accountings. Although most writers are satisfied with receiving the statements sent through the agent from various payment sources, you should have the right per your agency agreement to receive an accounting from the agent with respect to funds received and, on reasonable notice, to inspect the agent's records relating to your works. As your fiduciary, the agent is obligated to keep your financial affairs confidential.

Separate payments. If you can persuade your agent, add a statement in the agency contract to the effect that if either the agent or the author requests, the publisher will send separate checks directly to each. This option can give you control over your own earnings and peace of mind, which is especially important if the relationship were to end with hard feelings. It also protects you in the event the agency ceases doing business or files for bankruptcy (it happens). But this term is somewhat controversial. Some publishers object because they fear liability to the agent if they send only the commission to the agent and the author owes the agent for expenses. Publishers also do not like to send two checks and statements when they can satisfy their legal obligation by sending only one. But if the agent asks for it, publishers tend to agree to add the term.

Agents naturally have concerns about the issue of separate payments. Some agents have agreed to add it to their contracts, but others object to what they see as having their hands tied when they are owed for expenses. They also question its effect on the author-agent relationship, which is ideally built on trust. When you interview your agent and talk with her clients prior to signing, ask about this issue. The agency's track record, the agent's reaction to the request, and her clients' reports about the promptness of remittances to them and the thoroughness with which the agent reviews statements could sway your views on how important this term is. Still, it makes good sense to ensure you have the right to separate payments when the agency is terminated if not before then.

Termination. As with most contracts, including an at-will termination clause is perhaps the single most important protection you can provide for yourself. Essentially, it should say that you may end the agency agreement by giving advance notice (no more than thirty days should suffice) at will, or with or without cause (i.e., without having to give a reason). If the agent has lost interest in representing a work or you are displeased with the agent's representation, it is in both parties' interest to end the relationship quickly and cleanly. Of course, the agent is entitled to collect commissions on compensation earned for all works she has placed—and to some degree, where she has shown the work to a publisher that then licenses it—before the agency ended.[115]

A conflict could arise over whether a work shown to a publisher by a former agent entitles her to the full commission if the publisher decides to license it after the agency is terminated. An argument can be made that by marketing the work successfully, the former agent should be compensated as agreed. On the other hand, the former agent presumably will not negotiate the payment or contract terms, and so will not provide full service. Often, when the writer has retained a second agent, the new and the former agents can work out a satisfactory split of the commission, but to avoid this problem, it is helpful to set a time limit posttermination (such as four to six months) after which the former agent will be entitled to no commission even if a publisher she approached decides to offer for the book. In no event should you have to pay more than one full commission.

When the relationship is terminated, the agency clause in an existing publishing contract is unaffected—the agent generally continues to collect her commission on contracts already negotiated, executed, or earning money before termination. Most agents would understandably object, strenuously, to having any time period placed on their right to receive commissions on contracts they procured. As mentioned, commissions might be renegotiated if another agent is retained and she must do additional work to exploit certain rights, such as negotiate the underlying contract. Regardless of your former agent's success in placing a work, after the agency terminates, she should not be entitled to commissions on income from contracts and licenses she did not procure or negotiate. This includes new book contracts entered after the original publishing contract ends when the work goes out of print.

---

[115] The terms governing termination should be set forth in a separate author-agent contract but do not usually appear in the agency clause in a publishing contract. If you are only relying on the agency clause, this sticky subject needs to be raised during your interview with the potential agent.

CHAPTER 16

COLLABORATION AND

GHOSTWRITING AGREEMENTS

"**C**ollaboration is gelt by association." Playwright George S. Kaufman uttered this quip when describing his work with Moss Hart, Edna Ferber and others. You can be sure these professionals had collaboration agreements between them. If you are collaborating, either as a ghost or an "as told to" writer, an equal contributor to a project, or otherwise, you need one, too.

Under copyright law, the moment two or more creators begin working together on a single project, they might be subjecting themselves to legal obligations to each other that they do not intend. Whether or not you have a friendship or a highly productive creative relationship with your collaborator(s), a written agreement is absolutely necessary to ensure that your expectations regarding control over the work and the sharing of the rewards are mutually understood and binding. Ideally, your agreement should be finalized as soon as you decide that you will create an integrated work product together.

COPYRIGHT AND JOINT AUTHORSHIP

Under US copyright law, certain contributors share the copyright in a "joint work." A "joint work" is defined as a copyrightable work prepared by two or more authors with the intention, at the time the work is created, that their contributions be merged into inseparable or interdependent parts of a unitary whole. No contract is required to give rise to a joint work and all that it entails. In fact, unless they otherwise agree, authors who create a joint work are co-owners of the undivided copyright in the work, meaning that each of them owns all the rights in the work, but shares them equally with the other. Any coauthor may license the work on a nonexclusive basis without the others' consent, but she must share the proceeds equally among all other coauthors. On the other hand, no coauthor may grant an exclusive license without the consent of all other joint owners. These legal rules apply—unless agreed otherwise—to all participants who make a copyrightable contribution of any size if the collaborators intend at the time for their contributions to be merged into a unitary whole.[116]

For some collaborators, these terms might be acceptable, but there are many situations in which they are not ideal. Also, the law is silent about some important matters and is of no help in many potential scenarios—especially, although not only, when things do not go as planned. The fact that no joint owner can license exclusive rights in the work unless the other consents in effect gives each partner veto power over most deals to publish and otherwise exploit the work (because publishers and other licensees usually require exclusive rights). In the worst case scenario, one party could pull out of the partnership when the work is finished, or nearly so, leaving the other with limited rights to bring in a third party to help finish or revise the work and no meaningful way to market it.

Fortunately, you can alter the statutory rules by agreement. If you so choose, for example, you and your collaborator can agree that each retains a distinct copyright in your own contributions, or that the work will not be considered a "joint work" unless and until each party completes her part. You can provide that the term of the collaboration agreement will be the same as the length of copyright,[117] or make the term shorter (after

---

[116] Chapter 4 discusses the concept of "joint works" in more detail, including the judicial precedent in most jurisdictions, including New York and California, that requires each collaborator to make a copyrightable contribution in order to claim an interest in a joint work.

[117] The term of copyright in a joint work is 70 years after the death of the last surviving joint author.

which the default provisions under copyright or another arrangement can apply). You can give one (or both) the right to negotiate and sign licenses, exclusive and nonexclusive, and you can allocate to each other any share of the proceeds as you agree. You can—and should—also determine attribution protocols.

COLLABORATION AGREEMENTS

To devise your agreement, you will need to discuss and resolve the following issues: ownership and control of the rights in finished, unfinished, published, and unpublished works; editorial control over the final work product(s); competition and confidentiality; how earnings will be shared; authorial credit; and responsibility in the event of legal liability. Consider also including terms that address disputes, such as mediation and arbitration clauses, and the future, such as whether and when the agreement should end. Once your mutual understandings are settled, they should be reduced to a writing signed by both of you. It is a good idea to hire a knowledgeable attorney to draft the contract and negotiate on your behalf, especially if you do not know your collaborator well or if you have less negotiating leverage (for example, if you are ghostwriting). If your relationship is more equitable and your understanding is straightforward, you might both be able to hire one attorney to prepare the contract or possibly to write your own using a form.[118]

DEFINING THE JOINT WORK

The agreement should define and describe the nature of the project and the responsibilities of each collaborator in enough detail that a reasonable person (that is, a jury) could readily determine what each is responsible for and whether each has met her responsibilities. If you plan to create multiple specified works together, a list and description of each contemplated work that is separately appended to and referenced in the contract is a good idea. Alternatively, you could state that the terms of your agree-

---

[118] *Business and Legal Forms for Authors and Self-Publishers* by Tad Crawford (3d ed. Allworth Press, 2005) has a good collaboration agreement template; the Authors Guild can supply one also. Of course, it is always safer to have a competent attorney review your specific situation and prepare a contract.

ment will apply to any work you create together as long as the contract lasts. If feasible and desirable, lay out deadlines for each portion (and as applicable, sequential deadlines for each stage of the project, such as a book proposal and sections of the manuscript) to be contributed by each collaborator.

If you are ghostwriting or collaborating on an "as told to" book, make sure the contract requires the other party to grant you the necessary access to interview subjects (including herself) and materials such as letters, diaries, etc., on a timely basis. The more concretely you describe such access obligations in terms of number of hours and deadlines, the better.

CONTROL OF THE WORK

Ownership. By contract, the parties can provide that one contributor will own the copyright in the final work product, that each will own it jointly (as the Copyright Act provides), or that each will own the copyright only in her own contributions to the project (either permanently, or until the work is complete). What you decide should depend on the nature of your collaboration and of the project (and possibly on the parties' relative negotiating positions). Has one party been retained to ghostwrite the work? What are your collective plans to exploit the final product commercially? Are your respective contributions readily severable? Does it make sense for one or both of you to reserve the right to repurpose and reuse your contributions independently if the joint project does not sell or after it goes out of print?[119]

When each party retains the copyright to their contributions, the possibility of one collaborator competing with the joint work must also be addressed. If the joint work finds a publisher, each partner will be bound by the publishing contract not to reuse her contribution independently. But in case the project does not find a publisher, the parties should consider allowing for termination of the agreement under the circumstances, which would free each to revise and reuse or assign the rights to their contributions. (Termination is discussed more fully below.) If this would not be

---

[119] It is likely that the subject of an "as told to" or ghostwritten book will want the right to take her story to another writer and terminate your right to use your work if the joint project does not sell. Although this is understandable, make sure your contract guarantees you satisfactory compensation and credit for your time and work.

feasible given the nature of the project (for example, if the contributions are inseparable or would unacceptably compete with each other), you might agree that one party may buy out the other's interests in the project, freeing the buyer to use, revise, and market the entire work freely.

If relevant, also provide for possible future editions and prequels/ sequels. Ask yourselves: if one party no longer wishes to work with the other after the project is completed or abandoned, should either of them have the right to create sequels or new editions on their own? If so, to what extent, if at all, will the other party be compensated and what form of attribution should she receive? If you agree on a buyout clause, it should specifically address sequels and revised editions.

Depending on what you decide, the contract should indicate that the parties intend all contributions to the defined work either: to be merged into a single joint work(s) the copyright of which shall be jointly and severally owned by each contributor; or to be merged into a single work, the copyright of which shall be owned solely by one named party; or to remain separately owned by each contributor. No matter who owns the copyright, the matters of editorial control, marketing, sharing the proceeds, and attribution can and should all be separately addressed in the contract.

Editorial Control. The Copyright Act assumes a joint work is a collaboration of equal contributors, but in reality, it could be that one person has the greater vision, industry clout or reputational interest (such as in a ghostwritten memoir), and/or contributes the lion's share of the work comprising the project. Consider whether creative decisions over the project, including final approval of the proposal and the manuscript to be submitted to a publisher, should be made jointly by the coauthors or assigned to one. The collaboration agreement should state who will have decision-making authority during the process of creation and who will have final approval of works submitted to publishers. Also, consider providing that in the event either contributor dies after substantially delivering her share of the work, the survivor will have full editorial and licensing control over the work, subject to the obligation to remit the deceased's share of the proceeds to her heirs.

Competition and Confidentiality. The agreement should address the extent to which the coauthors may publish works that compete with the collaboration if the project is published (or while it is being marketed). A common practice among collaborators is to specify a period of time during which neither may publish any work that competes with the joint work; it is a good idea to define "competing work" in terms of format, market, and subject matter.

Regardless of the nature of the work, but especially if it is a ghostwritten book, each collaborator should agree to keep the project and the other party's information strictly confidential, except to the extent needed to carry out the intentions of the contract.

Marketing, Negotiating, and Administering Licenses. As a practical matter, the collaborators (or one of them) will probably have a literary agent who will exclusively market the work, but if there is no agent, it generally makes sense to state that the parties will coordinate in marketing the work (and that neither will commit the other to marketing expenses without consent). If only one writer has an agent or the inclination to negotiate, the contract might give that party the right and responsibility to negotiate the licensing of the work, though if the other party holds a copyright interest in the work, she will also need to sign any licenses. If one party does not hold copyright and thus will not sign licenses, the collaboration agreement might provide that the nonsignatory has the right to approve any proposed license prior to execution. In either case, it is a good idea to specify that one party's agreement to what the other party has negotiated will not be unreasonably withheld, delayed, or conditioned. Each collaborator should receive a copy of any executed license.

You should decide which coauthor (or whose agent) will be assigned to receive, account for, and distribute the proceeds earned. Some agreements provide that all funds will pass through one of the authors or agents, to be distributed according to the agreed shares, but it might be more practical and less burdensome to provide for direct payment by the publisher to each coauthor. If you agree, state in the contract that the parties will use their best efforts to ensure that any license will require the licensee to account directly to each collaborator for her share of any advances, fees, and royalties. Also provide that if either of the collaborators receives payments that should go to the other, she will forward them promptly with a written accounting.

INCOME AND EXPENSES

Shares of the Proceeds. Although the Copyright Act by default gives joint work contributors equal shares of the proceeds, collaborators are free to agree to alter that formula and allocate the earnings from a work in any way they wish. If each is an equal partner in the collaboration, then equal shares are typical. In some cases, the parties agree to divide the shares differently for specific types of exploitation (such as film/TV or audio rights). With ghostwritten or "as told to" works, where one party does most of the writing, that person often gets a larger portion of the advance and the other party then receives all earned royalties until each has received an agreed amount (after which royalties are shared).

If you are retained to help a celebrity or other nonwriter prepare a proposal for a ghostwritten or "as told to" book, make sure in your contract that you will receive a fee for writing the proposal whether or not it leads to a publishing agreement and some portion of the proceeds if it does. Provide also that any advance portion you receive will be nonrefundable. Such terms are some protection against being dropped from the project in favor of another writer after your proposal sells or having your collaborator pull out after you have worked on the manuscript.

Expenses. The parties should devise a system for authorizing and sharing expenses. One way to do this is to set a budget that lists specific expenses and allows for some miscellaneous costs. Expenses are often shared in the same proportion as the allocation of proceeds from the work. If expenses are to be shared, the agreement should provide who will own any tangible purchases as well as the results of such purchases, such as recordings of interviews, research notes, and photographs. Another expense involves obtaining permission to use copyrighted work. If fair, you might choose to make each party responsible for the costs of third party releases needed for her portion of the work.

ATTRIBUTION

Will the product(s) of your collaboration be credited as "by A *and* B," "by A *with* B," "by A, *as told to* B," "by A" alone, or in some other way? The copyright law says nothing about how a joint work should be credited, though a contributor who is wrongly omitted might be able to use unfair competition laws to remedy the bald misattribution of a work. You should decide on authorship credit and specify it in both your collaboration agreement and any contracts to publish or otherwise license the work. If the work is a book, specify the order, size, and prominence of the authors' names as they will appear in each edition and in all promotional materials and advertisements.

COPYRIGHT REGISTRATION

The copyright registration should mirror your agreement on who will own the copyright and the collaboration and publishing contracts should both specify in whose name(s) the work will be registered. If the work does not find a publisher, copyright should still be registered as the parties have agreed.

LEGAL RESPONSIBILITY

In general, it makes sense to hold each collaborator individually responsible if their contribution infringes a copyright or defames or otherwise injures a third party. But publishing contracts will likely make all signatories jointly and severally responsible for any liability the publisher incurs based on the book. Depending on the nature of the project, collaboration agreements typically provide that each coauthor warrants to the other that her contributions are original, that she is free to enter the contract and to license her contributions and that they do not infringe upon the copyright or violate any rights of any third party. Each party then agrees to indemnify the other for any expenses (including reasonable attorneys' fees and out of court settlements) suffered as a result of a breach of these warranties. Agreeing to this will be trickier for the ghost or "as told to" writer, because her work is controlled by the other party more than in an equal collaboration. If you are in this position, try to exclude specifically from your warranties any material provided or approved, in writing or verbally, by the other party.

THE FUTURE

Term and Termination of the Collaboration. Collaborators can allow the term of their contract to last as long as the copyright in the work,[120] or they can make it shorter. They might also agree that either party can terminate the agreement if, for example, the work is not published or subsequently goes out of print, or if one collaborator cannot or does not satisfactorily complete her contribution. The advantage of a shorter term and a right to terminate is that either party might, depending on the nature of the work, be able to reuse and market their contributions (but not the other's) without obligation to the other. The disadvantage is that it effectively kills any

---

[120] In effect, this is the default for a joint work under the Copyright Act; the length of the term is seventy years after the death of the last surviving coauthor.

future for the joint work, unless the contract also provides for a buyout of one party's rights in her contribution upon termination.

Mediation or Arbitration. The agreement should provide a method for resolving disputes between the coauthors, such as a disagreement over whether a contribution is satisfactory, whether the project is ready to market, which publishers to show the work, or whether to accept an offer. Disagreements arising between a surviving writer and the estate of a coauthor who has died can be especially thorny. An agreement to mediate disputes can save the parties considerably in anxiety, time, and legal fees. Using an independent mediator, who does not decide disputes but rather helps the parties reach a settlement, often results in amicable resolutions.

Arbitration is akin to litigation, but it is private, cheaper, simpler and less time-consuming than a lawsuit. Here, an arbitrator chosen and paid by the parties hears both sides of the dispute and decides in favor of one side or the other. The parties can present their cases without hiring lawyers (though in complex matters, lawyers might be necessary) according to rules set by the arbitrator or, if the parties choose, by a body such as the American Arbitration Association. They can also choose whether the decision will be legally binding or leave them free to pursue litigation.

Although the parties can decide on mediation and/or arbitration when a dispute arises even if their agreement does not require them, it is obviously better to include them in the contract. If you do not, then either party can decline to use them, possibly leaving the other with only the options to concede, see the project paralyzed, or deal with costly litigation.

Assignment and Succession. Without limiting the collaborators' obligations to each other, it is a good idea to allow each the freedom to assign her ownership interest and/or her right to receive income to a third party. It is also wise to state that the collaboration agreement will bind and inure to the benefit of the heirs, executors, administrators, representatives, and assigns of the coauthors.

THE PUBLISHING CONTRACT

If one collaborator holds the copyright, she alone will execute the publishing contract (and other licenses). If both own copyright, then either the collaborators will enter one publishing contract jointly or (less likely) they will sign separate contracts. In either case, negotiate realistic delivery deadlines for each collaborator because failing to meet them can lead to cancellation of the contract and a requirement that the advance be returned.[121] The publishing contract should incorporate, or at least not conflict with, the payment terms to which the collaborators have agreed and should include to the letter the agreed attribution provisions. The publisher will usually insist that all signatories jointly warrant and indemnify the publisher against legal claims. If only one signs the contract, make sure you have ensured in the collaboration agreement (as appropriate) the responsibility of each party to the other for a breach of warranty in her contribution.

---

[121] This is another argument for why a ghostwriter should get a higher portion—or all—of the advance, even if the parties agree to share the royalties in a different proportion. She might need the advance to live on while preparing the manuscript for timely delivery.

CHAPTER 17

FILM AND TELEVISION

CONTRACTS AND DRAMATIC

PRODUCTIONS

Film, television, and theatrical producers must draw together many financial and creative elements to put together a finished product. The process of gathering these resources is known as the development stage. One of the first things the producers undertake during development is to obtain control of the rights to the story line. In these industries, producers begin by optioning the rights to buy a particular book, script or treatment from the writer(s). An option gives the producer the exclusive right to shop and develop the work to determine whether there is sufficient financial and creative interest before deciding whether or not to actually purchase the work outright from the author.

If you are offered an option, you will be in effect negotiating two contracts: one (or more) for the length of the option period, including extensions, and the other for the purchase of the work in the event the buyer exercises the option. Film, television, and dramatic options and the purchase agreements that accompany them can be highly complex. This chapter can serve as a starting point to help you understand the basic terms and structure of transactions for films and television (for both book/freelance authors and screenwriters) and for dramatic, i.e., theatrical productions, but if you are contemplating any such deal, you need to retain an agent or attorney who specializes in the relevant field.[122]

FILM AND TELEVISION OPTIONS—BOOK AND FREELANCE AUTHORS

The process of turning your story into a motion picture or television program involves: (1) the option, which puts your rights on hold and guarantees the optioning party the right to purchase the rights in the future, and (2) the related purchase agreement, through which the rights to the work are actually transferred. The optioning party usually presents the two contracts to the writer in tandem.

The option secures for a negotiated period of time the exclusive right to purchase the film rights later. Payment for an option is usually much smaller than the payment to be made upon the exercise of the option and actual purchase of the property. The option agreement will attach or include the terms of the purchase agreement, including the price, that the parties will enter if the option is exercised. This practice of negotiating both contracts at the same time is common practice in the industry. Even the development phase of a film or television project can be very expensive, and a would-be purchaser needs to be able to analyze whether a project has potential before deciding to buy the story, and ought to know with some certainty what the story as an element of the project will cost to secure. The option serves these purposes for the buyer. But the option can be negotiated in such a way as to promote the writer's interests, too.

Once you give someone an option on your work, you can neither take it back nor interfere with the optioning party's ability to purchase your work during the option period. A binding option need not be formal; a letter or a simple memo memorializing a deal (often called a "deal memo") can be binding as a "short-form" option contract. Negotiate any such understanding, regardless of its length or informality, with care, even if you agree to enter into a more formal contract later.

---

[122] *Dealmaking in the Film and Television Industry* by Mark Litvak (3d ed. 2009) and *Hollywood Dealmaking: Negotiating Talent Agreements* by Dina Appleton and Daniel Yankelevits (2010) are two excellent books for authors by experts in the field that explain the components of these deals in detail.

What follows is a general explanation of terms you will see in option and purchase agreements for film and television productions.

THE GRANT OF RIGHTS

Be aware of the potential scope of what might appear at first glance to be a simple grant of rights. The phrases "all allied" or "ancillary" rights, for example, can be interpreted to include just about anything—not just the right to make a film based on your work, but the right to make sequels, television movies and series, the right to publish a special "movie version" of your book, even merchandising and advertising rights. The seemingly narrower phrase "motion picture and television rights" is in reality similarly broad.

Most option buyers will try to get all of the rights for one price, but sellers with leverage and good representation can retain some rights and negotiate additional royalties for them. For example, you should seek to retain the rights to print and online textual publication, novelizations, author-written sequels, audio rights, live TV and radio, and dramatic stage rights. Be aware that for any rights you reserve, the option purchaser might request a so-called "hold back," in which you agree not to exploit any of your reserved rights for a specified period of years after the motion-picture release date. The purchaser might also require that you refrain from writing more than one sequel to the story in a particular time period.

In addition to understanding and limiting the scope of your grant, you should explicitly reserve all rights not granted. Also, be aware that granting any of these broad rights can conflict with rights you might have already granted in a publishing contract; again, you should have professional help in negotiating these agreements.

Granting film or television rights will necessitate giving up creative control over the final product. Many writers who licensed their books to be made into films have expressed disappointment or dismay over the end product. If you are also agreeing to write the screenplay, you might have a bit more control, but it is unheard of for all but the most powerful players in a film—the director or a major star—to have final approval over the product. The best you can hope to achieve is the right to remove your name from the billing credits, and possibly to require a change in the film's title, or a change in the main characters' names if the film is based on your memoir or a biography.

TERM

The length of an option may vary considerably and is subject to negotiation. Many options range from six to eighteen months, with or without specified renewal terms. To make sure there is no confusion over the exact end date, provide expressly that "the term shall expire at midnight, on [X date] or [X] calendar months after the date of execution of this agreement." Option terms can be, and frequently are, extended or renewed automatically. Under an automatic renewal, all the purchaser has to do is give you notice and the specified payment in order to extend or renew her option. Understand that if the optioning party has made enough progress in development to want to continue to keep your story on hold, the rights have necessarily grown in value. Therefore, the fee for the second term should be higher than the original amount. By the same logic, it is generally better not to lock yourself into more than one automatic renewal. The purchaser can always come back to you to negotiate a new option term (for more money). As well, renewal periods should be successively shorter than the original. It is also a good idea to keep a flame burning under your purchaser by providing that renewal of the option is contingent on the demonstration of specific steps actually taken toward exercising the option. These steps might include, for example, having secured financing and/or the participation of one or more of the other essential players in creating a film: director, screenwriter, or actors.

THE OPTION PRICE

The odds are against the possibility that your option will ever be exercised, and the option price is therefore likely to be all that you will earn from this industry. It pays to negotiate accordingly. The price of an option is negotiable and will vary according to a number of common-sense factors: your reputation, bargaining power, and the scope of the rights you are granting. The average option fee probably falls somewhere around $10,000 for the standard term of one year (closer to $50,000 for authors with powerful representation), but the price of an option can vary enormously, from hundreds of thousands of dollars to almost nothing. A good ballpark figure for an option payment is approximately ten percent of the full purchase price.

Unless the situation dictates otherwise, you should probably push for the largest option price you can get. You might make an exception in certain cases, for example, where you are dealing in the arena of independent films, so there is less money to be had up front, or you have great confidence that the film will ultimately be made. If the purchaser claims not to be able to pay a large option fee, one way to grant the option but still protect your interests is to ask for what is known as a "lay off" or "set up" bonus. For example, if your purchaser offers $1,000 instead of the $10,000 you want, you can grant it for $1,000, but include a provision that if that purchaser transfers the option to a major party, such as a motion picture studio, the $1,000 option fee automatically increases (and is immediately due and payable) to $10,000 (or more) when the purchaser transfers the option. The following language provides another important precaution: "Whether or not notice is ever provided, any commencement of principal photography by the purchaser or its assignees will constitute exercise of the option, and will trigger the obligation to make immediate payment of the specified purchase price."

Much like an advance against future book royalties, the initial option payment is usually applied against the purchase price should the buyer exercise the option. However, extension or renewal fees are commonly not credited against the purchase price.

Sometimes, an optioning party purchases an option (and several renewals) with no intention of actually exercising it. Purchasers might do this for any number of reasons, including keeping potentially competitive stories or similar ideas from hampering projects they are already developing. Selling your rights without the possibility of developing them might be fine with you; there are more than a few writers earning money by selling options they do not expect to see exercised. Still, unless the option calls for generous renewal payments, it pays to be careful about the ultimate length of time your rights will be tied up. The option should state that if the purchaser fails to exercise the option during the specified time period (including renewals), the agreement will terminate automatically and all rights will revert to you (and all option money is retained by you). Writers with considerable clout are also sometimes able to stipulate that even after the exercise of the option, if the work has not been produced within a specified number of years, the rights will revert to the writer.[123]

---

[123] Such a reversion clause usually also requires that a lien be placed on the project that any future purchaser must satisfy to repay the amount originally invested in production.

By reclaiming your rights in this way, you improve the odds that a picture will ultimately get made.

THE PURCHASE PRICE

Ideally, you would be able to negotiate the purchase price at the time the purchaser wants to exercise the option. By then, she would have invested considerable time and money in the project and have made enough progress to want to buy the rights outright. She would know what kind of production might be done and have an idea of its budget, and this knowledge would help quantify the value of your rights. It is after she has this information and has made these investments that you are in the best position to negotiate the purchase price. Knowing this, of course, your purchaser is sure to insist on settling both the option and the purchase price up front. Your best alternative is to try to get a sense of the true value of the rights at the option stage. Interview the optioning party at length and research the entities and individuals she mentions as possible participants in development.

If you sense that the planned production is the type that might lend itself to a big budget, the best way to ensure you will partake fairly is to push for a percentage of the budget (3.5 percent is considered favorable), with a fixed floor and ceiling, in lieu of a fixed purchase price. You might begin by asking for a particular percentage of the budget, with a floor in the six figures and no ceiling. When the budget is uncertain and a fair purchase price is difficult to ascertain, the purchaser might be equally interested in a budget percentage-based purchase price, though she will likely insist on a ceiling.

Give no credence to any offer of a share of the film's "net profits." No matter how thrilling it sounds to be offered a percentage of the profits on a film, the movie industry's fantastic method of calculating "net" profits means they will always be less than zero, i.e., worthless. Writers with genuine clout can try—as the producer, director, and stars of the film will—to negotiate for a percentage of the *gross* profits (ideally 5 percent, although 2 or 3 percent is more likely). If a share in gross profits is out of reach, try asking for a percentage of "adjusted gross." It is not "true" gross, but it is better than "net profits." Working closely with an experienced agent or lawyer, your goal is to negotiate a combination of initial option price, renewal price(s), purchase price, bonuses, and a percentage of something real (i.e., not net profits). Unless you can get bonuses or a percentage of something real, then the option and purchase prices will constitute your total payment for your work, and you should negotiate accordingly.

WARRANTIES AND REPRESENTATIONS

As in a standard publishing contract, you will be asked to promise that your work does not infringe copyright, defame anyone, or invade anyone's privacy. The same general principles apply here as with book contracts—seek both to qualify your promises realistically and to limit the amount of your financial responsibility should someone bring suit to a percentage of your total payment.

FILM AND TELEVISION OPTIONS—SCREENPLAYS

Writers employed in the creation of television and film scripts usually must join the Writers Guild of America, the screenwriters' union, and there are excellent reasons to do so. The WGA periodically negotiates revisions of its collective bargaining agreement with most of the film and television production companies in the industry. Whether or not you are a member, before submitting a script or treatment to a third party for purposes of optioning it, you would do well to register the work with the WGA.[124] Before negotiating through your agent or directly with a production company, refer to the WGA's Theatrical and Television Film Basic Agreement, which you may obtain from the union. It provides minimum compensation levels for members of the guild and the producers who have signed the union's collective bargaining agreement, including a current list of scale rates for writers for all kinds of theatrical and film deals. If the producer interested in your work is a signatory to the WGA Agreement, then its minimum terms must govern your contract. Even if the WGA Agreement does not apply, its compensation levels, terms, and conditions are still important guidelines for writers in nonguild arrangements.

In a screenwriter's contract to sell film rights, the grant of rights will usually be quite extensive, but make sure it distinguishes between television and film production rights, which reach different markets. The practice

---

[124] See Appendix A to chapter 1 and chapter 7 for a description of the Writers Guild and the benefits of registering your work with the WGA.

with respect to artistic control is quite different from book publishing and dramatic plays and musicals. Screenwriters can expect to have little or no control over changes in the property and the final form it takes. If you wish, seek the right to perform the first and/or subsequent revisions of the script. Also, you will invariably have to give the production company the power to assign your contract to a third party (although the production company may remain liable if the recipient fails to fulfill its obligations), because financing arrangements require this. If you negotiate a share of receipts from the film's distribution, the contract should specify whose receipts you will share, as between the producer or the production company, and, as described above, how "receipts" are defined. Given the number of people and entities involved in creating the end product, be sure to negotiate specifically how you will be credited, and try to get the right to remove your name from the billing credits at your option. The WGA arbitrates disputes over billing credit among members and signatories to its agreement.

One fairly common occurrence is the simultaneous sale of a book to a publishing company and to a film studio, in which the writer's agent or a coagent negotiates screenplay rights with the production company. If the writer is a first-time screenwriter, she will usually be offered WGA scale to produce a first draft, and receive equal amounts for second, third, and final ("polish") drafts. The producer or production company will probably insist on the right to reassign the material to another writer if they deem the first or subsequent drafts unsatisfactory.

DRAMATIC PRODUCTIONS

Before negotiating an agreement for the use of your work in a dramatic (i.e., stage) production, you need to know the theatrical market in which the producer intends to stage the production. The Dramatists Guild provides good resources about particular theater markets and corresponding model contracts for the use of its members. Some of the Dramatists Guild contracts are commonly accepted in certain markets; others are not industry standard but serve as helpful guides. If you are marketing a dramatic play or musical, you should join the Dramatists Guild for all the benefits it offers playwrights.[125]

---

[125] You should also read Donald C. Farber's *Producing Theater: A Comprehensive and Legal Guide* (3d ed., 2005) for a comprehensive explanation of how this industry works.

Generally, theaters are classified in one of three markets: Broadway, Off-Broadway, and Off-Off-Broadway. These classifications reflect the overall theater market in New York City and other major cities and are based on the theaters' size, not their geographic location (most "Broadway" theaters, for example, are not actually on Broadway). Broadway theaters, also known as "First Class" theaters, have a seating capacity of five hundred or more. For the Broadway market, the Dramatists Guild and the League of American Theaters and Producers negotiated what is now known as the Approved Production Contract (APC), which many parties use, though it is not legally required. Other First Class producers and writers agree to terms and royalty shares different from what the APC provides.

Off-Broadway theaters (which may stage "Second-Class" productions) include theaters that seat between 99 and 499 people. Off-Off-Broadway theaters are generally those that seat fewer than 100 people, and include for-profit and nonprofit theater organizations. Agreements with smaller and nonprofit theaters can be quite different from those with First- and Second-Class producers. Often, the writer grants only nonexclusive licenses for dramatic productions, which do not include subsidiary rights, to small theaters. In exchange, the writer earns much less money (if any). The Dramatists Guild can give guidance about what is fair with such theaters, but the final terms will reflect what the theater can afford to give and what the writer will accept.

The Dramatists Guild has developed a Dramatists Bill of Rights (at www.dramatistsguild.com/billofrights/) that it recommends be used as a starting point for negotiations with producers of any class, large and small, that wish to produce a writer's work on stage. The bill of rights covers issues such as control over the script and all other theatrical elements ("artistic control"), the right to be present in all readings, rehearsals, and productions, appropriate billing credit, compensation and subsidiary rights shares, and ownership of the final script, including all changes and additions made by others. You should use the bill of rights to guide your contract review and negotiations for any theatrical production.

A producer interested in obtaining a playwright's script will request either an exclusive option or a nonexclusive license to produce the play or musical. The exclusive option is invariably used when the plan is for a First Class production. The option is typically paid for though an advance against future royalties, lasts for anywhere from six months to one year, and is usually renewable for additional specified terms under certain conditions, such as demonstrated progress in producing the work and/or additional payment.

The issues for negotiation of the option contract are similar to other exclusive licenses of literary property: the scope of rights granted, creative control over the production, royalties, who is entitled to shares of future proceeds and for how long, for example. The same issues arise in a non exclusive agreement with smaller theaters or producers. If you are a member, call on the Dramatists Guild for advice about what it calls standard industry royalties and other contract terms for various levels of production.

Royalties. If a producer successfully previews and opens a First- or Second-Class production before the option expires, the writer's compensation for granting dramatic production rights is often based on a percentage of the box office's weekly receipts ("receipts" are defined in the Dramatists Guild's standard contracts). Some producers have challenged the payment of straight royalties to the playwright because this method does not take into account whether the show is generating a profit for its investors. They have devised a different method based on "points" that ensures no additional royalties to the writer or other collaborators unless the investors are on track to recoup their investments.

For small productions, the Dramatists Guild recommends that playwrights receive royalties if any other participant in the production is receiving compensation or if any admission is charged to see the show. Your royalty might be small for a small- to medium-sized production, but you should receive something, unless no other player is getting paid.

Subsidiary Rights. Many exclusive contracts provide that when a production runs beyond a stipulated number of performances (e.g., twenty-one), additional rights are automatically granted to the producers to reward them for their investment. These might include the right to produce First Class-level tours, make a British production, move from Off-Broadway to Broadway, reopen the show after it has closed, share motion picture rights, and take a portion of proceeds from other subsidiary rights. These additional rights do not give the producers control over these subsidiary rights;

they instead receive a right to share in proceeds from these uses.[126] But it makes sense to specify that you retain control over the disposition of all other subsidiary rights, which can be quite valuable: worldwide motion picture rights, radio, television, Second-Class touring productions, foreign-language performances, concert tour versions, condensed and tabloid versions, commercial uses, play albums or records, stock and amateur performances, and musicals based on the play. Also, limit the producers' right to a percentage of income from subsidiary rights to a certain period of time after the original production closes. After that time, the right to share in proceeds from subsidiary rights should expire.

---

[126] The Dramatists Guild recommends that playwrights be permitted to choose to grant a limited, nonexclusive option to produce another work to the producer instead of giving up shares of subsidiary rights income.

CHAPTER 18

HOW TO AVOID AND

RESOLVE DISPUTES

P rofessional writers begin, maintain, and end many business relationships in the course of their careers. The nature of these relationships makes a writer vulnerable to disappointment, lost money, and career damage if the other side to the transaction does not live up to its promises, or worse. As this book tries to demonstrate, well-crafted and carefully negotiated contracts can protect you to a substantial degree from potentially harmful disputes and help foster mutually advantageous relationships. Even a clear, enforceable contract does not guarantee smooth sailing every time, however. People and organizations sometimes disregard their contractual obligations for various reasons, financial and otherwise. If that happens to you, you might eventually be able to enforce your contract, but it is obviously much better to keep a breach from happening in the first place. Your first line of defense, then, is to recognize warning signs that a potential partner might renege or perform poorly before committing, and to find another situation if you can.

DUE DILIGENCE

The more well versed you are about the business, the savvier you will be when choosing and negotiating with the other side of any transaction. Take advantage of the free and low-cost industry resources described in chapter 1 before you begin negotiating any publishing-related transaction. When a publishing house or an agent expresses interest in your work, investigate them thoroughly to ensure that they are not an unknown quantity and that they have not earned a reputation for unfair dealings with writers.

When dealing with editors, try to avoid anyone who shows a lack of interest in your project. An editor who is unenthusiastic about a book or article at the outset is unlikely to help you if difficulties with the publishing house arise down the line. Also, be wary of editors who do not have some experience in the field in which you write, especially if you cover specialized subjects or formats. An inexperienced editor can make unrealistic demands, not just of you but also of the publisher's other personnel involved in the project, and could well be incapable of giving you any meaningful editorial assistance.

Avoid publishers that have unrealistically low budgets, set unrealistic deadlines, or present you with unusually one-sided contracts. If a publisher that makes you an offer is unfamiliar to you, check it out with your writing colleagues, professional writers' group, editors or agents you know, even the local Better Business Bureau. The industry is small, and word of dishonorable behavior, payment problems, financial shakiness, and other inside information about a publisher usually spreads quickly. As well, you do not want an agent who will inquire with only a small number of editors regarding your work, who does not seem to understand your work (or the business), or who is difficult to reach, churlish, or evasive about answering your questions.

You should generally take a step back from anyone—freelance editor, publisher, agent, coauthor, or packager—who is reluctant to sign a contract that sets forth your mutual understanding of the deal. Once you have entered a contract, clear and timely communication between you and the party with whom you are working is paramount to avoid misunderstandings and maintain good relationships. Of course, you should not call or email your agent and editors too often or without a specific reason. Understand that they are very busy with other writers' business, too. And no matter how upset or alarmed you might be about a party's behavior, always maintain your composure and keep your tone cordial and professional. Remember that the industry is very small. Viral media can conceivably magnify throughout the industry any communication you make in writing or via voice mail. Unfair or not, the way you conduct yourself with your agent and editors—regardless of the provocation—will earn you a reputation, either neutral, good or bad. Writers who flame their agents or editors or lose their tempers could soon find their opportunities trickling away.

NEGOTIATING DISPUTES OUTSIDE COURT

What should you do if, despite your precautions and due diligence, a dispute arises between you and a third party with whom you are doing business? What if you believe the other party has clearly breached your contract or is otherwise harming your interests? At what point should you consider bringing a lawsuit? In almost every case, the best answer to that last question is "not yet." Litigation involves time, energy, and inordinately high costs, and you will almost certainly never again do business with the other side. Most of the time, litigation should be your last resort.

The best way to help yourself initially is to join the Authors Guild and contact its Legal Services Staff. They counsel approximately 1,200 writers annually about specific industry issues. A large portion of the inquiries they address involves writers with contract disputes. Often the Guild will intercede on the writer's behalf or help the writer prepare a demand letter or find qualified counsel when necessary. At the least, the Guild will review and assess your situation and tell you the most realistic prospects for resolving it.

Even if you are not a member, you should follow the basic steps the Guild legal staff employs in legal and business disputes. First, determine what your position is and what exactly you want or need to be satisfied. Then, if you cannot resolve the problem by talking about it, write a polite but firm letter to the appropriate person—usually the individual with whom you are having the problem. Set forth clearly and succinctly your version of the relevant events and why a certain course of action (i.e., your demand) is appropriate at this time. Request relief specifically, and always state in a demand letter and settlement communications that your letter is "without prejudice to any claims, privileges or defenses" so as to preserve all available legal arguments. Carbon copy anyone you think would be interested and helpful to you, but be politic about doing so. It is often better to give the individual at fault one opportunity to address the problem on her own before involving her supervisor or an outsider. Using this tactic allows you to escalate the pressure iteratively if the first request does not work.

Although in any given case you might be entitled to full relief, be realistic about the likelihood you will get it in light of the other side's current position and situation. Consider whether any compromises would be acceptable to you. Of course, do not disclose your final fallback position at the outset, but having one can help you avoid an impasse. If it becomes clear that no redress will be forthcoming without pressure, then try at least a second round of communications, through email, letter, phone calls, and eventually a promise to involve the Authors Guild, the Association of Authors' Representatives (for agents), or the Better Business Bureau. If these actions do not work to obtain relief or an acceptable compromise, then consider consulting a private attorney, who will escalate the communication, probably beginning with a demand letter.

MEDIATION AND ARBITRATION

Litigation should be the last resort for most writers with a business dispute. The costs, duration, and uncertainty are just too high for most people. Two popular alternatives to a lawsuit are mediation and arbitration.

Mediation involves a disinterested and trained third party who actively tries to help adversaries reach a settlement. The parties pay the mediator; sometimes she will negotiate for a "success fee" from the parties if the process results in a settlement. If they choose mediation, the parties will also agree that the information disclosed to each other and the settlement discussions will not be used against each other if there is no settlement and a lawsuit is brought. Courts sometimes order parties in litigation to mediate before their cases will be heard.

If the amount in dispute is higher than the small claims court limit but less than $15,000, it makes little sense to bring a lawsuit because attorneys' fees will probably devour the recovery, if any. Arbitration gives you an opportunity to obtain redress in disputes involving amounts that are too large for small claims court and too small to bring in a state court. Arbitration is akin to a private trial, but it is less formal, faster, and usually less expensive than a trial. The parties present their cases to one or more trained arbitrators chosen and paid by the adversaries. The arbitrator does not try to get the parties to settle; she rules for one party or the other and decides the amount of recovery.

Despite their advantages over litigation, arbitration and mediation are voluntary endeavors. While nobody has a choice about being haled into a lawsuit if jurisdictional requirements are met, both sides must agree to use mediation and arbitration, either at the contract stage or after the dispute arises. Often, the financially stronger party prefers to go to court instead, so as to wear down the other party.

If they appear in a contract, arbitration and mediation clauses are generally enforceable. Mediation clauses typically require both parties to submit any dispute to mediation for a specific period of time and describe how the mediator is to be chosen. Arbitration clauses require that any dispute must be addressed through arbitration according to particular terms and procedures. They usually specify that the arbitration is "binding," i.e., the arbitrator's decision is final and may be recorded in the appropriate court, where it has the force of a nonappealable verdict, or that it is "non-binding," allowing the loser to bring a lawsuit without reference to the arbitration.

To obtain additional information about mediation and arbitration, contact a nearby office of the American Arbitration Association, JAMS (formerly, Judicial Arbitration and Mediation Service, Inc.), your nearest bar association or volunteer lawyers group, or a writers organization.

SMALL CLAIMS COURT

Most small claims courts are very inexpensive; parties usually handle their cases without a lawyer, and a small claims court verdict is as enforceable as that of any official court. The maximum amount at stake allowed in small claims courts varies from a low of $1500 to $5000 or more depending on the locality. Call or check your local bar association or courthouse's website for information on the location of small claims court, complaint templates and instructions on procedures.

CHAPTER 19

TAXES: WRITING INCOME

AND EXPENSES

"To produce an income tax return that has any depth to it, any feeling, one must have Lived—and Suffered." The truth of this quip by author Frank Sullivan might be felt most vividly in April, when many writers who must report self-employment income scramble to gather the information, and sometimes the funds, to file their tax returns. Occasionally, taxpayers can take steps near the end of the year to relieve their tax burdens, but more often than not, the end of the year is too late. Chapters 19 and 20 are intended to help you to plan ahead, keep proper records on a regular basis, and pay your estimated taxes on time. Professional writers should keep their tax information current on a regular basis throughout the year. If you follow the fairly simple recommendations provided here, your tax preparation should be relatively simple, your tax bill might be smaller, and you should be well prepared to handle an IRS audit.

Please note that the advice given here is no substitute for the advice or tax preparation services of a qualified accountant or tax lawyer. Tax rules change continuously and few, if any, off the shelf resources can aspire to be comfortably accurate and current when it comes to income tax rules. It is penny-wise and pound-foolish for anyone earning self-employment income to prepare her own tax returns. You need a good accountant. These chapters are intended to give an overview of the issues most important to writers based on current federal tax law, so you can prepare and carry out a tax strategy that will make your accountant's job easier.

For tax purposes, a writer's taxable income typically includes all amounts received for sales and licenses of her written work, including advances and royalties paid by book publishers and licensees, royalties from sales of self-published ebooks,[127] lecture fees and honoraria, prizes, awards, and most grants. Regular wages also count, of course, though your wages reported by your employer on Form W-2 are distinct from self-employment income. All of this income is taxed as ordinary income by the federal government and, as applicable, by the state and municipality of the writer's residence. The business expenses incurred by a writer may be deducted from her income, thereby reducing the amount subject to taxation.[128]

Self-employed professionals, including professional writers, must include Schedule C, Profit or (Loss) from Business or Profession, as an addendum to their Form 1040 tax returns. Self-employment income and related business expenses are reported on Schedule C.[129] Schedule C is not terribly difficult to complete, especially if you work with a tax accountant, but you may use the even simpler Schedule C-EZ if you meet the following requirements: (1) you have only one sole proprietorship, (2) you have incurred no net business loss, (3) your business expenses are $5,000 or less, (4) you maintain no inventory at any time during the tax year, (6) you use the cash method of accounting, (7) you do not claim a home office expense, (7) you do not need to report depreciation on Form 4562, (8) your business has not previously claimed suspended passive activity losses, and (9) your business had no other employees during the year. You should discuss which form is best to use with your tax advisor. The official 2011 Schedules C and C-EZ are reproduced at the end of this chapter so you can follow them as you read this overview.

---

[127] The tax rules are different for publishers, so if you self-publish extensively, you might be subject to a different regime, but professional writers selling their works as ebooks should be able to count sales proceeds as self-employment income. Check with your accountant to be certain.

[128] A writer employed and earning a salary for writing services might be able to claim deductions for writing-related expenses if they are either not reimbursed or reimbursed but reported as income by the employer. Again, ask your accountant.

[129] If a writer earns both self-employment income and a salary from an employer, she must file two separate Schedule Cs so as to avoid paying self-employment tax twice on her wages.

General guides to federal taxation include IRS Publication 17, *Your Federal Income Tax*, for individuals and IRS Publication 334, *Tax Guide for Small Businesses (for Individuals Who Use Schedule C or C-EZ)*, each of which cover the rules in great detail. These and all other IRS publications can be downloaded from the IRS's website: at www.irs.gov/formspubs. (Some IRS forms, schedules, and publications are available in Spanish.) The IRS also provides advice on the phone via toll free numbers Monday through Friday (see www.irs.gov/contact). You can also contact your local IRS office for a face-to-face meeting. Be aware that IRS publications and advice represent the views of the IRS and have been known to conflict with precedent established by tax courts. Of course, tax policy is one of the most potent ways to regulate the economy and public policy, so Congress and the White House (as well as states and municipalities) are constantly amending the tax laws. Keep abreast of the changes through your tax accountant, one of many privately published guides, such as the *J. K. Lasser* line, or with a tax return software program.

In addition to income tax, you will also need to determine whether other kinds of state or local taxes, such as unincorporated business tax, must be paid. These taxes vary with each state and municipality and will not specifically be addressed here.

RECORD-KEEPING

Keeping clear and current records of your income and expenses not only makes the task of filling out tax returns and paying estimated tax much easier, it can also help you sail through an audit. If you are audited, the IRS will require you to back up all income and deductions claimed with credible and accurate documentation. Get into the habit of promptly recording all income and expenses generated from your writing in a ledger or spreadsheet regularly used for that purpose. The entries should specify the date and amount of money received and paid out, the character of the receipt or payout, the source or destination of the payment, and other relevant data. Keep copies or originals of all checks, bills, and receipts. The IRS favors self-employed taxpayers maintaining separate business bank accounts solely for their self-employment income and expenses, and it is a good idea to do that. IRS Publications 552, *Recordkeeping for Individuals*, and 583, *Starting a*

Business and Keeping Records, details the "permanent, accurate and complete" records the IRS requires.

To illustrate, the following example is one method of setting up an efficient ledger on paper (if you choose, Excel, Quicken, Quickbook and other computerized spreadsheets are even easier once you learn them). The first column is for the date, the second for a description of the kind of income or expense, the third for the check or receipt number, the fourth for the amount of income, the fifth for the amount of the expense, the sixth and subsequent columns for the specific kinds of expenses listed on Schedule C that correspond to a writer's typical deductible expenses. (Note that with this method, every expense is entered twice, once in the expense column and again under its particular category). If maintained regularly, a ledger like this greatly expedites the process of completing Schedule C, especially if you match your expense categories to it.

Date	Description	Check/ Receipt	Income	Expense	Expense Categories					
					1	2	3	4	5	6 etc.

To show how easy it is to keep records this way, suppose you paid $24 for office supplies on January 8. In your ledger, enter the following: the date, January 8; "office supplies" as the description; a check number if payment was by check as well as an assigned receipt number if you received one (number and file your actual receipts by month or category to locate them easily). If you receive payments from several sources, try creating income categories (such as royalties/advances according to book title, articles by name of publication, speaking appearances, and so on).

ACCOUNTING METHODS AND PERIODS

Like any other taxpayer, writers may choose either of two methods of accounting: the cash method or the accrual method. The cash method is simpler and most commonly used. It requires that you report all income actually received and deduct all expenses actually paid during the tax year. The accrual method requires that you report all income that you earned and have a right to receive in the tax year, even if you do not actually receive it until the following tax year, and that you deduct expenses for the year they are incurred instead of when they are paid.[130] For simplicity, this chapter assumes you are using the cash method.

The tax year used by most taxpayers is January 1 through December 31. Theoretically, one could use a different fiscal year, such as July 1 through June 30, but the IRS must accept a filer's reasons for not using a calendar year. More information on accounting methods and periods is available in IRS Publication 538, *Accounting Periods and Methods*. This chapter assumes you are filing based on a calendar year.

One basic tax-saving technique for filers using the cash method is to pay as many expenses as possible before year end and to put off the receipt of income until the following tax year. The idea is to decrease the current year's tax bill by offsetting income through expense deductions while deferring income until the following tax year. Or, if you anticipate that a significant increase in your income in the next year will put you into a higher tax bracket, or if the tax rate is set to increase in the new year,

---

[130] Under the cash method, there might be a few cases in which income not actually received in a tax year must nonetheless be reported. This would happen if the income is credited or segregated such that it is subject to the taxpayer's control, for example, if it is received by the writer's agent, unless the agent is legally restricted from forwarding the payment during the tax year.

try to receive as much income during the present year as you can, and to defer paying expenses until the following year. If you are negotiating an advance to be paid in installments, these considerations should enter into your calculations.

INCOME EARNED BY WRITERS

In general, all income earned by you from your trade—advances, royalties, payment for freelance contributions or works for hire, kill fees, speaking fees—must be reported as gross receipts from your trade or business, i.e., self-employment income.[131] Either the party that pays you or the one that pays your agent should send you a Form 1099-Misc by February 1 of the new year that reports all payments made to you in the previous year.[132] If you earn a salary, your employer should report that income on Form W-2 and you will complete a separate Schedule C for that income. An important distinction is made in the Tax Code between ordinary income and capital gains income. "Ordinary income" is that which is realized from all the income-producing activities of one's profession and is taxed at regular income tax rates. "Capital gains income" is that which is realized from the sale of capital assets, such as stocks, bonds, mutual funds, real estate, or precious metals. Capital gains from assets owned for longer than one year are classified as long-term gains and generally receive significantly better tax treatment (i.e., a much lower tax rate and no self-employment tax) than does regular income.

Unfortunately, copyrights and writings prepared by a writer are not considered capital assets of the writer. Income from copyrights, literary, musical, and artistic compositions, letters or memoranda, or similar property received by the taxpayer who created them are taxed as ordinary income.[133] Another important distinction is between earned and unearned income. The professional income of an author is considered earned income, but

---

[131] Self-employment income tax also includes the full amount of Social Security and Medicare tax that a salaried employee shares with her employer.

[132] A publisher or commissioning party that pays you less than $600 in a year does not have to send you a Form 1099, but you still must report the amount you received as income.

[133] If a writer sells her copyright or a manuscript to someone else, the buyer will own the work as a capital asset, and the buyer's profit from selling it can be taxed at the capital gains rate.

income from stock dividends, interest, rent, and capital gains, for example, is treated as unearned income.

BASIS

The cost of creating a work (or of acquiring a capital asset) is called its "basis" for tax purposes. An author who uses the cash method and deducts business expenses when they are paid may not double dip and deduct these costs from the basis when she sells a work. In other words, if you deduct expenses currently, then your work product has a zero basis and the entire amount of the proceeds to you from its sale or license is taxable income.

GRANTS

Grants awarded to writers are usually taxed as "other income" on Line 6 of Schedule C. Degree candidates may exclude scholarships or fellowships from reportable income only to the extent the award is used for tuition and course-related fees, books, supplies, and equipment at a qualified educational institution. To qualify as nontaxable, such grants or scholarships may not include expenses for meals, lodging, or travel. Nor may they include payments to the recipient for teaching, research, or any other services rendered in exchange for the scholarship. Nondegree candidates may not exclude scholarships or grants from income. More information on the taxation of grants and scholarships is in IRS Publication 970, *Tax Benefits for Education* (Section 1, Scholarships and Fellowships).

PRIZES AND AWARDS

Authors must report all prizes, monetary and nonmonetary, as "other income." Nonmonetary prizes should be valued at their fair market value. If you receive a prize for your achievement as a writer and you designate a tax-exempt institution to receive the prize, the prize and the donation are not treated for tax purposes as income and a deductible charitable contribution; the prize is treated as no receipt of income. Should you win and keep a monetary prize, you may choose to enter the amount received on Form 1040 as "other income" instead of on Schedule C, and thus avoid paying self-employment tax on the prize. On the other hand, if you are concerned about a home-office deduction or hobby loss challenge by the IRS (which are explained below), consider entering prizes as income on

Schedule C so as to offset penalties for underpayment of self-employment tax. Discuss how to treat a prize with your tax advisor.

BUSINESS EXPENSES

Deductible business expenses, which must be reported on Schedule C, include all of the ordinary and necessary expenditures you incur that help you earn income from your writing. They include, but are not limited to, advertising and promotional costs, writing materials and supplies, work-space rental, office equipment, professional books and journals, writers organization dues and conference fees, office and equipment repairs, travel and car use for business purposes, telephone, postage, agents' commissions, and legal and accounting fees. Expenses claimed must be reasonable, and certain kinds of major expenditures, such as computers, might not be fully deductible in the year they are incurred, but must be depreciated over the course of several years.

SUPPLIES AND OFFICE EXPENSES

Items with a useful life of less than one year are typically considered current expenses, fully deductible in the year purchased. They include writing materials and supplies such as paper, ink, pens, erasers, rental of computers, photocopying, stationery, and similar items. You may include sales tax paid in the expense calculation. Postage is deductible as soon as the expense is incurred. The cost of professional journals and books used to prepare specific works is deductible. Telephone bills and an answering service are deductible in full for a business telephone. Repairs to professional equipment are fully deductible in the year incurred. As with all expenses, however, if you use an item or service for both personal and business purposes, then you may only deduct the portion of the cost attributed to your business use. For phone expenses, the IRS expects clear and thorough records itemizing both long-distance and local message units expended for business purposes.

PROFESSIONAL DEVELOPMENT

Educational expenses are generally deductible if they were incurred to maintain or improve your writing skills, but are not deductible if incurred to learn or qualify for a new profession. Consult IRS Publication 529, *Miscellaneous Deductions*, for more information. Dues for membership in professional organizations (but not for clubs) are deductible, as are fees to attend workshops and programs sponsored by the organizations.

MOVING EXPENSES

If you move to a new residence, the pro rata share of the moving expenses attributable to professional equipment is deductible as a business expense. More substantial deductions for reasonable moving expenses can be taken if a self-employed person's new work location is at least fifty miles farther from her former residence than her old job location and certain other requirements are met. This deduction is explained in IRS Publication 521, *Moving Expenses*.

HEALTH INSURANCE PREMIUMS

Self-employed people may deduct 100 percent of their premiums for health insurance as an expense on Form 1040. This deduction may not be claimed for any month you are covered by an employer's (or your spouse's employer's) subsidized health plan. The health insurance deduction may not exceed your Schedule C income, but any health insurance premiums that may not be deducted on Form 1040 might be deductible on Schedule A if you itemize deductions.

WORKSPACE EXPENSES AND THE HOME-OFFICE DEDUCTION

If you rent workspace at a location different from your home, all of the rent and expenses in connection with that workspace are deductible. However, the tax code has strict rules about business deductions attributable to a home office or studio (and anecdotal evidence suggests that those claiming a home office deduction are more likely to be audited). The home office deduction is allowed only if the filer uses a discreet part of the home exclusively for her business and uses it on a regular basis as her principal place of business. Even if you have another profession, as long as your home office is the principal place of your writing business and is used regularly and for no other purpose, you may take the deduction. If you maintain a separate structure and use it exclusively and regularly in connection with your writing business, you may deduct the full expenses attributable to it. For employees (as opposed to the self-employed), the home-office deduction is available only if your exclusive use of it is for the convenience of your employer, in addition to the criteria described above. You must calculate and report the home office deduction on Form 8829, *Expenses for Business Use of Your Home.* Publication 587, *Business Use of Your Home,* explains the rules further.

You may deduct expenses related solely to the office portion of your home, such as repairs to that area, in full. Other expenses that benefit your whole home including the home office portion are deductible only in the proportion of the office to your entire home.

This means that you may deduct that portion of your expenses for utilities, insurance, and cleaning that are attributable to your home office. Likewise, repairs to maintain the home are deductible on a pro rata basis. Property taxes and mortgage interest are deductible if you itemize personal deductions on Schedule A of Form 1040 whether or not you claim a home office deduction. If you do not itemize, the home office portions of your property taxes and mortgage interest that are deductible business expenses can be claimed on Schedule C.

To determine the portion of deductible expenses attributable to a home office, first you must calculate the portion of the total space used as your exclusive workspace. If you rent your home, and one-fifth of the area is used as workspace, 20 percent of the rent is deductible. A homeowner makes the same calculation to find the amount of workspace used, but as a capital asset, the house must be depreciated. A house (but not land) has a basis for depreciation, which is usually what it cost plus any major improvement costs. The calculation used to determine the number of years over which depreciation is taken and the percentage of basis taken as a deduction each year depends on when the house was acquired. Depreciation of capital assets, including a home, is explained below and in IRS Publications 529, *Miscellaneous Deductions,* 946, *How to Depreciate Property,* and 534, *Depreciating Property Placed in Service Before 1987.*

If you qualify to take the home office deduction, your related business expense deductions may not exceed your gross income from writing, reduced by your Schedule A itemized deductions (i.e., deductions incurred outside of business use, such as real estate taxes and mortgage interest). In other words, the tax code disallows any home office business expense deduction to the extent that it creates or increases a net loss from your writing business. But any disallowed amounts may be carried forward and deducted in future years.

As an example: A writer earns income of $3,000 in a year from writing, while exclusively and on a regular basis using one-quarter of her home as the principal place of her writing business. She owns her home, mortgage interest is $2,000 and real estate taxes are $1,600, for a total of $3,600 in deductions that she may take on Schedule·A, whether or not incurred in connection with her business. Other home expenses, such as electricity, heat, cleaning, and depreciation, total $8,800. Allocating one-quarter of these expenses to the home office expense would attribute $900 of mortgage interest and real estate taxes and $2,200 of the other expenses to the business. The writer's gross self-employment income of $3,000 must be reduced by the $900 allocated to the home office portion of mortgage interest and real estate taxes, leaving $2,100 as the maximum amount of her workspace expenses that she may deduct.

Gross income	$3,000
Home office expenses allocated to the business	
Interest and property taxes	$900
Electricity, heat, cleaning, depreciation	$2,200
Total home-office expenses	$3,100
Expenses of writing business (excluding home-office expenses)	$2,400
Total expenses	$5,500

The writer will apply against her gross self-employment income (1) deductions for her business expenses (excluding expenses allocable to the home office), and (2) the taxes and interest allocable to her business use of the home. Since (1) $2,400, and (2) $900, total $3,300, her gross writing income of $3,000 would be reduced to a negative figure. A zero or negative figure means that no additional expenses may be deducted, so the other expenses allocable to the home office ($2,200) are lost for the year. She may carry forward the expenses that are not deductible this year as a deduction in future years when her income is sufficient. Mortgage interest and property taxes would remain fully deductible on Schedule A if she itemizes her deductions.

TRAVEL, TRANSPORTATION, AND ENTERTAINMENT EXPENSES

Travel, transportation, and entertainment expenses for business purposes are partly deductible, but keep careful records and deduct the amounts accurately. Travel expenses are defined as the ordinary and necessary expenses, including meals, lodging, and transportation, incurred for travel for more than an average workday spent away from home in pursuit of professional activities. You may deduct such expenses, for example, if you travel to another city to give a lecture series and stay several days to complete your work. If you are not required to sleep or rest while away from home on business, deductible transportation expenses are limited to the cost of travel. Meals and entertainment expenses, such as business luncheons, receptions, or similar, are currently 50 percent deductible but only if they are directly related to your writing business or involve a substantial business discussion.

If you use a car to make necessary trips for your work, such as travel to interview subjects or to do research, you might be able to deduct the expenses incurred in connection with the car, including gas, oil, insurance, license and registration fees, parking, tolls, repairs, and so on, or to take a standard mileage deduction. Several limitations apply, however. If you do not claim a home office deduction, you generally may not deduct your driving expenses. Costs of commuting to your office are not deductible. You may, however, deduct driving expenses between different work locations. If you claim driving expenses, be meticulous about recording every trip, including date, mileage, and the business reason, and keep all receipts. If you use your car solely for business, you can claim all the expenses on Schedule C. If you use it for personal reasons as well, you must prorate the expense deduction according to the percentage of business use. Some taxpayers find that taking the standard mileage deduction (55.5 cents per mile for 2012) more advantageous, but you must use that method in the first year of business use of the car; if you deduct actual driving expenses the first year, you may not switch in later years to the standard mileage method. If you use the standard mileage record, you cannot also depreciate the cost basis of the car; depreciation is included in the standard mileage rate.

Accurate and contemporaneous records detailing your business purposes (and the business relationship to any person entertained or receiving a gift), date, place, and cost are especially important for all these deductions. Get into the habit of writing these details on copies of bills or credit card charge receipts. IRS Publication 463, *Travel, Entertainment, Gift and Car Expenses*, gives more details, including the current permissible mileage charge. Self-promotional items, such as advertising, business cards, and sending holiday greetings to professional associates, are also deductible expenses.

COMMISSIONS, FEES, AND SALARIES

Your agent should provide you with Form 1099s that will show your writing income earned through her; note that it will properly report your gross income and not what you earned net of her commission. The proper way to deduct her commission is as a business expense. As well, fees paid to lawyers or accountants for business purposes are tax deductible, as are payments made to typists, researchers, freelance editors, and other service providers. If you can, it is better to employ and pay people as independent contractors rather than employees, so you can avoid liability for social security, disability, and withholding tax payments. The IRS applies a multifactor test to determine who is an employee and who is an independent contractor. It explains these factors in IRS Publication 15-A, *Business Expenses*. Treating an employee as an independent contractor could result in liability for back taxes and substantial penalties. If you have any concerns that someone who works for you is an employee rather than an independent contractor, discuss it with your tax advisor. If you use independent contractors, you must file with the IRS and give to the contractor Form 1099-MISC, Statement for Recipients of Miscellaneous Income, if you paid the contractor at least $10 in a year in gross royalties or at least $600 for their services.

PROFESSIONAL EQUIPMENT

Traditionally, the cost of professional equipment having a useful life of more than one year (cars, computers, homes, and the like) could not be fully deducted in the year of purchase. Its value had to be depreciated over a certain number of years at a certain rate, with corresponding deductions allowed in each year. Over the years, the law has significantly changed the method by which depreciation is determined. With some exceptions, the method of depreciation that you must use is based on when the property was placed in service. IRS Publication 946, *How to Depreciate Property*, aids in the computation of depreciation. Form 4562, *Depreciation and Amortization*, applies for all types of depreciation discussed here. Following is a brief overview of the different relevant time periods and the current expensing method:

1) 1987 to the Present: The Modified Accelerated Cost Recovery System (MACRS) applies to property placed in service from 1987 to the present. MACRS depreciates property using several different depreciation methods.

It places assets into different classes with different class "lives." "Five-year property" includes cars; "seven-year property" includes office furniture and fixtures. Residential real property has a twenty-seven-and-one-half year "life." These classifications, and the methods of depreciation, determine how quickly the cost of this property may be expensed. The law restricts the use of MACRS for cars (and other personal transportation vehicles), entertainment and recreational property, and computers, unless these types of equipment are used more than 50 percent for business purposes. If they are used less than 50 percent for business purposes, other depreciation rules apply. Publication 962 and Form 4562, *Depreciation and Amortization,* explain the rules in more detail.

2) 1981 to 1986: Almost all equipment placed in use from 1981–1986 must have depreciation computed under the Accelerated Cost Recovery System (ACRS). ACRS provides different categories for depreciation, which depends on the nature of the equipment acquired. Instead of using the ACRS percentages, it is possible to choose an alternate ACRS method, which allows the basis simply to be divided out over a specified number of years. Consult IRS Publication 946, and for every depreciation issue, consult your tax advisor.

Section 179 Deduction: An alternative to depreciating your big-ticket items over time is to take a one-time deduction, called a "Section 179 deduction," which allows you to take the entire basis of your depreciable business property in one year. Depending on your situation, a Section 179 deduction might be better for you than depreciating a capital asset. The amount you can deduct under Section 179 is limited to $500,000 for 2011 (but is only $3,060 for a car) and it cannot exceed your annual business income, though any excess may be carried forward to subsequent tax years. IRS publication 946 describes the Section 179 deduction in detail.

SCHEDULE C (Form 1040) Department of the Treasury Internal Revenue Service (99)	**Profit or Loss From Business** (Sole Proprietorship) ▶ **For information on Schedule C and its instructions, go to www.irs.gov/schedulec.** ▶ **Attach to Form 1040, 1040NR, or 1041; partnerships generally must file Form 1065.**	OMB No. 1545-0074 20**12** Attachment Sequence No. **09**

Name of proprietor		Social security number (SSN)

A	Principal business or profession, including product or service (see instructions)	**B** Enter code from instructions ▶		

C	Business name. If no separate business name, leave blank.	**D** Employer ID number (EIN), (see instr.)

E	Business address (including suite or room no.) ▶
	City, town or post office, state, and ZIP code

F Accounting method: **(1)** ☐ Cash   **(2)** ☐ Accrual   **(3)** ☐ Other (specify) ▶

G Did you "materially participate" in the operation of this business during 2012? If "No," see instructions for limit on losses ☐ Yes ☐ No

H If you started or acquired this business during 2012, check here . . . . ▶ ☐

I Did you make any payments in 2012 that would require you to file Form(s) 1099? (see instructions) . . . . ☐ Yes ☐ No

J If "Yes," did you or will you file required Forms 1099? . . . . ☐ Yes ☐ No

Part I Income

1	Gross receipts or sales. See instructions for line 1 and check the box if this income was reported to you on Form W-2 and the "Statutory employee" box on that form was checked . . . . ▶ ☐	**1**	
2	Returns and allowances (see instructions)	**2**	
3	Subtract line 2 from line 1	**3**	
4	Cost of goods sold (from line 42)	**4**	
5	**Gross profit.** Subtract line 4 from line 3	**5**	
6	Other income, including federal and state gasoline or fuel tax credit or refund (see instructions)	**6**	
7	**Gross income.** Add lines 5 and 6 . . . . ▶	**7**	

Part II Expenses   Enter expenses for business use of your home only on line 30.

8	Advertising	**8**		18	Office expense (see instructions)	**18**	
9	Car and truck expenses (see instructions)	**9**		19	Pension and profit-sharing plans .	**19**	
				20	Rent or lease (see instructions):		
10	Commissions and fees .	**10**		a	Vehicles, machinery, and equipment	**20a**	
11	Contract labor (see instructions)	**11**		b	Other business property . . .	**20b**	
12	Depletion	**12**		21	Repairs and maintenance . . .	**21**	
13	Depreciation and section 179 expense deduction (not included in Part III) (see instructions)	**13**		22	Supplies (not included in Part III) .	**22**	
				23	Taxes and licenses	**23**	
				24	Travel, meals, and entertainment:		
14	Employee benefit programs (other than on line 19) . .	**14**		a	Travel	**24a**	
15	Insurance (other than health)	**15**		b	Deductible meals and entertainment (see instructions) .	**24b**	
16	Interest:			25	Utilities	**25**	
a	Mortgage (paid to banks, etc.)	**16a**		26	Wages (less employment credits) .	**26**	
b	Other	**16b**		27a	Other expenses (from line 48) .	**27a**	
17	Legal and professional services	**17**		b	Reserved for future use . . .	**27b**	

28	**Total expenses** before expenses for business use of home. Add lines 8 through 27a . . . . . ▶	**28**	
29	Tentative profit or (loss). Subtract line 28 from line 7	**29**	
30	Expenses for business use of your home. Attach **Form 8829.** Do **not** report such expenses elsewhere . .	**30**	
31	**Net profit or (loss).** Subtract line 30 from line 29.		
	• If a profit, enter on both **Form 1040, line 12** (or **Form 1040NR, line 13**) and on **Schedule SE, line 2.** (If you checked the box on line 1, see instructions). Estates and trusts, enter on **Form 1041, line 3.**	**31**	
	• If a loss, you **must** go to line 32.		
32	If you have a loss, check the box that describes your investment in this activity (see instructions).		
	• If you checked 32a, enter the loss on both **Form 1040, line 12,** (or **Form 1040NR, line 13**) and on **Schedule SE, line 2.** (If you checked the box on line 1, see the line 31 instructions). Estates and trusts, enter on **Form 1041, line 3.**	32a ☐ All investment is at risk. 32b ☐ Some investment is not at risk.	
	• If you checked 32b, you **must** attach **Form 6198.** Your loss may be limited.		

For Paperwork Reduction Act Notice, see your tax return instructions.   Cat. No. 11334P   Schedule C (Form 1040) 2012

Schedule C (Form 1040) 2012   Page **2**

Part III	Cost of Goods Sold (see instructions)

33 Method(s) used to
value closing inventory: **a** ☐ Cost   **b** ☐ Lower of cost or market   **c** ☐ Other (attach explanation)

34 Was there any change in determining quantities, costs, or valuations between opening and closing inventory?
If "Yes," attach explanation . . . .   ☐ **Yes**   ☐ **No**

35 Inventory at beginning of year. If different from last year's closing inventory, attach explanation . . . | 35 |

36 Purchases less cost of items withdrawn for personal use . . . . | 36 |

37 Cost of labor. Do not include any amounts paid to yourself . . . . | 37 |

38 Materials and supplies . . . . | 38 |

39 Other costs. . . . . | 39 |

40 Add lines 35 through 39 . . . . | 40 |

41 Inventory at end of year . . . . | 41 |

42 **Cost of goods sold.** Subtract line 41 from line 40. Enter the result here and on line 4 . . . . | 42 |

Part IV	**Information on Your Vehicle.** Complete this part **only** if you are claiming car or truck expenses on line 9 and are not required to file Form 4562 for this business. See the instructions for line 13 to find out if you must file Form 4562.

43 When did you place your vehicle in service for business purposes? (month, day, year) ▶ ___ / ___ / ___

44 Of the total number of miles you drove your vehicle during 2012, enter the number of miles you used your vehicle for:

a Business _____   **b** Commuting (see instructions) _____   **c** Other _____

45 Was your vehicle available for personal use during off-duty hours? . . . . ☐ **Yes**   ☐ **No**

46 Do you (or your spouse) have another vehicle available for personal use?. . . . . ☐ **Yes**   ☐ **No**

47a Do you have evidence to support your deduction? . . . . ☐ **Yes**   ☐ **No**

b If "Yes," is the evidence written? . . . . ☐ **Yes**   ☐ **No**

Part V	**Other Expenses.** List below business expenses not included on lines 8–26 or line 30.

48 **Total other expenses.** Enter here and on line 27a . . . . | 48 |

Schedule C (Form 1040) 2012

SCHEDULE C-EZ **(Form 1040)**	**Net Profit From Business**	OMB No. 1545-0074
	(Sole Proprietorship)	**20**~~**12**~~
Department of the Treasury Internal Revenue Service (99)	▶ Partnerships, joint ventures, etc., generally must file Form 1065 or 1065-B. ▶ Attach to Form 1040, 1040NR, or 1041. ▶ See instructions on page 2.	Attachment Sequence No. **09A**

Name of proprietor	Social security number (SSN)

Part I   **General Information**

You May Use Schedule C-EZ Instead of Schedule C Only If You:	• Had business expenses of $5,000 or less. • Use the cash method of accounting. • Did not have an inventory at any time during the year. • Did not have a net loss from your business. • Had only one business as either a sole proprietor, qualified joint venture, or statutory employee.	**And You:**	• Had no employees during the year. • Are not required to file **Form 4562,** Depreciation and Amortization, for this business. See the instructions for Schedule C, line 13, to find out if you must file. • Do not deduct expenses for business use of your home. • Do not have prior year unallowed passive activity losses from this business.

A Principal business or profession, including product or service	**B** Enter business code (see page 2) ▶

C Business name. If no separate business name, leave blank.	**D** Enter your EIN (see page 2)

E   Business address (including suite or room no.). Address not required if same as on page 1 of your tax return.

City, town or post office, state, and ZIP code

F   Did you make any payments in 2012 that would require you to file Form(s) 1099? (see the Schedule C instructions) . . . .   ☐ Yes   ☐ No

G   If "Yes," did you or will you file required Forms 1099? . . . .   ☐ Yes   ☐ No

Part II   **Figure Your Net Profit**

1	**Gross receipts. Caution.** If this income was reported to you on Form W-2 and the "Statutory employee" box on that form was checked, see *Statutory Employees* in the instructions for Schedule C, line 1, and check here . . . . ▶ ☐	**1**	
2	**Total expenses** (see page 2). If more than $5,000, you **must** use Schedule C	**2**	
3	**Net profit.** Subtract line 2 from line 1. If less than zero, you **must** use Schedule C. Enter on both **Form 1040, line 12,** and **Schedule SE, line 2,** or on **Form 1040NR, line 13** and **Schedule SE, line 2** (see instructions). (Statutory employees, **do not** report this amount on Schedule SE, line 2.) Estates and trusts, enter on **Form 1041, line 3**	**3**	

Part III   **Information on Your Vehicle.** Complete this part **only** if you are claiming car or truck expenses on line 2.

4   When did you place your vehicle in service for business purposes? (month, day, year) ▶ _____ .

5   Of the total number of miles you drove your vehicle during 2012, enter the number of miles you used your vehicle for:

a   Business _____   **b** Commuting (see page 2) _____   **c** Other _____

6   Was your vehicle available for personal use during off-duty hours? . . . .   ☐ Yes   ☐ No

7   Do you (or your spouse) have another vehicle available for personal use? . . . .   ☐ Yes   ☐ No

8a   Do you have evidence to support your deduction? . . . .   ☐ Yes   ☐ No

b   If "Yes," is the evidence written? . . . .   ☐ Yes   ☐ No

For Paperwork Reduction Act Notice, see your tax return instructions.   Cat. No. 14374D   Schedule C-EZ (Form 1040) 2012

SCHEDULE C-EZ
(Form 1040)

Department of the Treasury
Internal Revenue Service (99)

Net Profit From Business
(Sole Proprietorship)

▶ Partnerships, joint ventures, etc., generally must file Form 1065 or 1065-B.
▶ Attach to Form 1040, 1040NR, or 1041. ▶ See instructions on page 2.

OMB No. 1545-0074

20**12**

Attachment
Sequence No. **09A**

Name of proprietor

Social security number (SSN)

Part I **General Information**

You May Use Schedule C-EZ Instead of Schedule C Only If You:

- Had business expenses of $5,000 or less.
- Use the cash method of accounting.
- Did not have an inventory at any time during the year.
- Did not have a net loss from your business.
- Had only one business as either a sole proprietor, qualified joint venture, or statutory employee.

And You:

- Had no employees during the year.
- Are not required to file **Form 4562**, Depreciation and Amortization, for this business. See the instructions for Schedule C, line 13, to find out if you must file.
- Do not deduct expenses for business use of your home.
- Do not have prior year unallowed passive activity losses from this business.

A Principal business or profession, including product or service

B Enter business code (see page 2)
▶

C Business name. If no separate business name, leave blank.

D Enter your EIN (see page 2)

E Business address (including suite or room no.). Address not required if same as on page 1 of your tax return.

City, town or post office, state, and ZIP code

F Did you make any payments in 2012 that would require you to file Form(s) 1099? (see the Schedule C instructions) . . . . ☐ Yes ☐ No

G If "Yes," did you or will you file required Forms 1099? . . . . ☐ Yes ☐ No

---

Part II **Figure Your Net Profit**

1	**Gross receipts. Caution.** If this income was reported to you on Form W-2 and the "Statutory employee" box on that form was checked, see *Statutory Employees* in the instructions for Schedule C, line 1, and check here . . . . ▶ ☐	**1**	
2	**Total expenses** (see page 2). If more than $5,000, you **must** use Schedule C	**2**	
3	**Net profit.** Subtract line 2 from line 1. If less than zero, you **must** use Schedule C. Enter on both **Form 1040, line 12,** and **Schedule SE, line 2,** or on **Form 1040NR, line 13** and **Schedule SE, line 2** (see instructions). (Statutory employees, **do not** report this amount on Schedule SE, line 2.) Estates and trusts, enter on **Form 1041, line 3**	**3**	

Part III **Information on Your Vehicle.** Complete this part **only** if you are claiming car or truck expenses on line 2.

4 When did you place your vehicle in service for business purposes? (month, day, year) ▶ _____ .

5 Of the total number of miles you drove your vehicle during 2012, enter the number of miles you used your vehicle for:

a Business _____ **b** Commuting (see page 2) _____ **c** Other _____

6 Was your vehicle available for personal use during off-duty hours? . . . . ☐ Yes ☐ No

7 Do you (or your spouse) have another vehicle available for personal use? . . . . ☐ Yes ☐ No

8a Do you have evidence to support your deduction? . . . . ☐ Yes ☐ No

b If "Yes," is the evidence written? . . . . ☐ Yes ☐ No

For Paperwork Reduction Act Notice, see your tax return instructions. Cat. No. 14374D Schedule C-EZ (Form 1040) 2012

CHAPTER 20

THE HOBBY LOSS RULE

The government does not consider every writer to be "in the business" of writing. If you do not report an annual profit (that is, income exceeding expenses) from your writing on a reasonably regular basis, the IRS might disallow some of your Schedule C business deductions by issuing a "hobby loss" challenge. The hobby loss rule, embodied in Section 183(D) of the tax code, prohibits taxpayers from fully deducting their business losses if the IRS finds their related activity is in pursuit of a hobby and not for profit. If the IRS concludes that you are writing as a hobby as opposed to for profit, then your deductions for related business expenses are limited to the amount of income you earned that year from your writing; you may not report a loss. By contrast, a writer deemed to be actively engaged in the business or trade of writing—that is, one who clearly pursues writing with a profit motive—may deduct all her ordinary and necessary business expenses, even if they exceed her income earned from writing in a given tax year.

The explanations and examples in this chapter are intended to illustrate how you can give yourself the best chance of prevailing in a hobby loss challenge. Organized and current record-keeping that shows you are engaged in seeking a profit from your writing is the key to succeeding. Before deciding to file Schedule C showing writing income and expenses, discuss what is needed to show you are writing with a profit motive with your accountant or a tax lawyer, and if you receive an audit notice, get your advisor involved immediately.

The tests employed by the IRS to determine whether a taxpayer with self-employment income is in business or is engaged in a hobby are relatively straightforward. You do not need to make a profit from writing year after year, but you do need to show that you are actively working to earn a profit from your writing. The IRS provides a thorough explanation of Code Section 183, which it calls "Activities not engaged in for profit," at its website.[134]

THE THRESHOLD TEST: PROFIT IN THREE YEARS OUT OF FIVE

The IRS employs a threshold test, which, if you pass, could end a hobby loss challenge. If a writer earns a net profit (i.e., income exceeding expenses) from her writing activity in any three of the previous five consecutive tax years, she is presumed to be in business. The IRS can overcome this presumption, but the burden of proof rests on it. Even if a writer does not meet this test, the IRS cannot disallow her business losses on that basis alone. Many writers who have experienced both good and bad years financially (as most writers have) are readily able to demonstrate a profit motive despite some years with losses.

The threshold test does not mean you are safe from a challenge until you have been reporting writing activity for five years. The IRS may audit individuals' tax returns for only three years after filing, so it cannot and does not have to wait for your business to exist for five consecutive years before it can challenge your loss in any given year. If you have not yet engaged in writing for profit for five consecutive years, you may file Form 5213 and elect to defer the IRS's determination as to your profit motive until after five consecutive years have passed. The risk of doing so is that if you are at that time determined to be writing as a hobby, you could owe back taxes, interest, and penalties for all five years. To bolster your defenses against a hobby loss challenge, if you use the cash method of accounting, and if it is reasonable and fair, try to defer the year end

---

[134] http://www.irs.gov/Businesses/Small-Businesses-&-Self-Employed/IRC-%C2%A7-183:--Activities-Not-Engaged-in-For-Profit-%28ATG%29

receipt of writing income and accelerate the payment of expenses to show that you have profited in some years. You might be better off reporting three years of profit and two years of larger losses than five straight years of small losses.[135]

PROFIT MOTIVE: NINE FACTORS

If you do not pass the threshold test of earning a profit in three years out of the past five, (or if you pass but the IRS seeks to rebut the presumption) you can still win a hobby loss challenge if you show a genuine profit motive. The tax code employs an objective standard based on all the facts and circumstances surrounding an activity. The code lists nine factors used to determine profit motive. Like many legal tests calling for consideration of several factors, the weight of each will vary depending on the unique case, and no single factor will necessarily trump the others. This is good news, because you can control to a significant degree whether you can demonstrate a pursuit of profit from your writing in a businesslike manner. Here are the nine factors used:

1. *The manner in which the taxpayer carries on the activity.* To satisfy this requirement, demonstrate that you have maintained effective business routines since you began reporting writing income on Schedule C. Thus, you should be able to present an organized and accurate bookkeeping system in which you have recorded all relevant receipts and expenses. A programmed system for engaging in regular relevant correspondence, submissions, follow-ups, contracts, deadlines, even rejection slips, will also be significant in showing your profit motive. However, the IRS disfavors a taxpayer's continued use of the same business practices that lead to continuous annual losses. Try to show that you have worked to identify and change what has contributed to your losses and to make your writing profitable. This might include tailoring your work to existing markets genres or exploring new markets. A word of caution here: if you make too drastic a change, the IRS could see the new method as a new and distinct business, and weigh this factor against you.

---

[135] Be cautious about using this technique. The IRS frowns on unreasonable manipulation of the timing of the receipt of income and payment of expenses.

2. *The writer's expertise, or that of her advisors.* Significant indications of expertise include your educational background, publication credits, encouragement by agents or publishers, awards, prizes, membership in professional organizations, recognition in critical publications, and the retention of business advisors such as lawyers and accountants who are known to advise writers on a regular basis—so long as you follow their advice. Teaching and speaking engagements, if at least partially based on your writing expertise, can also help.

3. *The time and effort expended on writing and marketing your writing.* Can you show that you devote several hours daily on a regular basis to your writing and to selling your work? As most working writers well know, employment in another occupation hardly shows that you lack a writing profit motive, but if you earn a significant amount of overtime income from another job, for example, the IRS might conclude that you do not have enough time to devote to a separate writing business.

4. *The expectation that assets used in the activity will appreciate in value.* This factor is less relevant to writers than to other professions that make large capital or investment expenditures. The IRS does not consider your own copyrights to be capital assets.

5. *Past business success from other activity, similar or not.* Past literary successes, whether financial or critical, can show a present profit motive even if you have been inactive in publishing recently. Although somewhat counterintuitive, the IRS also favors past business success even if unrelated to writing, as long as you can show that it was regularly profitable.

6. *Your history of income or loss in the writing activity.* Use this factor to your benefit by showing your writing generated profits in most years, even if it also incurred losses in other years. This is less likely to help if you incurred significant losses in most years, interspersed with smaller profits in fewer years. But the IRS expects a start-up business to incur substantial losses in its early years. If you can show a significant reduction in your losses over the first several years, this can weigh in your favor.

7. *The amount of occasional profits, if any, earned from your writing.* Just as the IRS is realistic about early losses, it might consider receipt of a large advance or significant writing fees in one or intermittent years to offset the negative implication of losses in other years.

8. *Your financial status/dependence on writing income for your livelihood.* If you do not have substantial income or capital from sources other than your writing, it is more likely your activity has a profit motive. Substantial income from sources other than your writing, especially if your reported losses against your writing income earn you substantial tax benefits, might show you do not have the requisite profit motive.

9. *Elements of personal pleasure or recreation you derive from your writing.* If you are being audited, you will not help yourself by telling the examiner that you are writing for love and not money. The IRS wants evidence that you are working to earn a profit. You do not have to prove that the work is a bore and you are only writing to earn a living, but you should indicate that, even if you enjoy your work, you are still conducting it as a business, marketing yourself and your work, negotiating the best possible contracts, and the like.

THE BOTTOM LINE

The IRS does not want to give professional writers a hard time. The hobby loss rule is in place to prevent nonprofessionals from taking deductions to which they are not entitled. Writers who devote much of their time to their writing and to selling their work, who have demonstrable expertise, who have received recognition for their writing, or for whom the expenses of writing are financially burdensome are more likely to be found to be engaged in business rather than a hobby. This holds true even more for newer authors who demonstrate that they have made financial sacrifices to begin a writing career. Younger authors are often found to have a profit motive even if they need other employment to survive during the early years of their writing careers. Keep good records, seek advice from your tax advisor and follow it, and if you are acting as a professional, you should be able to overcome a hobby loss challenge.

ILLUSTRATIVE CASES

The IRS is not the last word on a hobby loss ruling (or other tax determinations). A taxpayer who disagrees with an IRS determination can challenge it in court. A look at some typical hobby loss cases will illustrate the approach of the courts to the nine factors. Although these cases are not recent, they employ analyses that still apply.

CASE I: THE DILETTANTE—NO PROFIT MOTIVE

John Baltis graduated from college in 1948 and commenced work in the newspaper field. In 1967 and 1968, he was a copyeditor for the *San Francisco Chronicle*. During the same two years, he took deductions as a freelance writer—$1,968 in 1967 and $1,974 in 1968. Between 1948 and 1968, he had sold only three articles for a total of $550. Many of his claimed expenses involved family visits. The result: No profit motive could be shown. Significantly, the tax court also pointed out "there was almost a complete failure to substantiate the specific items which the Commissioner disallowed." Do not forget to keep accurate records to substantiate deductions.

CASE II: THE WEALTHY SCHOLAR—NO PROFIT MOTIVE

Corliss Lamont, a philosopher who taught at Columbia University, lectured across the country on philosophy, civil liberties, and international affairs. He also wrote numerous books and pamphlets about these subjects. He had independent wealth, so he could afford the continuous losses from his writing over a thirty-year period. The court concluded, "Although continuity and efficiency of operations are criteria which would tend to support the existence of a trade or business . . . the totality of circumstances surrounding Lamont's background, his interest in the wide dissemination of his ideas, his activities and financial status justifies the conclusion of the Tax Court that a profit motive was lacking."

CASE III: THE ESTABLISHED AUTHOR TRAVELING FOR RESEARCH—PROFIT MOTIVE

Stern, a writer of numerous articles and screenplays and a resident of Los Angeles, spent 335 days in New York City during 1965. He had been writing for almost forty years. The author was an expert on the film director D. W. Griffith and spent the time in New York researching Griffith's papers at the Museum of Modern Art. The results of his work provided the basis for an issue of *Film Culture Magazine* published in 1965, and the contents of the magazine were then to be used in a hardcover book scheduled for future publication. Stern received no income from the magazine, but had a contract providing for standard author's royalties on the hardcover book.

The court found a profit motive because the author had "participated in that endeavor with a good faith expectation of making a profit," despite the lack of immediate profits.

CASE IV: A WRITING VANDERBILT—PROFIT MOTIVE

Cornelius Vanderbilt, Jr. commenced his writing career in 1919 and pursued it with great success for two decades, despite his wealthy family cutting off his allowance. He published numerous books and articles in addition to founding newspapers and a news service syndicate. Motion picture producers purchased a number of his stories, and he began a successful lecture career in 1929. World War II and health problems curtailed his writing. He resumed his writing and lecturing career after the war and often wrote about travel and current foreign affairs. Much of Mr. Vanderbilt's writing, including several books, was devoted to these topics.

His writing-related activities, especially a substantial amount of travel, caused his deductions to far exceed his writing income. The IRS sought to disallow the entire amount of business deductions claimed in 1951— $30,175.90—on the rationale that Mr. Vanderbilt was not in the business or trade of being a writer in that year. It argued that his large losses over several years, inherited wealth, inattention to practical business details and even "his general propensity towards engaging in this field of endeavor whether it resulted in profit or not . . ." showed no profit motive.

The court disagreed with the IRS's characterization of Vanderbilt's career as bearing "a strong resemblance to that of a romanticist and adventurer." His past commercial success and continued devotion to his writing demonstrated his profit motive more than adequately.

CHAPTER 21

TAXES: BEYOND SCHEDULE C

Like all US taxpayers, professional writers are affected by special tax issues outside of those presented in income and expense filings. Although they are not addressed neatly in one place as income and expenses are on Schedule C, these issues are important to know about and understand.

SELF-EMPLOYMENT TAX

Virtually all employed Americans (with the exception, ironically, of our federal lawmakers) contribute from their earnings to, and are entitled to the benefits of, Social Security and Medicare. Social Security provides workers with retirement and disability income and dependent benefits in the event of their death or disability. Medicare currently provides guaranteed health care insurance for all citizens beginning at age sixty-five. Payroll taxes are automatically withheld from employees' regular paychecks to cover their mandatory Social Security and Medicare contributions, and employers pay one-half of these taxes. These taxes are not, however, withheld from payments received by the self-employed. Therefore, all self-employed people, including professional writers, must file Schedule SE, Computation of

Social Security Self-Employment Tax, with their Form 1040 and must pay the self-employment tax shown on Schedule SE.

Your self-employment income subject to the self-employment tax is basically your net income from writing as reported on Schedule C, subject to certain adjustments. If you have more than one business, your combined business earnings must be totaled on Schedule SE to calculate your self-employment tax. If you receive wages from an employer from which the payroll tax is withheld, you may subtract the wages from your total taxable income to calculate the tax on your self-employment income. If you and your spouse both earn self-employment income, each must file a separate Schedule SE.

To qualify for Social Security benefits, a worker must have worked and contributed for forty quarters (that is, ten full years) during her working life. The amount of one's Social Security (but not Medicare) benefits is based on the amount she has paid into Social Security. The more one earns, the more one pays into the system, and the larger the amount of monthly benefits from Social Security to which one is entitled.

For all workers, employed and self-employed, there is a ceiling on the amount of annual income on which Social Security taxes are paid. The maximum amount of taxed income has steadily increased over the years—from $14,000 in 1975 to $106,800 in 2011 (there is now no ceiling on the amount of income subject to Medicare tax)—and the rate of taxation has also increased to 15.3 percent in 2010, but was temporarily reduced for 2011 and for part of 2012 to 13.3 percent (10.4 percent for Social Security, plus 2.9 percent on all income for Medicare). Fortunately, a portion of your self-employment taxes is deductible from your gross income on Form 1040.

More information about the computation of self-employment tax can be found in IRS Publication 334, *Tax Guide for Small Business (For Individuals who use Schedule C or Schedule C-EZ)*. Additional information about the benefits available under Social Security is available at the Social Security Administration's website (www.socialsecurity.gov) or through its toll-free number (1-800-772-1213.) The Administration also offers a helpful pamphlet titled *Understanding Social Security* and an information sheet called *If You're Self-Employed*. Once you have paid into the system for the requisite forty quarters, the Administration must send you an annual report that explains your earnings history and your projected benefits based on credits earned. If you do not receive this report, contact the Administration.

ESTIMATED TAX PAYMENTS

The federal government needs funds to operate year-round. Employers withhold (and remit to Uncle Sam) both income and payroll taxes from their employees' regular paychecks on an ongoing basis throughout the year. By the same token, self-employed people must pay their federal income and self-employment taxes in quarterly installments, which are computed on Form 1040-ES, Estimated Tax for Individuals. If you will owe $1,000 or more in taxes in a given tax year from self-employment, you must send your quarterly estimated tax payments for the tax year to the IRS on or before April 15, June 15, September 15, and January 15 (of the year following the tax year). The $1,000 threshold for 2012 is net of any employment income tax withholding and refundable credits from your total tax (but not net of any estimated tax payments). Failure to pay sufficient estimated taxes can expose you to liability for penalties and interest on top of the tax deficiency. To avoid the penalties from underpayment, you may pay as estimated tax in the current year the amount equal to your actual tax bill for the prior year (110 percent of that amount if you will earn more than $150,000). IRS Publication 505, *Tax Withholding and Estimated Tax*, gives more detailed information about estimated tax payments and how to avoid penalties for underpayment.

RETIREMENT PLANS FOR THE SELF-EMPLOYED

Self-employed sole proprietors can use several types of deferred tax savings plans for retirement: a Keogh, or qualified plan, a Simplified Employee Pension ("SEP"), a traditional IRA and/or a Roth IRA. Keogh, SEP, and traditional IRA plan contributions can be deducted from income on Form 1040. For some plans, you might need to file additional forms; check with your plan's administrator.

You should also strongly consider setting up a Health Savings Account, similar in operation to a traditional IRA. If you anticipate medical costs that will not be covered by your insurance, including deductibles, a HSA allows you to set aside pretax money to cover them. See IRS Publication 969,

Health Savings Accounts and other Tax Favored Health Plans, for more details on this excellent option.

QUALIFIED PLANS

A "qualified" (also called "Keogh") plan permits self-employed people to contribute to a retirement fund and deduct the amount of the contribution from their gross income when computing income taxes. The Keogh deduction is allowed in a given year only if you invest it in one of a specified kind of retirement fund, described in IRS Publication 560, *Retirement Plans for Small Businesses (SEP, SIMPLE and Qualified Plans)*. Even if you are employed by a company with a retirement program, you might still be able to set up a tax deferred Keogh plan covering your writing income. If you have employees, any retirement plan you set up for yourself will also require contributions for the benefit of your employees.

A financial institution can help you set up and administer the Keogh plan. There are several ways to determine the maximum amount of contributions you may make to a Keogh plan, which are limited by certain caps. As with other tax deferred retirement plans, contributions to a Keogh plan must be made before the filing date of the tax return (usually the following April 15), but unlike other plans, the Keogh plan itself must be set up during the tax year for which your deduction is taken. You must pay a tax penalty for withdrawing from the plan prior to age fifty-nine and one-half (unless you become permanently disabled), but no taxes are incurred on the growth of a Keogh fund until the funds are withdrawn. Distributions are taxed when made.

Keoghs are good plans for self-employed people. Your tax bracket upon retirement age could be much lower than it is while you are working and contributing to the fund, so income tax on the distributions would be at a lower rate than you are paying today. Meanwhile, the funds will have grown tax-free. If you create a trust to hold the Keogh, you can act as trustee and administer the investments. One-participant Keogh accounts of less than $250,000 are exempt from annual filings, except in the last year of the plan. More information about Keogh plans can be obtained from the institutions that administer them.

SEPS

A self-employed person may also create a Simplified Employee Pension (SEP), which is simpler and has fewer requirements than a Keogh plan. SEPs do not need to be set up by the end of the year for which the contribution is made and do not have the same annual filing requirements as some Keoghs. If you want to make the largest possible deductible contributions to your retirement funds, however, a Keogh plan is better than a SEP. IRS Publications 560, *Retirement Plans for Small Business (SEP, SIMPLE and Qualified Plans)* and 4334, *Simple IRA Plans for Small Businesses,* explain the various plans in more detail.

TRADITIONAL IRAS

In addition to either a Keogh plan or a SEP, you might be able to open a traditional IRA (Individual Retirement Account). An IRA allows you to contribute up to a certain amount of your pretax income per year (assuming that your wages and professional earnings amount to at least that much) into a retirement fund. To qualify to make deductible contributions to an IRA, either you must not be covered by another retirement plan, such as an employer-sponsored 401(k), Keogh, or SEP, or if you do participate in another retirement plan, you must earn less than a certain amount in adjusted gross income. The custodial fees charged by a plan administrator (but not commissions paid on transactions) may be deducted as investment expenses on Schedule A if these fees are separately billed and paid.

THE ROTH IRA

Even if you participate fully in another retirement plan, you might also qualify to establish and make after-tax (i.e., nondeductible) contributions to an individual retirement plan called a Roth IRA. (You cannot invest in a Roth IRA if you earn more than a specified amount in adjusted gross income.) To qualify as a Roth IRA, the account or annuity must be designated as such when it is set up, but you may convert a traditional IRA (but not a SEP) to a Roth IRA (and back again) if you are willing to pay income tax on your original contributions to it. Roth IRAs are generally subject to the same rules as traditional IRAs, except that you cannot deduct contributions to your Roth IRA. The great benefit of a Roth IRA is that it grows tax-free, *and* qualified distributions from it can be tax-free when they are made. You may withdraw your original contributions to it at anytime without having to pay a tax or penalty (because you have already paid income tax on them). More information may be obtained from the institutions administering Individual Retirement Accounts, as well as IRS Publication 590, *Individual Retirement Arrangements* (IRAs).

OTHER TAX CREDITS AND DEDUCTIONS

Certain tax credits that apply to any individual taxpayer, both those employed by another and the self-employed, are explained below.

CHILD AND DISABLED DEPENDENT CARE

Anyone who maintains a household including either a child under age thirteen or a disabled dependent and who must pay for their care in order to gainfully pursue employment or self-employment might qualify for the child and dependent care tax credit.[136] The credit is 35 percent of what you pay to employ a caretaker in order to be gainfully employed. IRS Publication 503, *Child and Dependent Care Expenses*, describes in greater detail the rules and limitations of this credit.

BAD DEBTS

Although bad debts might be deducted as a loss against business income for those using the accrual method, a party's failure to pay you as agreed for your work may not be deducted as a bad debt. The reason is simple: the unpaid fee is not counted as taxable income. As stated in Publication 334, *Tax Guide for Small Businesses (For Individuals Who Use Schedule C or C-EZ)*, "Cash method taxpayers normally do not report income until they receive payment. Therefore, they cannot take a bad debt deduction for payments they have not received or cannot collect." But cash basis taxpayers can deduct certain types of business or nonbusiness bad debts. A loan to a customer or a friend that is never repaid, for example, qualifies as a bad debt. (Such a loan must be legally enforceable against the borrower.) Nonbusiness bad debt deductions are taken in the year in which the debt becomes worthless, and may be carried forward to subsequent years' returns, if it exceeds the yearly limit ($3,000 in 2011).

NET OPERATING LOSSES

A self-employed person who experiences a business loss as determined on Schedule C may carry the loss to Form 1040, where it is eventually subtracted from gross income to calculate taxable income. If the loss is

---

[136] Tax credits are subtracted directly from your tax bill. Their impact is much greater than are deductions from income in the same amount.

large enough to wipe out other taxable income for the year, the excess loss may first be carried back to reduce taxable income in up to two to five prior years (depending on the type of income) and then carried forward for future taxable years. This type of loss is likely to arise for a professional writer when they change from salaried employment to full-time writing. One favorable result could be a tax refund for previous years' payments and/or a lower tax bill in future years. IRS Publication 536, *Net Operating Losses*, describes the net operating loss deduction in detail. You will most likely need an accountant's help to compute your losses.

AMERICAN WRITERS LIVING ABROAD

American citizens living abroad are taxed by the United States government on all their income earned from anywhere in the world, but they are entitled to take an exclusion (the "foreign earned income exclusion") for income earned from foreign sources in the amount of up to $92,900 (for 2011). This exclusion can result in substantial tax benefits when the tax rates of the foreign country such as Ireland, where a qualified writer might live tax-free, are lower than the tax rates in the United States. Certain foreign housing costs might also be excluded or deductible from income.

The basic requirements are either a minimum one-year residence or physical presence in a foreign country and income earned from work done in the foreign country. "Residence" is a flexible concept based on the circumstances of each individual. While the residence must be uninterrupted (for example, by owning or renting a home continually), remaining abroad for the entire taxable year is not necessary. Brief trips to other countries do not affect one's tax status as a resident abroad.[137] "Physical presence" requires the taxpayer to be present in a foreign country or countries for at least 330 days during a period of twelve consecutive months. Regardless of which test is met, the foreign earned income to be excluded must be received no later than the year after the year in which it was earned.

---

[137] Some or all of your foreign earned income exclusion might be lost if you travel in countries restricted to US citizens under certain sanctions rules. Check with your local US consulate for more details. Publication 54, *Tax Guide for US Citizens and Resident Aliens Abroad*, explains the guidelines for eligibility for the exclusions.

If you wish to benefit from the exclusion for income earned abroad and foreign housing costs, consult with a tax lawyer or an accountant about your particular situation. If you live abroad, ask the US consulate whether any treaty regarding taxation between the United States and your residence nation affects your tax status.

In addition to the foreign earned income exclusion, some taxes paid to a foreign government on income that is also subject to US taxation might be eligible for a tax credit or deduction on your US return. IRS Publication 514, *Foreign Tax Credit for Individuals*, explains these provisions.

FOREIGN WRITERS IN (OR EARNING IN) THE UNITED STATES

Foreign writers who are residents of the United States are generally taxed in the same way as citizens. Foreign writers who are not residents of the United States are taxed on income earned from US sources under special rules, including a mandatory withholding tax of 30 percent on royalties earned on US sales. A foreigner who is merely visiting or whose stay is limited by immigration laws is usually considered a nonresident. A foreigner who intends, at least temporarily, to establish a home in the United States and has a visa permitting permanent residence, will probably be considered a resident for tax purposes. For a more extensive discussion of their tax status, foreign writers in the US should consult IRS Publication 519, *United States Tax Guide for Aliens*.

Non-US nationals earning royalties from US book sales that are subject to the 30 percent withholding tax might be able to claim a full or partial exemption from that tax. Whether and to what extent a foreign writer is entitled to the exemption depends on her country's tax treaty with the United States.[138] If the withholding rate in your country is 0 percent (as in the United Kingdom), you may claim the full exemption. But note that to the extent you take the exemption, you must declare it as foreign income and pay the tax imposed by your home nation. The downside of trying to qualify for the exemption is the inordinate amount of paperwork and filing time required. First, you must obtain a tax ID number. For an individual, this is the ITIN (Individual Tax Identification Number). Getting an ITIN is

---

[138] The IRS website lists the countries with which the US has a tax treaty at www.irs.gov/ Businesses/International-Businesses/United-States-Income-Tax-Treaties—A-to-Z

easier said than done.[139] After getting your ITIN, you can send the proper IRS form (W8-BEN) to your US publishers. This form allows them to pay your royalties without withholding the 30 percent tax as your country's tax treaty with the United States provides.

---

[139] Getting an ITIN takes many weeks and requires that your US publishers write a letter addressed to the IRS on your behalf, and that you submit the letter and other forms and proof of your identity and nationality to the nearest American Embassy. The wait for the ITIN to come from the IRS after you take these steps is several weeks. Your agent or publishers might be willing to help you navigate this process. It is best to start it significantly before royalties might be due, and to ask your publisher to withhold paying you until you have gotten the exemption.

CHAPTER 22

ESTATE PLANNING FOR

WRITERS

In 1945, Eugene O'Neill entrusted the original manuscript of *Long Day's Journey Into Night* to his editor, Bennett Cerf of Random House. In a written contract, Random House agreed to O'Neill's request not to publish the play until twenty-five years after his death. Within two years of his death in 1953, O'Neill's widow Carlotta demanded that Random House publish the play. Cerf felt honor-bound not to do so, so Carlotta withdrew the manuscript from Random House and had it published by Yale University Press. O'Neill also left an unfinished manuscript of *More Stately Mansions*. He had told Carlotta shortly before his death that "Nobody must be allowed to finish my play. . . . I don't want anybody else working on my plays." On a flyleaf placed in the manuscript of *More Stately Mansions*, he had written "Unfinished work. This script to be destroyed in case of my death!" Despite his demands, Carlotta had the work revised, published, and produced on Broadway as a new play by Eugene O'Neill. As the executrix of O'Neill's estate, his widow had every right in both instances to ignore the playwright's wishes because they were not formalized in his will.

Estate planning is too often neglected by many, but it is essential in order to protect a person's loved ones and, for writers, to ensure that their wishes regarding the treatment of their literary works will be posthumously honored. Every adult should have a will that appoints an executor (and if needed, a guardian for their children), disposes of their estate assets and ties up their affairs. Everyone should also consider obtaining a health care proxy, living will, and power of attorney in case they become incapacitated, naming beneficiaries of their investment and bank accounts, and getting life insurance that covers estate-related costs. It is not difficult to do any of these things. If you want to leave your assets to your spouse, children or other family members outright, then unless you have a complicated estate or are wealthy and want to limit your estate tax liability, you can prepare a serviceable will and other estate planning documents yourself using one of many online software programs.[140]

The main objectives of your will should be to efficiently distribute your assets at death to your chosen people and institutions, pay your outstanding debts, and limit the amount of taxes and other burdens to your heirs. Writers have additional concerns because of the nature of their intellectual property as an estate asset. This chapter will give you some general information to help you plan to make your will and take other estate planning steps. The information here is necessarily general, so if you have questions or if the disposition of your estate could raise complications, it is best to find a good probate lawyer or accountant.

BEQUESTS THROUGH A WILL

The most meaningful opportunity you have to control the use of your literary work after your death is through a will or a trust. A will is a written document, signed and witnessed under strictly observed formalities, that provides for the disposition of the maker's (that is, the "testator's") property upon his or her death. A probate court, to which every will is referred, must enforce the testator's intentions as expressed in the will unless there is a legal reason not to do so (such a case is quite rare).[141] Individual state laws govern the proper drafting and interpretation of wills, as well as the disposition of the property of a person who dies "intestate," that is, without a proper will.

---

[140] The best, with very helpful explanations, are at Nolo Press, www.nolo.com.

[141] One exception to this rule is where a will disinherits the decedent's spouse completely. Most states allow a spouse to choose a "statutory share," that is, a significant fraction of the estate assets, in lieu of what the will leaves to the spouse.

If no will is made, property passes to the decedent's heirs by the laws of intestacy. Intestacy laws vary from state to state, but generally provide that the estate assets pass in full to the decedent's relatives in order of preference: to the deceased's spouse if there is one, equally to the deceased's children if there is no spouse, to the parents if no spouse and no children, and so on. An administrator is appointed by the court to manage the estate of one who dies intestate. Dying without a will leaves the decedent's family in a bad position because they will be tied up in probate court for much longer and expend much more time than if there had been a will, and they will have limited legal rights to reverse the actions of the court appointed administrator. As a writer, you would do your literary estate no favors by dying intestate; the administrator will decide what to do with your copyrights and it is unlikely that a family member would be able to change what the administrator decided to do or not to do with your work.

Your will allows you to distribute your property to specified persons or institutions. For literary properties such as manuscripts and copyrights, this is usually done by bequest or predeath gift either to specific individuals or institutions or to a class (such as all your children or grandchildren). Estate taxes and administration costs are typically paid from the "residuary" estate, that is, the property not specifically distributed under the will, or from life insurance naming the will beneficiaries as the policy beneficiaries.

Items such as life insurance proceeds and your bank, pension, and investment accounts can be left directly to named beneficiaries instead of passing into your estate for disposition under the will. This has the advantage of getting those assets to your beneficiaries much more quickly and without the red tape involved if they were to be transferred to the estate and distributed according to the will.

EXECUTORS AND LITERARY EXECUTORS

When planning your will, think carefully about who should administer your estate, and who should have control over the management of your literary works. The will must designate one or more executors who will have fiduciary responsibility to act in the best interests of the estate and its beneficiaries. If you appoint coexecutors, each will bear equal responsibility for your assets unless you indicate otherwise. Although it makes sense to name your spouse as an executor, also consider appointing a coexecutor who does not have a personal interest in your estate property. One option is to retain the trust department of a bank or other financial institution for this important role.

An executor has certain unique responsibilities when administering a writer's estate. A preliminary duty is to notify the testator's publishers and licensees that royalties are to be paid to the estate during probate period (i.e., prior to final settlement of the estate). Under the Copyright Act, a writer may not bequeath by will any of her copyright renewal rights that arise after death. Rather, these rights flow directly to the author's spouse and/ or children. The executor should file the renewal of those copyrights in the name of the estate if the author's spouse and children, if any, are deceased. Similarly, the writer's inalienable right to terminate licenses and grants under copyright after 35 years (for post-1997 works) and 56 years (for pre-1977 works) does not pass through the estate, but rather passes directly to the writer's spouse and children, or if they are deceased, to the grandchildren.[142]

Should you appoint a literary executor in addition to the primary executor(s)? Although the law does not recognize a "literary executor" as such, you can and should make sure that at least one of your coexecutors is familiar with your work and ideally has some experience in the publishing industry. If willing (and young enough), a trusted agent, editor, or fellow writer could fit the bill. Your will could divide the duties between coexecutors, allowing one to handle general financial matters and the other to handle the disposition of the literary works. But because financial and literary matters are likely to intertwine in estate administration, the will should carefully delineate the duties of the literary executor and give to one of the executors the authority to decide disputed matters, whether over the literary estate or otherwise. After it names the general executor and gives her authority to act in all matters related to the will and estate, the literary executor appointment clause might read as follows:

> I appoint [name executor] to be the literary executor of my estate (hereinafter referred to as my "Literary Executor"), to have custody of, act with respect to, and be empowered to make all determinations concerning the use, disposition, retention, and control of the literary works that I have created or own, my letters, correspondence, documents, private papers, writings, manuscripts, and all other literary property of any kind created by

---

[142] See chapter 2 for explanations of copyright renewal and the author's inalienable rights to terminate licenses and transfers.

me, whether or not any such items are unfinished or are completed but not yet divulged to the public. Should a dispute arise between Literary Executor and General Executor concerning my literary property, the determination of the General Executor shall be final and binding.

Unless you make very clear in your will that your literary executor has the authority to determine how your literary and related property are to be used (or not) after your death, the primary executor will have control. In most cases, the estate will likely be administered more efficiently and leave more assets for the beneficiaries if the primary executor does have final decision-making authority even over your literary works. The estate assets, including literary works, must be assigned a fair market value, which, if the estate is very rich (or is in a state with a low estate tax threshold), could affect the tax bill even when the estate lacks sufficient funds to pay taxes. The beneficiaries might be better off if the executor's authority to dispose of assets trumps the literary executor's authority to make aesthetic decisions about your work. You might think differently about your literary legacy, however, as Eugene O'Neill did. If so, learn from his mistake and address how you want your works to be used, or not used, in the will.

In drafting your will, be very clear about your literary properties. Specify the person(s) or organization(s) to whom the rights under copyright are granted; identify unambiguously the property conveyed, both tangible, such as manuscripts and letters, and the copyright to your published and unpublished work, whether or not currently under contract; the rights under copyright conveyed, including their scope and duration; assign the right to receive the benefits from any contracts in force; and list your finished and unfinished manuscripts. Avoid ambiguous language, which could subject your disposition to attack. If you do not unambiguously dispose of specific property or rights, they might pass under the will to the recipient of the residuary estate, (or if there is no residuary clause, through intestacy laws).

An example of a bequest of manuscripts and the copyrights to a specific individual follows:

I give and bequeath all my right, title, and interest, including but not limited to all rights under copyrights and all other intellectual property rights, in my manuscripts entitled [describe manuscripts] to my daughter, Jane, if she shall survive me.

An example of a bequest of tangible manuscripts but not the copyright in literary works to a class follows:

> I give and bequeath to my son, Dick, my daughter, Jane, and my daughter, Sally, or the survivors or survivor of them if any shall predecease me, all my tangible manuscripts [describe manuscripts], but not the rights under copyright thereto, [which are bequeathed elsewhere in the will]. If they shall be unable to agree upon a division of the said property, my son Dick shall have the first choice, and my daughter Jane shall have the second choice, and my daughter Sally shall have the third choice, the said choices to continue in that order so long as any of them desire to make a selection.

Leave a clear and complete inventory of your assets, passwords, etc., and provide unambiguous written instructions to your executor(s) and heir(s) detailing your desired posthumous treatment of your work. After consulting with your executors and advisors, you can decide whether to put these instructions in a separate letter or in your will. You should also clarify whether your instructions are binding on your executor(s) or are merely advisory. In preparing instructions, consider how much posthumous control you really want to exercise over how your literary work is treated. For example, should your unpublished works be published after your death? If they are published, who may edit them? May another author complete your unfinished works? If so, who may decide who will finish them and how may authorship be credited? The publisher, format, the extent to which subsidiary rights may be exploited are all questions that somebody must answer, and all of these creative decisions can impact the estate financially.

You can direct the publication of some or all of your unpublished works in your will. The executor is not responsible to your beneficiaries, however, if he or she fails after diligent efforts to find a publisher for your work. The scope of the executor's duty to dispose of your literary works extends to entertaining offers fairly and granting licenses that would serve your beneficiaries, unless you expressly prohibit that in the will. There is usually no legal requirement, however, that your executor permit others to reproduce your work. By contrast, you may if you choose restrict certain types of publication and use of your work and provide for a period of time to elapse before posthumous publication.

DONATING YOUR PAPERS

You might want to donate copies of books, manuscripts, letters and other personal papers to a library, university, or another institution. Every institution maintains its own policies on accepting private archives. Many cannot accept all that is offered to them. Be sure to consult with the institution before naming it in your will and identify unambiguously the works to be donated and the institutions to receive them. You should also state in the will whether or not the institutions should receive any copyright interests in the works, or whether you are leaving the copyright to others and wish the proceeds from photocopying, etc., to be given to your heirs.

Related issues involve your personal papers. Who, if anyone, will be allowed to publish letters you have written? In what manner should publication be made? Who will have permission to look at your drafts, notebooks, and diaries? Who will have access to letters you received from others? If you designate an official biographer, how will that affect your estate's willingness to make information available to other researchers and the public? The writer who donates manuscripts and personal papers to a university or museum might want to know in advance the treatment the donated materials will receive. What should your executor do if the institution does not treat your papers as promised? You can address all these questions in your will or in separate instructions to your executor. If you do not, your executor will be operating without knowing what your preference would have been.

TRUSTS

Proper administration of any estate requires funds. If the testator does not set aside enough money to cover costs, the executor might have no choice but to dispose of estate property, even if the will directs otherwise. To avoid these headaches for your executor and loved ones, you could either set aside funds during your lifetime or maintain a life insurance policy for this specific purpose. Another interesting choice is to consider establishing an *inter vivos* revocable trust. Trusts are a valuable estate-planning device under which title to property is given to a trustee who is to use the property (or income from the property) for the benefit of certain named beneficiaries. You may create a trust during your life and/or by will. Trusts created during life can be revocable by the creator of the trust, or irrevocable, in which case the creator cannot dissolve the trust. *Inter vivos* literally means "during life," and an *inter vivos* trust is a legal instrument in which you transfer title to any of your assets to the trust while you are alive. As trustee, you control what is done with those assets. During your lifetime, you are the beneficiary of the trust. After death, your assets will pass directly to those named in the trust as beneficiaries.

The establishment of an *inter vivos* trust has one great advantage—the avoidance of probate. Property transferred to the trust might or might not be included in the gross estate subject to federal estate tax, but the assets are transferred to your beneficiaries without any of the formalities and delay of probate. Trusts are frequently used to skip a generation of taxes, for example, by giving the income of a trust to children for their lives and having the grandchildren receive the principal. In such cases the principal would not be included in the estates of the children for purposes of estate taxation. The tax law, however, severely restricts the area of generation-skipping trusts and other similar transfers and it is subject to constant change. Consult a tax specialist or estate planning attorney on whether an *inter vivos* trust is a good option for you.

ESTATE TAXES

Estate planning allows you to anticipate and control the amount of estate taxes to be levied by the state (if any) and the federal government. A writer who lives in more than one state risks having a so-called double domicile and being taxed by more than one state, so plan to avoid this result. You will also wish to benefit from a number of deductions, discussed below, that can substantially reduce the taxable estate if properly planned. Tax planning is especially necessary for authors with sizeable estates because copyrights and manuscripts must be given their fair market value in computing the gross estate. Thus, the projected earnings of your works, based when possible on their past earnings, are figured into their fair market value, even though the earnings have not yet been realized. The valuation process creates uncertainty as to the size of the estate (because the valuation might be high or low) and raises the possibility that the estate will lack the ready cash it needs to pay estate expenses and taxes on time.

THE GROSS ESTATE

The gross estate includes the value of all the property in which the testator had an ownership interest at the time of death. Complex rules, depending on the specific circumstances of each case, cover the inclusion in the gross estate of such items as life insurance proceeds, property the testator transferred within three years of death in which she retained an interest, property over which she possessed a general power to appoint an owner, annuities, jointly held interests, and the value of property in certain trusts.

VALUATION

The property included in the gross estate is valued at fair market value as of the date of death or, if the executor chooses, as of an alternate date (typically six months after death). "Fair market value" is defined by the Internal Revenue Code as "the price at which the property would change hands between a willing buyer and a willing seller, neither being under any compulsion to buy or to sell and both having reasonable knowledge of relevant facts." Expert appraisers are used to determine the fair market value of copyrights and manuscripts. But whether the estate is large or small, the opinions of experts can exhibit surprising variations. Fair market value is not only important for determining the value of an estate, but also for determining the value of gifts and charitable contributions.

Prior to the Tax Reform Act of 1969, writers could donate copyrights or manuscripts to universities or museums and take a charitable deduction for income tax purposes based on fair market value. Since 1969, such a donation by the author of the work would create a charitable deduction in the amount of only the cost of the materials comprising the work—a negligible amount. (The Authors Guild is supporting legislation that would reverse that regulation.) By contrast, one who inherits the work from an author's estate may make a charitable contribution and deduct its full fair market value.

TAXABLE ESTATE

The executor calculates the taxable estate by reducing the gross estate by the amount of certain deductions. Allowed deductions currently include funeral expenses, some administration expenses, casualty or theft losses during administration, debts and other enforceable claims against the estate, mortgages and liens, the value of property passing to a surviving spouse (subject to certain limitations), and the value of property donated to a qualified tax-exempt nonprofit organization. Charitable deductions might be of particular interest to an author. One could bequeath copyrights and manuscripts to tax-exempt charitable or educational institutions and reap intangible benefits, including perpetuating the author's reputation. But they do not help reduce the taxable estate because the fair market value of such works is part of the gross estate.

UNIFIED ESTATE AND GIFT TAX

If an author makes gifts of copyrights, manuscripts, or other assets while alive, the value of the gross estate at death will be reduced by their fair market value. If, however, these or other gifts given during life are valued at more than $10,000, a gift tax applies to the amount over $10,000. The government allows everyone a tax credit against gift and estate taxes cumulatively, meaning that any amount of the unified estate and tax credit used during life to avoid gift tax will decrease the credit allowed to the estate upon death. The amount of tax on the cumulative total of the taxable gifts and the taxable estate is reduced by the tax credit, so an estate is subject to federal tax only if the cumulative total of taxable gifts and the taxable estate is greater than the maximum unified credit in the year of death. The unified credit on the basic exclusion amount for 2011 is $1,730,800 (exempting $5 million from tax) and is $1,772,800 for 2012 (exempting $5,120,000 from tax). The complexity of the rules in this area makes legal and tax advice necessary to ensure that the gifts you give are effective for tax purposes.

LIQUIDITY

Most relatively simple estates (cash, publicly traded securities, small amounts of other easily valued assets, and no special deductions or elections, or jointly held property) do not require the filing of an estate tax return. A tax return is required for estates with combined gross assets and prior taxable gifts exceeding $5,000,000 or more for decedent's dying in 2010 or later (note: there are special rules for decedents dying in 2010). If estate taxes are due, they normally must be paid within nine months after death, at the time the estate tax return is filed. For estates that cannot make full payment immediately, it might be possible to spread payment out over a number of years.

One simple way to ensure there is cash available to pay estate taxes is to take out a life insurance policy. The proceeds of life insurance payable to the estate are included in the gross estate, as are the proceeds of policies payable to others if the decedent retained any ownership or control over the policies. Policies payable to other people and not owned or controlled by the decedent will not be included in the gross estate. Therefore, if your spouse or children are the beneficiaries under both a life insurance policy and the will, they may use the life insurance proceeds to pay estate taxes and other administrative fees and preserve the assets of the estate. This arrangement could especially help heirs of creators of valuable intellectual property. Consult with an insurance agent to obtain life insurance to cover your estate taxes and fees.

APPENDIX A

PROFESSIONAL AUTHORS ASSOCIATIONS

THE AUTHORS GUILD, INC. (WWW.AUTHORSGUILD.ORG)

If you are a published book or freelance author, have been offered a publishing contract or are a self-published book author, you should seriously consider joining the Authors Guild. (The Authors Guild is a co-publisher of this edition of *The Writer's Legal Guide*.) The Guild has more than 9000 members writing in every genre, and is the only organization that offers members individual business and legal advice, including contract reviews and advocacy, from experienced publishing attorneys at no additional charge. Members receive its Model Trade Book Contract and Guide with helpful negotiating tips. Its quarterly *Bulletin* and frequent Advocacy Alerts keep authors up-to-date on key legal and business developments. The Guild lobbies for legislation favorable to writers and engages in grass roots and direct advocacy against unfair businesses practices by publishers, agents, and retailers. It offers print-on-demand republishing service, seminars and workshops on negotiating contracts and industry trends, and superior and economical web and blogging site design software to members. The online edition of this book is available exclusively to Authors Guild members at *www.authorsguild.org*.

AMERICAN SOCIETY OF JOURNALISTS AND AUTHORS
(WWW.ASJA.ORG)

ASJA is a national organization of independent nonfiction professional writers. It offers benefits and services focusing on professional development, including regular confidential market information, meetings with editors and other field professionals, an exclusive referral service, seminars and workshops, discount services, and the opportunity for members to explore professional issues and concerns with their peers. Membership is open to established nonfiction writers who meet the organization's high standards, but ASJA advocates industry wide for freelancers' interests. Based in New York City, the Society has active regional chapters in Northern and Southern California, the Rocky Mountain area, the Southeast (Atlanta area), the Upper Midwest (Minneapolis area), upstate New York, Long Island, and Washington, DC.

THE AUTHORS REGISTRY
(WWW.AUTHORSREGISTRY.ORG)

The Authors Registry is a nonprofit organization formed by a consortium of writers groups to help expedite the flow of royalty payments and small reuse fees to authors, particularly for new media uses. As a payment clearinghouse for certain categories of royalties and fees, the Registry lifts the burden from publishers and delivers checks to freelancers. The Registry also distributes fees to U.S. authors for photocopying of their work abroad.

THE NATIONAL WRITERS UNION
(WWW.NWU.ORG)

The National Writers Union is a trade union of freelance writers in all genres, formats, and media who work for American publishers or employers. A local of the United Auto Workers, it bills itself as an activist organization committed to improving the economic and working conditions of freelance writers through the collective strength of 1,500 members in 15 local chapters throughout the country. It offers grievance assistance, industry campaigns, contract advice, a jobs hotline, health and professional liability insurance plans, member education, and networking. The NWU aims to challenge corporate media against unfair treatment of writers, lobbies Congress to pass legislation that protects the rights of writers, creates viable solutions to provide publishers fair alternatives to unfair practices, and educates and empowers its members.

P.E.N. AMERICAN CENTER
(WWW.PEN.ORG)

P.E.N. American Center is an international community of writers, editors, translators, and others interested in the field of literature who work to defend free expression worldwide, support persecuted writers, and promote and encourage the recognition and reading of contemporary literature. Its 3,400 Professional Members include published writers, translators, and editors. The organization also includes Associate Members who come from other parts of the literary community—booksellers, librarians, students, and "passionate readers." P.E.N. advocates for the free expression rights of writers and readers. It has member committees and groups focusing on translation, children's/young adult authors, and a women's literary workshop. Benefits include a journal, discounts to P.E.N.'s prominent public programs, such as its World Voices Festival of International Literature, health insurance at group rates in certain states, and a discounted subscription to its online database of Grants and Awards available to American Writers.

CANADIAN AUTHORS ASSOCIATION
(WWW.CANAUTHORS.ORG)

The Canadian Authors Association (CAA) is a national organization with local branches in nine geographic regions and a "virtual branch," dedicated to promoting a flourishing community of writers across Canada and to encourage works of literary and artistic merit. The CAA does this by establishing and maintaining professional standards, promoting professionalism, providing opportunities for professional development, and advocating for fair and equitable treatment of writers.

PROFESSIONAL WRITERS ASSOCIATION OF CANADA
(WWW.PWAC.CA)

PWAC is a nationwide non-profit organization that plays a leading role in the Canadian freelance publishing industry. It has more than 600 members who write professionally in every arena: magazine and newspaper articles, books, speeches, newsletters, media releases, white papers, annual reports, advertising and brochure copy, sales and marketing material, web content, training manuals, film scripts, radio and television documentaries, and any other material on a freelance basis. PWAC develops and maintains professional standards in editor-writer and client-writer relationships, encourages higher industry standards and fees for freelance writing, publishes current freelance payment rate information, provides networking opportunities and professional development workshops and materials for members, and lobbies for freedom of the press and freedom of expression in Canada.

GENRE-SPECIFIC ASSOCIATIONS

HORROR WRITERS ASSOCIATION
(WWW.HORROR.ORG)

The Horror Writers Association is a nonprofit organization of more than 500 writers and publishing professionals, dedicated to promoting horror and dark fantasy literature and the interests of those who write it. In addition to sponsoring the annual Bram Stoker awards for superior achievement in horror literature, HWA provides networking, a mentoring program, information trading, and promotional resources to aspiring and established horror writers, including a monthly newsletter with publishing and market news and a timely, comprehensive listing of markets. It has local chapters in the United Kingdom, Ontario (Canada), New England, New York City, Hudson Valley, New Jersey, Mid-Atlantic Region, Florida, Michigan, Chicago Area, Missouri/ Lower Midwest, and Los Angeles. Full members must be published professional writers of horror, but aspiring authors who demonstrate an intention to become a professional writer may join as affiliate members.

MYSTERY WRITERS OF AMERICA
(WWW.MYSTERYWRITERS.ORG)

The Mystery Writers of America is an organization of and for mystery writers and those allied to the crime-writing field. MWA is dedicated to promoting respect for crime writing and for those who write it. It provides scholarships for writers, sponsors a youth literacy program and symposia and conferences, presents the annual Edgar Awards, and conducts other activities to further a better appreciation and higher regard for crime writing. MWA also works to educate writers and those who aspire to write regarding their rights and interests, and to make writers and readers aware of developments that could affect crime writing such as legislation, publishing industry practices, judicial decisions, and in other ways. Membership includes writers of books, short stories, plays, and screenplays; publishers, editors, agents, librarians, booksellers, and other in allied fields; aspiring writers and others devoted to crime writing.

MWA has eleven regional chapters, and members are automatically enrolled in the appropriate regional chapter. All chapters have a newsletter and most have regular meetings; increasingly, chapters also have an online presence. Benefits include ten issues annually of the national newsletter, internal listservs focused on practical issues such as touring, contracts, publicity, agents, foreign rights, movie options, and other business questions, help for traditionally published writers who have been dropped by their publishers, access to health, vision, and dental insurance, and discounts on resources such as Writer's Digest books and magazine, Publishers Weekly, invitation to the Edgar Awards, a one-day writing conference, and exclusive databases of bookstores and libraries interested in mystery writers and books.

NATIONAL ASSOCIATION OF SCIENCE WRITERS
(WWW.NASW.ORG)

NASW was formed to "foster the dissemination of accurate information regarding science through all media normally devoted to informing the public." Its mission is to fight for the free flow of science news. Members include freelancers and employees of most of the major newspapers, wire services, magazines, and broadcast outlets in the country. NASW offers an array of benefits to professional science writers and practitioners in related fields: a quarterly newsletter, reports on trends, issues and controversies, news of regional events, practical advice on freelancing, teaching, public affairs, and other professional specialties, annual workshops, a jobs mailing list, educational resources and mentoring programs, the annual Science in Society awards, free website hosting, insurance plans, and travel fellowships. Applicants for regular membership must be established science writers and have two sponsoring members. Student memberships are available.

NOVELISTS, INC.
(WWW.NINC.COM)

Novelists, Inc. is a coalition of working writers dedicated to serving the needs of multi-published writers of popular fiction and to improving the status of career novelists. NINC helps its members connect and communicate with each other and to stay informed, with a focus on "the business of the business." It provides a popular members-only e-mail loop that is considered a go-to resource for research and the latest industry information, a monthly newsletter, a well-attended annual conference, a legal fund and advocacy, and a discount on personalized Nielsen BookScan reports, among other benefits.

OUTDOOR WRITERS ASSOCIATION OF AMERICA
(WWW.OWAA.ORG)

OWAA represents a diverse group of professional communicators dedicated to sharing the outdoor experience. Its mission is to improve the professional skills of its members, set high ethical and communications standards, encourage public enjoyment and conservation of natural resources, and be mentors for the next generation of professional outdoor writers. Members include writers, editors, book authors, broadcasters, film and video producers, photographers, artists, and lecturers. OWAA promotes responsible outdoor reporting by providing workshops and seminars, setting professional standards, a monthly publication, annual membership directory and other publications, and an annual conference. It provides online lists of various outdoor publishers' needs and current job listings. The national office provides information, liaison services, and assistance with business problems. OWAA sets professional standards and business guidelines and offers health insurance coverage at competitive rates.

ROMANCE WRITERS OF AMERICA
(WWW.RWA.ORG)

Romance Writers of America is dedicated to advancing the professional interests of career-focused romance writers through networking and advocacy. Open to published and unpublished romance writers, it has more than 10,000 members in 145 chapters that offer local or special-interest networking and education opportunities. RWA works to support the efforts of its members to earn a living, to make a full-time career out of writing romance, or a part-time one that provides fair compensation. RWA hosts an annual conference that allows writers to increase their understanding of the industry and to network with industry professionals and fellow writers. It sponsors awards, which get the attention of editors, recognizing excellence for published and unpublished romance writers. RWA advocates for best publishing practices for its members, including fair contracts from publishers and agents, publishes a monthly report and a bi-monthly newsletter, and provides a private online community and many chapter contests and conferences for published and unpublished works. It also offers discounted subscriptions to Nielsen BookScan. One of the key benefits of membership in RWA is the local RWA chapters. They generally meet once a month and many offer critique-partner or critique-groups.

SCIENCE FICTION AND FANTASY WRITERS OF AMERICA (WWW.SFWA.ORG)

SFWA includes published science fiction and fantasy writers, artists, editors, and allied professionals. Its mission is to inform, support, promote, defend, and advocate for its members. SFWA helps writers promote their works, provides a grievance committee to help resolve contractual and royalty disputes, has an emergency medical fund, and offers private discussion forums for members to communicate with their peers. The organization takes on industry issues that individual writers cannot, such as confronting mass copyright infringement, reviewing new publishers' standard contracts, and negotiating directly with publishers to improve industry standards. It publishes the popular Writer Beware blog that alerts the community to scams, schemes, and bad actors who take advantage of aspiring writers.

THE SOCIETY OF CHILDREN'S BOOK WRITERS AND ILLUSTRATORS (WWW.SCBWI.ORG)

SCBWI is a professional organization specifically for people writing and illustrating for children and young adults in the fields of children's literature, magazines, film, television, and multimedia. It calls itself a network for the exchange of knowledge between writers, illustrators, editors, publishers, agents, librarians, educators, booksellers, and others involved with literature for young people. It advocates to effect changes within the field and lobbies on copyright and for the fair treatment of authors and artists, including in contract terms. SCBWI sponsors two annual International Conferences on

Writing and Illustrating for Children and dozens of regional conferences and events. It publishes a bi-monthly magazine, gives awards and grants to writers and illustrators, provides market information, and prides itself on giving individualized advice, information, and counsel to its members. Joining the national organization automatically makes members part of their local chapters, which offer critique and "shoptalk" groups, newsletters and social events.

SCBWI's members-only discussion boards deal with current marketing information, upcoming events, and the goings-on of fellow members. Posting forums include Critique Groups; Publishing Tips, Techniques & Questions; Portfolios, Contracts, Art Submissions & Other Biz; Public Speaking Resources; and Classifieds.

TEXT AND ACADEMIC AUTHORS ASSOCIATION
(WWW.TAAONLINE.NET)

The Text and Academic Authors Association (TAA) provides professional development resources, industry news, and networking opportunities for textbook authors and authors of scholarly journal articles and books. Established in 1987, TAA is dedicated solely to assisting textbook and academic authors. Benefits include listservs that allow members to post questions and get expert answers, a mentoring directory, annual conference, local chapters, audio podcasts and webinars, and a newsletter.

DRAMATISTS AND SCREENWRITERS

THE DRAMATISTS GUILD
(WWW.DRAMATISTSGUILD.COM)

The Dramatists Guild of America advances the interests of playwrights, composers, lyricists and librettists writing for the stage by helping them protect the artistic and economic integrity of their work. The Guild has more than 6,000 members nationwide, from beginning writers to the most prominent authors represented on Broadway, Off-Broadway and in regional theaters. Membership is open to any writer who has completed a dramatic script regardless of production history. The Dramatists Guild maintains model contracts for all levels of productions, (including Broadway, regional and smaller theaters) and encourages its members to use these contracts when negotiating with producers. The Guild is an advocate for dramatists' interests and assists dramatists in developing their artistic and business skills with publications and educational programs.

THE WRITERS GUILD OF AMERICA—EAST
(WWW.WGAEAST.ORG)

THE WRITERS GUILD OF AMERICA—WEST
(WWW.WGA.ORG)

The Writers Guilds of America, East and West, are affiliated but separate labor unions comprised of the thousands of writers who write the content for television shows, movies, news programs, documentaries, animation, and Internet and mobile devices (and other new media). Membership is open to any writer who has a contract with a signatory to a WGA-endorsed contract. If you are interested in writing professionally for screen, television, or new media, a visit to these unions' websites is a must. Qualified writers join the WGA-East if they live east of the Mississippi, and the WGA-West otherwise.

The WGA's key purpose is to represent their members in negotiations with film and television producers to ensure members' financial, creative, and legal rights are protected. Once a contract is in place, the WGA enforces it. The long-term efforts of the unions have led to screen writers receiving pension and health coverage and to protection of their fundamental financial and creative rights. The Guilds adjudicate proper writing credits for feature films, television, and new media programs, and monitor, collect, and distribute residuals (payments for the reuse of movies, television, and new media programs) for their members. Each also sponsors seminars, panel discussions, and events. A major benefit, open to members and nonmembers, is the unions' registration service for screenplays, scripts, and treatments, which provides legal evidence of the authorship of material and when it was written.

APPENDIX B

The Bent Agency: http://jennybent.blogspot.com/

Joshua Bilmes (JABberwocky Literary Agency): http://brilligblogger.blogspot.com/

Books & Such Literary Agency: http://www.booksandsuch.biz/blog/

Brenda Bowen (Sanford J. Greenburger Associates): http://bowenpress.blogspot.com/

BookEnds: http://bookendslitagency.blogspot.com/

Nathan Bransford: http://nathanbransford.blogspot.com/

Terry Burns (Hartline Literary Agency): http://www.terryburns.net

Nadia Cornier: http://agentobvious.livejournal.com/

Kimberley Cameron & Assoc: http://www.kimberleycameron.blogspot.com

Jill Corcoran (Herman Agency): http://jillcorcoran.blogspot.com/

Sarah Crowe (Harvey Klinger): http://acrowesnest.blogspot.com/

Sarah Davies (The Greenhouse Literary Agency): http://greenhouseliterary.com/index.php/blog/

Doyen Literary Services: http://www.barbaradoyen.com/articles

DHS Literary: http://dhsliterary.blogspot.com/

Dystel & Goderich: http://www.dystel.com/

Scott Eagan (Greyhaus Literary Agency): http://scotteagan.blogspot. com

Elaine English: http://elainepenglish.blogspot.com/

FinePrint Literary: http://confessionsofawanderingheart.blogspot.com/

Natalie Fischer (Sandra Dijkstra Literary Agency): http:// adventuresinagentland.blogspot.com

Daisy Frost (Edward Cecil Agency (London)): http://www. missdaisyfrost.com

Folio Literary Management: http://foliolit.blogspot.com

Diana Fox: http://foxliterary.blogspot.com

Full Circle Lit: http://fullcirclelit.blogspot.com/

Rachelle Gardner: http://cba-ramblings.blogspot.com/

Barry Goldblatt: http://bgliterary.livejournal.com/

Ashley Grayson: http://graysonagency.blogspot.com

David Hale Smith: http://dhsliterary.blogspot.com/

Hartline Literary Agency: http://hartlineliteraryagency.blogspot.com/

Mandy Hubbard (D4EO Literary Agency): http://mandyhubbard. livejournal.com/

Jennifer Jackson: http://arcaedia.livejournal.com/

John Jarrold (London): http://jjarrold.livejournal.com/

Knight Agency: http://knightagency.blogspot.com/

Lucienne Diver (The Knight Agency): http://varkat.livejournal.com/

Mary Kole (Andrea Brown Literary Agency): http://kidlit.com/

Michael Larsen (Larsen-Pomada Literary Agency): http://sfwriters. info/blog/

Steve Laube: http://www.stevelaube.com/blog/

Jennifer Laughran (Andrea Brown Agency): http://literaticat. blogspot.com/

Colleen Lindsay: http://theswivet.blogspot.com/

Lyons Literary: http://lyonsliterary.blogspot.com/

Cameron McClure (Donald Maass Literary Agency): http:// bookcanibal.blogspot.com/

Laurie McLean (Larson-Pomada Agency): http://www.agentsavant. com/

MacGregor Literary: http://chipmacgregor.com/

Tracy Marchini (Curtis Brown Ltd): http://www.tracymarchini.com

Mortimer Literary Agency: http://perilsofpublishing.com/

Kristin Nelson: http://pubrants.blogspot.com/

Bree Ogden (Martin Literary Management): http://agentbree.wordpress.com/

Kathleen Ortiz (Lowenstein Associates): http://kortizzle.blogspot.com/

Lori Perkins: http://agentinthemiddle.blogspot.com/

Jenny Rappaport: http://litsoup.blogspot.com/

Janet Reid (FinePrint): http://jetreidliterary.blogspot.com/

The Rejecter: http://rejecter.blogspot.com/

Kate Schafer: http://ktliterary.com/archives.html

Eddie Schneider (JABberwocky Literary Agency): http://eddieschneider.com/

Wendy Sherman Associates: http://www.wsherman.com/blog/

Miss Snark: http://misssnark.blogspot.com/ (sadly retired but well worth reading)

The Strothman Agency: http://www.strothmanagency.com/articles

Scott Treimel NY: http://scotttreimelny.blogspot.com/

Simon Trewin (United Agents): http://simontrewin.com/

Upstart Crow Literary: http://upstartcrowliterary.com/blog/

Matt Wagner: http://www.fresh-books.com/blog/

Scott Waxman Literary: http://waxmanagency.wordpress.com/

Adrian Weston (Raft Representation): http://raftpr.blogspot.com/

Tina Wexler: http://blog.myspace.com/tinawexler

Wylie-Merrick: http://wyliemerrick.blogspot.com/

Andrew Zack: http://www.zackcompany.blogspot.com/

APPENDIX C

Copyright Duration and Renewal		
Date of Copyright	When to Renew	Duration of Copyright
Pre-1923		Copyright has expired*
1923–1963	Copyright must have bean renewed during the 28th year of copyright, otherwise it has lapsed.	95 years from the original copyright year, if renewed in 28th year
1964–1977	Copyright holder may renew during the 28th year of copyright, even if a renewal registration was not filed, the copyright automatically renewed.	Author's life plus 70 years
1978 or later	No renewal necessary	Author's life plus 70 years
Works created before 1978 but neither published nor registered**	No renewal necessary	Author's life plus 70 years. (However, the copyright did not expire until at leasat December 31, 2002. If the work was published between Jan. 1, 1978 and Dec. 31, 2002, the copyright will not expire before December 31, 2047.)

Continued on next page

Copyright Duration and Renewal		
Date of Copyright	**When to Renew**	**Duration of Copyright**
Joint works created on or after January 1, 1978	No renewal necessary	95 years from the year work was first published or 120 years from the year of creation, whichever comes first
Anonymous works, pseudonymous works, and works for hire created in or after 1978, or created but neither published nor registered before 1978	No renewal necessary	95 years from the year work was first published or 120 years from the year of creation, whichever comes first
*If not published or registered for copyright before 1923, copyright may not have expired. See ** above*		

INDEX

Books from Allworth Press

Allworth Press is an imprint of Skyhorse Publishing, Inc. Selected titles are listed below.

The Pocket Legal Companion to Copyright: A User-Friendly Handbook for Protecting and Profiting from Copyrights
By Lee Wilson (5 x 7 ½, 320 pages, paperback, $16.95)

The Business of Writing: Professional Advice on Proposals, Publishers, Contracts, and More for the Aspiring Writer
Edited by Jennifer Lyons; foreword by Oscar Hijuelos (6 x 9, 304 pages, paperback, $19.95)

Starting Your Career as a Freelance Writer, Second Edition
By Moira Anderson Allen (6 x 9, 192 pages, paperback, $24.95)

Starting Your Career as a Professional Blogger
By Jacqueline Bodnar (6 x 9, 240 pages, paperback, $19.95)

Starting Your Career as a Freelance Editor: A Guide to Working with Authors, Books, Newsletters, Magazines, Websites, and More
By Mary Embree (6 x 9, 240 pages, paperback, $19.95)

Publish Your Book: Proven Strategies and Resources for the Enterprising Author
By Patricia Fry (6 x 9, 264 pages, paperback, $19.95)

Promote Your Book: Over 250 Proven, Low-Cost Tips and Techniques for the Enterprising Author
By Patricia Fry (5 ½ x 8 ¼, 224 pages, paperback, $19.95)

Talk Up Your Book: How to Sell Your Book through Public Speaking, Interviews, Signings, Festivals, Conferences, and More
By Patricia Fry (6 x 9, 320 pages, paperback, $19.95)

The Author's Toolkit, Third Edition
By Mary Embree (5 ½ x 8 ½, 224 pages, paperback, $19.95)

The Writer's Guide to Queries, Pitches, and Proposals, Second Edition
By Moira Anderson Allen (6 x 9, 288 pages, paperback, $19.95)

Writing the Great American Romance Novel
By Catherine Lanigan (6 x 9, 224 pages, paperback, $19.95)